How Britain

Broke the World

First published by Canbury Press 2022
This edition published 2022

Canbury Press
Kingston upon Thames, Surrey, United Kingdom
www.canburypress.com

Printed and bound in Great Britain
by CPI Group (UK) Ltd, Croydon
Typeset in Volkorn/Interface
Cover: Alice Marwick

This is a work of non-fiction

FSC® helps take care of forests for future generations.

ISBN
Hardback: 978-1-912454-60-0
Ebook: 978-1-912454-61-7

How Britain Broke the World

Arthur Snell

*To Charlotte,
Matilda, Edward and Peggy*

CONTENTS

INTRODUCTION

There was a brief silence after the bomb blast. Then shouting, and nervous laughter. The Iraqi official gestured to the shattered window and stammered: '*Shay 'aadi*,' a 'normal thing.' We were both uninjured, but I learned later that several guards had died outside the office where we were meeting. It was 2005 and I was in Baghdad, working as a British diplomat. Car bombs were normal. As I left the building I noticed a charred hand on the ground, probably the bomber's.

In 2003 I had been open to persuasion that the invasion of Iraq could leave the country better off in the long-term. But the coalition had lost control. Every indicator, every piece of evidence, pointed to that fact. This was an unwelcome truth, so we tried to ignore it. Senior officials told us that the problem was foreign terrorists infiltrating Iraq to attack the international soldiers. Being a suicide bomber was not in the 'Iraqi character.' Once these foreign jihadists were taken care of, the problem would go away.

Others claimed that the only barrier to progress was the lack of an Iraqi army (the previous one had been disbanded carelessly by the US in the first days of the occupation). Once the new army was up and running, it would all be fine.

These excuses were wearing thin. The attacks were increasing in frequency and severity. That day, in the bombed building, I could no longer deny to myself that the Allied powers had unleashed a terrible whirlwind. Now, as I write in the early 2020s, the existence of Islamic State is a direct consequence of the 2003 invasion. But the impact of that terrible mistake stretches far wider: from regional chaos in the Middle East, to shredding the credibility of Western governments, to the renewed power of autocratic countries, chiefly Russia and China.

A FAILING WORLD ORDER

The unsteady rules-based international order finally collapsed on 24th February 2022, when Russia launched a full-scale invasion of Ukraine. Under stress for some time, this system – international law, accepted national borders, with the United Nations as global police chief – had delivered peace and security for most Western democracies from World War II into the 1990s. Admittedly, many countries, particularly in the Global South, missed out on the upsides. But a world without this framework is volatile. We are living in a period of global disorder, conflict and uncertainty.

As I write in 2022, major conflicts are laying waste to the large and geopolitically sensitive states of Ukraine, Libya and Yemen, and civil wars are raging in the large countries of Ethiopia and Syria. In addition, an arc of instability runs across the entire

Sahel region of Africa and widespread civil strife continues in Myanmar, Afghanistan and Iraq. Running alongside these flashpoints is the spectre, once more, of great power conflict. Russia may be economically weak and facing chronic under-population, but it still has an expeditionary military that can transform a conflict. It proved its ability to do so in Syria where, by committing war crimes with indiscriminate bombing campaigns, it destroyed much of Syria's opposition and shifted the war in President Assad's favour. It applied similar brutality to the towns and cities of Ukraine. Perhaps just as impactful are Russia's irregular forces – the 'little green men' who overran the Crimea; the hackers whose 'Solar Winds' attack penetrated US government computers; the GRU assassins who deployed chemical weapons on the streets of the sedate British city of Salisbury against a defector. Above all, Russia's willingness to break the rules of the game, to interfere in foreign politics, gives it disproportionate power. Across Europe, Moscow's money funds far-right political movements. In the United States in 2016, Russia manipulated the American presidential election campaign in favour of Donald Trump. In 2020, its efforts to provide kompromat on Joe Biden's son did not change the election outcome but was a reminder of its continued willingness to pull democratic strings from the shadows. Here in Britain, oligarchs of Russian origin with clear links to the ruling elite are major donors to the governing Conservative party. The leading financial backer of Brexit – Britain's exit from the European Union – was offered business opportunities by the Russian Ambassador in London (though there is no evidence he took them up.) Whether Russia interfered in the Brexit referendum campaign at large is unknown, because the pro-Brexit British government has ensured that this has never been investigated by its security services.

China is also challenging the existing order. The world's most populated nation is likely to overtake the US as the world's largest economy before the end of the 2020s. China is building new islands to lay claim to the western side of the Pacific Ocean. It is investing rapidly in its military, particularly its navy, and is becoming a world leader in information technology. Historically, it is rare for one leading world power to overtake another without conflict between them. In the case of China and America, numerous flashpoints, particularly over Taiwan, could potentially escalate into full armed conflict. Even if this is avoided, a global struggle for economic and diplomatic influence is under way.

The United States has itself weakened the structures of international security and economic growth, often referred to as the liberal international order. Donald Trump transformed America's Republican party into a far-right nationalist political movement which pitted nationalism against internationalism. His America First approach was expressly opposed to multilateralism, co-operation and a rules-based global order. President Trump set about trying to destroy many of America's global alliances: questioning his military commitments to Japan and South Korea. He undermined NATO, the North Atlantic Treaty Organisation, Europe's military and security bulwark against an increasingly-aggressive Russia. Other international organisations appear equally shaky. The United Nations Security Council, supposedly the ultimate guarantor of international peace, could become a meaningless talking shop because of vetos held by leading nations. In December 2018, Trump's US threatened to veto a long hoped-for ceasefire in Yemen unless language guaranteeing humanitarian aid deliveries was removed, to placate its Gulf allies, Saudi Arabia and the United Arab Emirates. (Russia exercised its veto 16 times from 2011 to 2021 to block action on Syria.)

Trump's administration plunged a G7 summit in Quebec in June 2018 into rancour and disorder. The G7 is the talking shop for the world's largest democratic economies (in economic size order – USA, Japan, Germany, France, UK, Italy and Canada). As the *New York Times* reported: '[l]iterally moments after [Canadian Prime Minister] Mr Trudeau's government proudly released the joint statement, noting it had been agreed to by all seven countries, Mr Trump blew apart the veneer of cordiality.' As Trump's plane headed for a one-to-one meeting with North Korea's dictator Kim Jong-Un, itself an unprecedented event, the President lashed out with insulting tweets accusing Canada's Prime Minister of giving 'false statements' and being 'very dishonest & weak.'

Some of these developments can be classed as part of the ebb and flow of modern politics. At the 2020 Presidential election, Donald Trump lost to Joe Biden, a Democrat with a reputation for consensual, 'big-tent' politics. However, this in no way means the threat to America's democracy has disappeared. At the time of writing, Trump remains effective head of the Republican party, and even were he to stand aside, as a political movement the Republicans appear to have embraced authoritarianism, political violence and the contesting of election results that do not suit them. Most Republican supporters have concluded, against all the evidence, that the 2020 election was rigged against Donald Trump. The same group appear, according to June 2021 polling, to have a higher opinion of Vladimir Putin, who was transparently hostile to America, than of their own President Joe Biden.

In 2021, President Biden ensured there were no American flounces at the G7, but underlying tensions remained. Britain was under pressure from all of the other attendees to adhere to its international commitments under the Northern Ireland Protocol, an international agreement it had signed but did not to want to honour. And Biden's focus was on generating a concerted stand against China. They could not reach an agreement.

Things aren't much better in Europe. The 27 members of the European Union surprised many British politicians by maintaining a united front on the Brexit negotiations, frustrating those hoping for a stitch-up orchestrated by German car-makers. But in recent history, Brexit was about the only thing that the EU member states agreed on. Two of its members, Hungary and Poland, are facing unprecedented disciplinary procedures in response to the anti-democratic actions of their respective governments. The European principle of free movement within the borderless 'Schengen' zone has effectively broken down in the face of a migration crisis fed by instability in North Africa and the Middle East, as well as longer term trends such as climate change in Africa's Sahel region. In 2018, Italy's right-wing populist strongman, Matteo Salvini, declared Italian ports closed to migrants rescued from people smuggling operations in the waters off Libya, triggering a crisis between Italy, Malta and the wider EU. Similarly, Greece, on the frontline of Europe's border with Turkey, appears to have been conducting illegal operations to push refugees back into international and Turkish waters. It does this because other European countries don't want to cope with the influx. The pan-European migration crisis is always someone else's problem.

'PUNCHING ABOVE OUR WEIGHT'

As a British diplomat active from the late 1990s until 2014, I have been a first-hand observer of the way the UK's foreign policy has contributed to this mess. Since Tony Blair's first election victory in 1997, Britain has contributed to the fracturing of the global order. Brexit is a symptom of that fissure. Britain has often acted in a way that has reduced global security, increased instability, and undermined trust between nations and between individuals and their governments. Put bluntly, a lot of the bad stuff happening right now is happening because of Britain. Britain talks self-centredly of 'punching above our weight,' strangely stimulated by the idea that its virility depends partly on its ability to be disproportionately powerful. But it doesn't seem very interested in whether it is punching the right people in the right places, or whether it should be punching at all. Is Britain using its considerable influence and capabilities to good effect, to promote international stability, progress, and peace? Or is it part of the problem, desperately clinging to a declining status, acting incoherently, with little or no thought for the long-term impact?

Its foreign policy is constantly shaped by imperial hubris, the strange belief that Britain knows best, that it can dispense wisdom and guidance, often forcefully, around the world, when recent actions should give it pause for thought. This book seeks to learn the lessons from the cracked world we live in and explain Britain's role in breaking it. The unwelcome truth is that Britain bears an outsized share of the blame for the current wave of crises. The United Nations, an organisation co-founded by the UK and whose first meetings took place in London in 1946, has been fatally undermined by Britain's insistence that the UN's role as final arbiter of global conflict can be ignored when it is convenient to do so, as happened with Kosovo, Iraq and Libya. In 2022, the British government appears to take pleasure in breaking international law, whether over the Northern Ireland Protocol of the Brexit agreement, or its treatment of refugees attempting to reach Britain in small boats across the English Channel. And Britain operates the world's largest network of offshore financial institutions, ensuring that criminal money can be laundered across the world, and corporate tax avoidance denies sovereign governments their rightful resources.

But it is not just about 'rules': nations, even allied ones such as those in Europe and North America, appear unable to work together to solve geopolitical challenges. Britain came close to breaking up the world's leading intelligence alliance because of a refusal to take the risk of an aggressive China seriously. Britain's insistence on pursuing a certain type of Brexit risks renewed conflict in Ireland and makes co-ordination with Europe on a range of major global issues much harder. This has further undermined the idea of a liberal global order of democracies working together.

It is not that geopolitical crises, or challenges to world order, are a new phenomenon. What is new is the way that Britain has responded. During both the Cold War and the immediate post-Cold War era, Britain understood its role as a defender and upholder of a Western alliance, founded on a belief in liberal democracy and global security, overseen by international institutions. Britain may have been a significant power, but it knew who it had to work with to get things done. By contrast, since 1997, Britain's foreign policy has been guided by an underlying theme: a misplaced British belief that it has a better understanding of what is good for most people outside Britain than those people have themselves. In the same period, Britain has starved its diplomatic and foreign policy machinery of resources, jettisoning expertise and slimming down its overseas presence. As a result, just when Britain has needed a confident, competent foreign policy delivered by well-resourced professionals, it has ended up pursuing an incoherent set of objectives, rarely in full co-ordination with its allies, sometimes ignoring them altogether (as was the case with China and Brexit). Britain got steadily worse at managing its overseas entanglements just as it needed to be better than ever. This helped to create the new global disorder. Countries large and small pursue increasingly uncoordinated and contradictory policies, driven by short term political aims and limited understanding of consequences.

Britain's impact has been felt from southeastern Europe to the Middle East, from London's offshore financial centres to the impoverished countries whose kleptocrats use these centres to launder their wealth. It has largely been the unintended consequence of slapdash incompetence, in part reflecting dysfunctional foreign policy structures that persist in generating the same results, even after repeated failures. Britain has not cynically acted to make things worse. I do not regard Tony Blair as the embodiment of evil. British policy-makers have not pursued the sort of zero-sum thinking associated with Russian President Vladimir Putin, in which whatever increases his immediate power and authority is the guiding light of Russian policy, whatever the consequences for everybody else. (Donald Trump favoured this approach, albeit less effectively because he is a poor negotiator.)

MOTIVATION

So while explaining the overall failure of the rules-based world order, this book zooms into Britain's foreign policy, its ideologies, structures, and shibboleths. At the moment, Britain doesn't seem to believe in funding its foreign policy machinery appropriately. Nor does it believe in having experts guide foreign policy choices. Having got others into a mess, Britain, with Brexit, undermined its national credibility, undermined international law and undermined the integrity of the country itself.

I fully expect that some will mistake my criticism of Britain for a lack of affection or feeling for my country. Suffice to say that I hope those that accuse me of a lack of patriotism have been similarly willing to risk everything, as I did, in service of their country.

My motivation is to try to improve things. I want Britain to do better as a country in the future, for the egregious failings of governance to become distant memories, learning points, rather than awkward facts of the present. Regrettably, we live in an age of polarisation, enabled by self-selecting online bubbles. Disagreements of policy and approach are greeted with cries of 'traitor' and 'quisling.' I may be caricatured as a 'Remoaner.' (For the record, as much as I regret Brexit, I don't believe that Britain will or should ever re-join the European Union.

In my career, I have had the immense privilege to work alongside fantastic, hardworking, brave and patriotic British public servants. These soldiers, diplomats, intelligence officers and countless others are the best of this country – yet they are often underappreciated, misrepresented and ignored. I have spoken to many of them for this book. It is intended to give voice to those who must remain silent.

But the ultimate judgements are my own. Who am I to be making them? I joined the British Foreign Office more or less directly from Oxford University at a time when most of my contemporaries were gliding into well-paid jobs in the private sector. I did not have any family background in diplomacy or international affairs. Once in the Foreign Office I volunteered to serve in Zimbabwe where British diplomats were being harassed and targeted by President Robert Mugabe's thugs, and Nigeria, where violent crime was a daily hazard. On the day of the 9/11 attacks I volunteered to be put onto a rapid Arabic language programme and, having learned the language in half the time normally allotted to British diplomats, I was deployed to Yemen to work on counter-terrorism in an embassy that was targeted by an active Al-Qaeda cell. From Yemen I volunteered again to serve in Baghdad, at that time by some margin the most dangerous city in the world. In Baghdad my work took me daily outside the fortified Green Zone to Iraqi government buildings and other locations under constant threat from suicide bombings. A few years later I volunteered, again, this time to be in a Forward Operating Base in Afghanistan's Helmand province, where my duties included regular visits to the military frontline.

I could go on, but suffice it to say I know how mistakes in wood-panelled rooms at the Foreign Office in London, or in the headquarters of the Ministry of Defence nearby, can detonate bombs in dusty streets.

How did we get here? Optimism was in the air when Tony Blair, the youthful leader of the Labour party, walked through the imposing black door of No 10 Downing Street on 2nd May 1997. His government, we thought, would not be like the others.

1. AN 'ETHICAL FOREIGN POLICY'

In May 1997, Robin Cook, Foreign Secretary to the newly-elected British Prime Minister Tony Blair, gave a speech outlining the government's approach to foreign policy. Cook made no mention of warfare, terrorism, famine or extremism. He had no need to: 1997 was one of the most peaceful years of the entire 20th Century. Instead, he was able to focus on the New Labour government's priority 'to make Britain once again a force for good in the world,' insisting that foreign policy 'must have an ethical dimension and must support the demands of other peoples for the democratic rights on which we insist for ourselves.' Predictably enough, Cook was attacked by right-wing commentators. *The Spectator* harrumphed that it was 'bad for Britain' and 'piffle.' But the idea that democracy and peace were the inevitable end-point of human development was already widely accepted, even in conservative political circles.

Writing eight years earlier in 1989, Francis Fukuyama, a senior analyst in Republican President George H W Bush's State Department, had been able to announce the 'End of History' and the victory of the liberal international order across the world. His broad thesis was that, with the West's triumph in the Cold War, the debate over how societies should organise themselves was now over. The standard that all major states had achieved, or were aiming for, was liberal democracy. In Fukuyama's words, 'liberal insofar as it recognises and protects through a system of law man's universal right to freedom, and democratic insofar as it exists only with the consent of the governed.'

Fukuyama's article has been much criticised by those that haven't read it. As a result, his nuanced and cautious points are often overlooked: notably his far-sighted observation that 'Russia and China are not likely to join the developed nations of the West as liberal societies any time in the foreseeable future.' Also, he points out that while history appeared to have ended for the wealthy countries of the West, 'the vast bulk of the Third World remains very much mired in history.'

In the 2020s we are all mired in history. We have seen major warfare, great-power rivalry, international terrorism, cyber attacks, the collapse of the liberal order, and the rise of populist nationalist politics in every continent. As this book shows, Britain has played an outsized and inglorious role in this process.

WHY ARE THINGS SO BAD?

We all know things are bad. But why are so many things so bad at the moment? Part of the answer is contained in the question.

Too often, international crises are considered in isolation. We study the war in Syria, examining who supports Bashar al-Assad and who supports the dwindling band of rebels. Then we turn to China and Russia's increasingly antagonistic relations with the democratic world. These are often viewed as unrelated issues, whereas in fact they are interwoven like a carpet bought in the suq of Aleppo before it was flattened by Assad's bombs. Since the late 1990s, and in an accelerated manner since 2001, Western foreign policy has been dominated by an idea and an activity. The idea, a continuation of Fukuyama's thesis, was liberal hegemony, 'an ambitious strategy in which a state aims to turn as many countries as possible into liberal democracies like itself.' Liberal hegemony, and the liberal international order, was an appropriate ideology for the end of history. That is why it appealed to Robin Cook who espoused it as a cornerstone of New Labour's foreign policy in 1997 (although he did not use the term explicitly). Liberal dominance is an attractive concept, particularly if one chooses to believe the often-repeated claim (broadly true) that no two democracies have fought a war against one another. While the global liberal hegemon has undoubtedly been the United States, Britain has often propelled this movement. As we shall see, it was Tony Blair's forceful advocacy that pushed the United States into a 'liberal intervention' in Kosovo aimed at protecting human rights, a key moment in shaping this concept.

On 11th September 2001, Al-Qaeda terrorists flew hijacked airliners into crowded buildings in New York and Washington, killing 3,000 people. It soon became clear that the so-called '9/11' attackers, motivated by a twisted version of militant Islam, were directed by fugitive international terrorists based in the lawless anarchy of Afghanistan. Suddenly, the value and importance of spreading the liberal international order became more urgent. This turned the idea into a febrile activity. The liberal hegemon forced countries to take sides. As President George W Bush himself put it: 'Every nation, in every region, now has a decision to make. Either you are with us, or you are with the terrorists.'

As we will see, the activity was intervention, first in Afghanistan, then in Iraq and across much of the Middle East. These operations consumed and dominated America's national security policies from 2001 to the 2020s, but Britain also played a key role. British special forces were in Afghanistan from the start. It was Britain that led the way collecting intelligence that apparently justified the invasion of Iraq. Just as his predecessor Blair had over Kosovo, David Cameron played the role of chief advocate for the Libya intervention. All this activity has directly affected the West's relations with Russia and China. China is controlled by the Communist Party and Russia controlled by Vladimir Putin. As authoritarian states, they cannot be reconciled to the ideology of liberal hegemony that contains an assumption of representative democracy. And, distracted by military interventions elsewhere, Western countries have devoted insufficient energy to their relationships with China and Russia, allowing these relations to deteriorate over time. In the same period, Russia and China have built up their own military and strategic capabilities, learning from Western mistakes. Russia has directly intervened in conflicts to counteract America in Syria and, more recently, in Ukraine, where it has staged a full-scale invasion. China's role has been more subtle, taking advantage of America's preoccupations to expand its trade and diplomatic networks in Asia-Pacific and the Americas. As the military strategist David Kilcullen has observed, China has been 'simultaneously accelerating their development of new military capabilities.' Everything is connected.

RISE IN NUMBER OF CONFLICTS

The breakdown of our liberal international order is not merely a feeling of insecurity and danger. In hard numerical terms, the world of the 2020s is more violent, more dangerous and more divided than at any time since the end of the Cold War in 1991. The number of deaths from conflict encompassing warfare, terrorism and other forms of political violence has been consistently higher since 2012 than at any period since the end of the Cold War. The number of individual conflicts worldwide (encompassing state and non-state violence) has risen to unprecedented highs – from 116 conflicts in 1997 to 167 in 2020, according to a database maintained by the University of Uppsala. Put simply - more people are dying in more wars and conflicts.

One of the most devastating conflicts has been in Afghanistan, where Western powers, led by the United States, made a rushed exit from the country in 2021, leaving their Afghan allies at the mercy of a resurgent Taliban. We will see how in 2006 Britain's military sought to create a success story in Helmand province, Afghanistan, in part to draw attention away from its failures in southern Iraq. Instead, this manoeuvre ran out of control, creating a major new front in Afghanistan's seemingly endless civil war.

Britain is seemingly happy to see some conflicts continue. As we shall see in Chapter 9, the United Kingdom is a hawkish outlier on supplying arms to the kingdom of Saudi Arabia, enabling it to continue its war on Yemen, even after the Biden administration scaled back its support for it.

But it's not just armed violence. 'War is the continuation of politics by other means,' wrote Carl von Clausewitz, the military theorist, in *On War*. And wars take many forms. Trade warfare occurs when a country raises taxes (known as tariffs) on imports of a certain product or commodity to put pressure on the exporting country and to protect domestic industries from international competition ('protectionism'). Unsurprisingly, the exporting country usually responds by slapping its own tariffs on exports of the first country, resulting in a trade war. Until 2018, these wars were considered something best left to history, best not revived. One simplistic reading of the history of the 1930s is that a trade war started by the United States led to the Great Depression, the rise of nationalism, Hitler and, ultimately, World War II. The truth is more complex and debate continues over the role of trade wars, exchange controls, and economic contraction in fuelling the Great Depression. But all serious analyses agree that the imposition of trade barriers in the pre-war period amounted to 'the strongest adverse shock to international trade in modern history.' Once again, the numbers are very clear: world trade plummeted from $68 billion in 1929 to $26 billion in 1932. As the League of Nations observed at the time: 'These figures show clearly, not only the extraordinary shrinkage of world trade, but the acceleration in the rate of decline from year to year.' Douglas Irwin, an economist and historian, noted that it was foreign retaliation to the United States' decision to impose tariffs, as much as the tariffs themselves, which caused the slump in world trade in the 1930s.

President Donald Trump was proud to advertise his unorthodox views on trade. Perhaps the most jarring of these was his assertion in March 2018, on Twitter, that 'trade wars are good, and easy to win.' However little historical evidence exists for this claim, Trump's actions suggested he believed it was the case. Six days after Trump's bold tweet he imposed tariffs on aluminium and steel imports from all countries except for Argentina, Australia, Brazil and South Korea (a temporary exemption for the EU lapsed at the end of May 2018). Predictably, the affected countries responded, with the EU and Canada imposing retaliatory tariffs and bringing the dispute to the World Trade Organization (WTO). In response, Trump refused to appoint a judge to the WTO's Dispute Settlement Body, rendering it inoperative. In future, trade disputes would be settled by power and threat, not by rules or judgements.

A month after his steel and aluminium tariffs, Trump announced approximately $50 billion in proposed tariffs on imports from China in response to findings that China had repeatedly stolen America's intellectual property. The allegation was almost certainly correct; but a trade war was probably not the correct remedy. China retaliated and by December 2018 the US was threatening $200 billion of tariffs on imports from China if agreement was not reached by the 'hard deadline' of 1st March 2019. There have been other sallies and feints in this war:

- threats to impose tariffs on European car exports to America
- a forced renegotiation of the North American Free Trade Agreement (NAFTA) between Mexico, Canada and the United States
- withdrawal from the Trans-Pacific Partnership (TPP)

Again, the numbers don't lie: world net trade reached a high point in 2017. It fell sharply the following year, before plummeting as the Covid-19 pandemic stunted the world economy. Disentangling the effects of the pandemic from the wider trade crisis is difficult. But there can be no doubt that global trade faces severe challenges, particularly from China.

Britain's own approach to world trade is less confrontational than Donald Trump's, but one can hear echoes. In deciding to leave the EU via a 'hard' Brexit (leaving the EU's Single Market and Customs Union), Britain sought to negotiate an agreement that would make it harder to trade with its number one trading partner and world's largest economic bloc. It was a trade deal whose desired outcome was to erect new barriers to trade. Inevitably, the process was fraught with tension and rancour. A new trade war between the UK and EU over certain food products cannot be ruled out. We shall examine these factors in greater detail later.

RISE IN AUTHORITARIANISM

Other numbers demonstrate the dangers facing the liberal world order that we have taken for granted for so long. According to

Freedom House, a US non-governmental organisation that has tracked the progress of democracy worldwide for decades: 'In 2020, the number of Free countries in the world reached its lowest level since the beginning of a 15-year period of global democratic decline, while the number of Not Free countries reached its highest level.'

Even in countries with robust democratic systems, respect for the rule of law and the institutions of democracy has declined. There is no longer any debate over whether Russia attempted to interfere in the 2016 US presidential election campaign that Donald Trump won. According to a court filing from Robert Mueller, the Special Counsel investigating Russian interference in the 2016 presidential election, Trump's campaign manager, Paul Manafort, shared internal polling data with a political consultant, Konstantin Kilimnik, who was 'assessed to have ties to a Russian intelligence service.' Earlier, Trump was forced to accept the resignation of his first National Security Adviser General, Michael Flynn, who was found to have lied about his contacts with senior Russian diplomats with whom he had shared sensitive information. Trump's bombastic style, prone to extraordinary statements, exaggerations and outright falsehoods, makes it hard to assess the seriousness of much of what he says (this may be intentional). Notoriously, on 27th July 2016, Trump said to a large crowd at a Florida campaign rally: 'Russia, if you're listening, I hope you're able to find the 30,000 emails that are missing.' On exactly the same day, 'conspirators attempted after hours to spearphish for the first time email accounts at a domain hosted by a third-party provider and used by [Presidential candidate Hillary] Clinton's personal office. At or around the same time, they also targeted 76 email addresses at the domain for the Clinton Campaign,' according to an indictment from Special Counsel Mueller against a group of officers of Russia's military intelligence service (the 'GRU').

Were President Trump's actions the equal of President Richard Nixon, who resigned in 1974? As the *New York Times* reported then, the fatal blow to Nixon's presidency came when his own Republican congressmen decided to vote to impeach him on charges of obstruction of justice. Forty-four years later, Trump's presidency was kept alive by members of his own party; partisan support for 'their' man transcended any desire to hold him to account. They supported Trump even after he had refused to accept the clear results of the 2020 presidential election. On 6th January 2021 – incited by an incendiary Trump speech nearby – a mob of armed Trump supporters stormed the US Capitol, in a thwarted attempt to prevent the certification of the election results. As a result of persistent lies by Trump and his acolytes, most Republican voters now believe, against all the available evidence, that Joe Biden's victory in the 2020 election was rigged.

What is the health of British democracy? The British Electoral Commission, the watchdog supposed to investigate voting malpractice, is largely toothless. In 2017, after investigating the campaign finances of the three major political parties during the 2015 general election, the Commission fined the Conservatives, Liberal Democrats and Labour the maximum amounts allowed under the regulations. The Commission's Chairman, Sir John

Holmes, pleaded to be allowed to impose more impactful fines: 'This is the third investigation we have recently concluded where the largest political parties have failed to report up to six figure sums following major elections, and have been fined as a result. There is a risk that some political parties might come to view the payment of these fines as a cost of doing business; the Commission therefore needs to be able to impose sanctions that are proportionate to the levels of spending now routinely handled by parties and campaigners.' Sir John's plea was ignored. In 2021, the Prime Minister, Boris Johnson, announced plans, 'to strip the Electoral Commission of the power to prosecute law-breaking, just weeks after it launched an investigation into his controversial flat refurbishment [Johnson had undertaken an expensive upgrade to his private quarters and sought funding from unidentified private donors].'

The ability for hidden money to dominate British politics is built into its ramshackle, make-it-up-as-you-go-along system. In Britain, the 'unincorporated association,' effectively an ad hoc group whose membership, finances and purpose are not disclosed, is able to make political donations. The association must register with the Electoral Commission if it makes political donations of more than £25,000 in a calendar year, but these unincorporated associations are under no obligation to reveal their membership, source of funds, or objectives. Each one that is created can donate £25,000 under the radar. In a supposedly transparent, democratic country there is nothing to prevent significant donations by special interests passing completely unnoticed.

BRITAIN STILL MATTERS

Everything is connected. To understand the new turbulence, we need to understand the historic decisions that pitched us into its midst. Part of this is people in Britain being realistic about the country. Some on the left in Britain take pleasure in referring to Britain as a 'small island' (as we shall see, this is not geographically or strategically correct) with little impact or autonomy. On the right, the opposite is often the case, with overblown statements declaring that Brexit will make Britain 'Great again' as it takes its rightful place as a commercial and political leader of the world. This second aggrandising approach is summarised in the tone of a campaign promoted by the Department of Education for children to celebrate 'One Britain One Nation Day,' a new national festival taking place on 25th June. The chorus of a song to be trilled out by patriotic schoolchildren has the lyrics 'Strong Britain, Great Nation' (repeated four times.)

The reality is that Britain is a large economy, has a powerful military, and is rich and highly influential. Many of its policies and actions have had an impact that has been lasting, sustained and disproportionate. These policies have demonstrated Britain's ability to make a difference on the world stage. Britain has often played the equivalent role of a 'marginal buyer,' the figure that is willing to pay the highest price, and therefore define the market for a given commodity. Repeatedly, Britain has been the geopolitical player without whom certain events or incidents would not have happened. Britain has not been the sole actor, nor has it necessarily been the most significant, but it has, surprisingly often, been the one that tipped the balance.

In the following chapters we shall look at British foreign policy choices since the New Labour era, starting with Tony Blair's approach to the breakdown of Yugoslavia in the 1990s. Some distance from the events of the past 25 years allows us a greater sense of perspective than available to some politicians and commentators in the thick of things. British leaders have often argued that, in relation to America, they take the role of 'Greeks in this American empire.' A more considered, intellectual, far-sighted contrast to America's 'great big vulgar, bustling people, more vigorous than we are and also more idle, with more unspoiled virtues, but also more corrupt,' to quote Harold Macmillan, British Prime Minister between 1957 and 1963.

Whether justified at the time, Macmillan's sense of superiority does not hold up in the present day. Britain's foreign policy structures and institutions have let the country down: its insistence on underfunding its foreign policy system has made it harder to reach the right decisions at the right times, as we saw with the UK's intervention in Libya. A lack of geopolitical thinking was seen in the Cameron government's approach to China. Unable to take a nuanced position on increasing economic engagement, its willingness to kowtow to every aspect of China's national interest led to an unprecedented crisis within Britain's oldest and closest intelligence alliance, the 'Five Eyes.' Britain's financial institutions, including its network of offshore tax havens, make the UK the global leader in money laundering. By doing this Britain helps prop up the thieving regimes of corrupt countries such as Russia. And the UK parliament, fixated on short-term tactical gain and media posturing, shows itself incapable of taking strategic decisions. This was demonstrated comprehensively in the vote over military action in Syria in 2013, where politicians fought over near-identical proposals where the apparent objective was to embarrass the other side, rather than to address the tragedy of Syria's civil war.

Finally, Britain's fixation with its colonial past and its misplaced national self-importance has been a constant and unhelpful factor in foreign policy with former colonies such as India. There, Britain is desperate to agree a trade deal with the ethno-fascist government of Narendra Modi, which has shown itself to be both incompetent and morally repugnant. The UK prioritised a trade deal with distant Australia, with whom it has minimal trade, for the same post-imperial cultural reasons, in place of key trade markets on the doorstep in Europe.

How did we get to this point? The answers are not to be found in dry foreign policy reports, in the texts of international treaties or in theoretical concepts about international relations. Having worked in this field for more than 20 years, I have repeatedly seen that dysfunctional institutions smother the hard work of talented people. The most important factor remains leadership: individual choices made by national leaders, senior diplomats and heads of intelligence agencies. While I draw on contemporary reports, academic journals and published memoirs, a lot of this book is based on unique sources: activists who have shared their experiences directly with me, policy practitioners, rebel fighters, expert analysts. I also have an insider's analytical perspective from years in public service, including on the front lines in Iraq and Afghanistan, at other times attending National Security

Council meetings, witnessing government on the ground. But I also want to give space to the people at the receiving end. Those whose lives have been upended and transformed by the wave of conflict and instability created by the leaders of distant and powerful countries. From my experiences in Zimbabwe, Nigeria, Yemen, Iraq, Afghanistan and the Caribbean, I know that it is these people, who don't get to give press conferences and broadcast interviews, who bear the brunt of Britain's foreign policy choices.

To understand ordinary people's lives is to understand the impact of Britain's foreign policies. One of these ordinary people is a midfielder in a second-tier Kosovan football team called KEK. His name is Bler Thaci and his story is at the centre of the next chapter.

2. KOSOVO: WAR IN EUROPE

'Every footballer has a bad moment to go through.'
Footballer Bler Thaçi, interviewed by Panorama Sport Albania,
21st November 2018

AN ALBANIAN FOOTBALLER

FOR BLER THAÇI, 2019 was an eventful year. Let go by his
Albanian team Besa Kavajë after a solid, but not stellar season,
he returned to his native Kosovo and the team he had played with
as a junior, KEK. As a 20-year old, Thaçi had his best playing years
ahead of him. But he had hit a rut at Besa, where he struggled to
secure a place on the starting lineup. He explained the reasons
with disarming honesty: 'This is what happened to me and to be
honest... I was a bit overweight. I developed a boring training
routine, but again without reaching my optimal physical shape.
But in football it is more difficult to get back into the lineup than

to leave it. Already, there are a few weeks that I feel very fit and I will fight hard to convince the staff that I am getting into the shape I was in last season.'

The significance of a mid-tier Balkan footballer's struggles to stay in shape may not be obvious. But Thaçi is a child of Kosovo's turbulent years at the turn of the millennium when ethnic Albanian Kosovars were being driven from their homes by a Serbian-led campaign of ethnic cleansing. His mother, Remzije Thaçi, slept in forests and dodged sniper fire to try to get food. Her journey was typical of many Kosovar Albanians. With her family, she moved into a refugee camp in Macedonia in early 1999, but by August she was back in Kosovo. There, she gave birth to a son, on 4th August 1999. She named Bler Thaçi, after Tony Blair.

Bler Thaçi's name is not unique. The practice of naming young Kosovars 'Bler' (or in some cases 'Tonibler') reflects the reverence with which the former British Prime Minister is held in Kosovo. What feels like a quirky historical footnote tells us something important about Blair's central role as the leading advocate of Western intervention, both in Kosovo and in general, at the turn of the millennium. Robin Cook may have signalled his government's foreign policy approach in principle in 1997, but it was Blair who explained what it meant in practice. In Chicago in April 1999, Tony Blair set out his 'doctrine of international community,' centred around the idea of military intervention in other countries for humanitarian reasons. As Blair delivered his speech, the Serbs were refusing to capitulate and internal support for their leader, Slobodan Milošević, was hardening. NATO jets were bombing the headquarters of Serbia's state television station, killing civilian journalists. NATO argued that this attack on the media counted as a legitimate military operation against 'the very brains of Milošević's military apparatus and leadership.'

Yugoslavia was formed in 1918, bringing together several Balkan peoples who had been living in the Austro-Hungarian empire. As Yugoslavia disintegrated during the Croatian and Bosnian wars of the 1990s, Kosovo, with its majority ethnic-Albanian population, had been sullenly peaceful. Yugoslavia's biggest new nation, Serbia, controlled the province. By 1997, however, the determinedly non-violent Kosovo Albanian leadership of Ibrahim Rugova was under pressure from the increasingly active Kosovo Liberation Army (KLA). The KLA, a nationalist paramilitary force, had received a significant boost in 1997 when the collapse of law and order in neighbouring Albania led to thousands of weapons seeping across the border into its hands. As the situation deteriorated, Serbian security forces responded with escalating violence to KLA operations, which often targeted Serbian police and officials. In March 1998, Serbian police killed 22 Kosovar Albanian fighters in Drenica and most of the civilian population abandoned the area. Increasingly, Kosovars fled into neighbouring Macedonia, upsetting the delicate ethnic balance there and destabilising that impoverished nation. By the end of 1998 more than 300,000 Kosovars had fled their homes, various ceasefire agreements were systematically being flouted and negotiations between the Federal Yugoslavia and Kosovar leaders had stalled. The KLA was determined to achieve independence, but the international community rejected this idea, fearing further regional destabilisation. There were also serious and legitimate questions about the nature of the KLA's leadership. As late as February 1998, Robert Gelbard, the US special envoy to the former Yugoslavia, asserted that the KLA 'is, without any questions, a terrorist group.'

In January 1999, 45 Kosovar Albanians were killed by Serbian security forces in the village of Račak. Serbian claims that the dead were all KLA fighters were undermined by the presence of a woman and elderly men among the dead. An EU Forensic mission concluded: 'There were no indications of the people being other than unarmed civilians.' Public opinion in NATO countries began to shift behind an armed intervention to end human rights abuses against Kosovar Albanians. An attempt to find a diplomatic solution through negotiations in Rambouillet in France proved unsuccessful and NATO forces began bombarding Serbia and Serbian targets in Kosovo. This was a significant moment: 'The first sustained use of armed force by the NATO alliance in its 50-year existence.' NATO, which had been formed to protect Europe against Soviet aggression, was trying to keep the peace in southeastern Europe, in a conflict that had nothing – at least directly – to do with Russia.

The air campaign did not deliver the expected results. As the distinguished scholar of international relations, Professor Sir Adam Roberts, noted, 'the most extraordinary miscalculation of the whole Kosovo campaign [was] ... that Belgrade would be likely to give in after a short period, perhaps only a few days, of bombing. This illusion appears to have been widely held in NATO headquarters and national capitals.' Instead, NATO appeared to be bombing increasingly soft targets, unrelated to Serbia's military or security apparatus, in an attempt to break the Serbs. In May 1999, five US laser-guided bombs hit the Chinese embassy in Belgrade, killing three civilians. While China had, with Russia, opposed any military action against Serbia, this was not a deliberate or justified target. President Clinton apologised for the mistake which was later attributed to incorrect CIA intelligence and the use of outdated maps to direct the guided munitions (an explanation revealing such extraordinary incompetence that many Chinese did not believe it). The incident led to frostier relations between China and America and huge crowds of protesters besieging the US Embassy in Beijing.

Milošević was not surrendering and NATO's airstrikes had not stopped the Serbian repression of Kosovar Albanians: on the contrary, they appeared to be speeding it up. As Blair made the case for a ground invasion publicly and privately to President Clinton, the US President became frustrated by the British leader's apparent enthusiasm for deploying an army that would largely comprise American troops. The fact that most of the military hardware involved in the aerial campaign was American did not detract from the fact that, 'Blair and his leading government ministers became NATO's propagandists-in-chief for [the Kosovo war] in general, and for the "ground option" in particular, at a time when President Clinton's support for such an offensive was restricted by unfavourable congressional and public opinion.' It was Blair's war, not Clinton's.

Eventually, after 78 days of aerial bombardment by NATO, a land invasion took place. But it was not a contested fight: Serbian security forces retreated from Kosovo in June 1999, handing over authority, if not formal sovereignty, to a large multinational army known as the Kosovo Force (KFOR), combining NATO members in an uneasy cohabitation with Russia. The province was in chaos with hundreds of thousands of Kosovars, including Bler Thaçi's mother Remzije, ejected from their homes by Serbian security forces during the air campaign, now sleeping rough in the countryside and many more in hastily assembled refugee camps in neighbouring countries.

Blair's Chicago speech and 'his' liberal intervention in Kosovo arguably defined British foreign policy for the next two decades. So his speech is worth detailed study. However, given that it is regarded as the birth of a foreign policy 'doctrine,' Blair's original text is not particularly clear. Writing eleven years later in his memoirs, Blair summarised his speech as: 'A very simple notion: intervention to bring down a despotic dictatorial regime could be justified on the grounds of the nature of that regime, not merely its immediate threat to our interests.' But in his speech, the notion is never spelled out simply. While describing the situation in Kosovo, Blair drew heavily on the precedent of World War II: 'We have learned twice before in this century that appeasement does not work. If we let an evil dictator range unchallenged, we will have to spill infinitely more blood and treasure to stop him later.' Blair then cites three cases that could justify intervention: genocide, oppression causing a migration crisis that destabilised neighbouring countries, and states based on unjust minority rule, for which he cited the example of South Africa. Blair was keen to stress that military action might not be appropriate in all of these cases and offered five considerations when considering interventions:

First, are we sure of our case? War is an imperfect instrument for righting humanitarian distress, but armed force is sometimes the only means of dealing with dictators.

Second, have we exhausted all diplomatic options? We should always give peace every chance, as we have in the case of Kosovo.

Third, on the basis of a practical assessment of the situation, are there military operations we can sensibly and prudently undertake?

Fourth, are we prepared for the long term? In the past we talked too much of exit strategies. But having made a commitment we cannot simply walk away once the fight is over; better to stay with moderate numbers of troops than return for repeat performances with large numbers.

And finally, do we have national interests involved? The mass expulsion of ethnic Albanians from Kosovo demanded the notice of the rest of the world. But it does make a difference that this is taking place in such a combustible part of Europe. I am not suggesting that these are absolute tests. But they are the kind of issues we need to think about in deciding in the future when and whether we will intervene.

These tests add to the confusion. Asking 'do we have national interests involved?' appears to contradict Blair's guiding principle that action could be justified even were there was not an 'immediate threat to our interests.' Blair himself was self-aware enough in his memoirs to acknowledge that applying those tests to the decision to invade Iraq in 2003 shows that it was a 'finely-balanced' decision. And perhaps the most important question of all isn't even mentioned: who operates these tests? Who decides whether the conditions have been met?

Blair's 'doctrine of international community' formed part of a wider speech that touched on the centrist domestic policies he shared with US President Bill Clinton (at the time described as the 'Third Way'), a discussion of globalisation, and wider observations on relations with Russia. On Russia, he urged: 'We must not let our current differences set us on a route towards the mutual hostility and suspicion which has too often characterised our relationship in the past.'

In 1999, Blair was still relatively newly-elected and had a need to present himself and his ideas on the world stage. But with his comments on intervention, Blair was reflecting his and his country's position at the hawkish end of the argument. Britain was not part of the consensus but was pushing other countries to adopt new norms. This process had unfolded during the previous year as the United Nations Security Council debated the appropriate response to increasing violence in Kosovo. During these debates it became clear that military action would not be authorised by the Security Council because it would be blocked by Russia and China. To counter this, as early as October 1998 the British Foreign Office circulated arguments to NATO allies that acknowledged existing norms: 'Security Council authorisation to use force for humanitarian purposes is now widely accepted (Bosnia and Somalia provided firm legal precedents). A UNSCR [United Nations Security Council Resolution] would give a clear legal base for NATO action, as well as being politically desirable.' However, the paper continued, 'force can also be justified on the grounds of overwhelming humanitarian necessity without a UNSCR.' The paper argued that 'military intervention by NATO is lawful on grounds of overwhelming humanitarian necessity.'

Perhaps the most interesting thing about Blair's 1999 speech was that he singled out only two national leaders for criticism, implying that they were eligible for ousting under the Blair doctrine. One was obvious: Slobodan Milošević was the target of the Kosovo operation. In 1999, the second was jarring: Saddam Hussein. Blair was speaking four years before allied troops invaded Iraq and 30 months before the horrific events of 9/11 that provided the questionable *casus belli* for that operation. And yet the seeds of that conflict were already being sown. Less than six months earlier, the Iraq Liberation Act had passed the United States Congress with overwhelming levels of support. It stated: 'It should be the policy of the United States to support efforts to remove the regime headed by Saddam Hussein from power in Iraq and to promote the emergence of a democratic government to replace that regime.'

THE RISE OF INTERVENTIONISM

In spite of the Foreign Office advice and Blair's Chicago speech, humanitarian military intervention without authorisation by the UN Security Council had little precedent in 1999. The

UN Security Council exists to be the supreme guarantor of international peace and security. As the United Nations itself explains:

> **Under the Charter of the United Nations, all Member States are obligated to comply with Council decisions.... In some cases, the Security Council can resort to imposing sanctions or even authorize the use of force to maintain or restore international peace and security.**

It is true that other countries had previously taken military action without UN Security Council authorisation. But these were always justified as acts of self-defence, perhaps the oldest principle governing international military operations. Even when these justifications stretched credibility, such as the United States' invasion of Panama in 1989, the argument of self-defence was rigorously relied upon. By contrast, the Kosovo operation was justified purely on humanitarian grounds. There was no self-defence argument. NATO countries did not claim to be under serious threat or risk. Instead, the action was legitimised by its intended outcome - the destruction of Milošević's security and military system to prevent a humanitarian crisis in Kosovo. Indeed, most of NATO's leaders insisted it was not a war (contrary to Tony Blair's words in Chicago): both the British defence secretary George Robertson and NATO Secretary-General Javier Solana maintained this stance, with Robertson repeatedly stating in parliament 'this is not a war,' preferring to use the term 'conflict.'

The British view was markedly different to that of other European partners, notably France and Germany. As Ivo Daalder, who would later serve as the US Ambassador to NATO, observed in March 1999, the French view on the use of force by NATO was clearly that it should only happen under the auspices of a UN resolution.

The British idea that a UN Security Council resolution was unnecessary for humanitarian military action was a radical departure from agreed international norms. Yet this was barely discussed at the time. There was no serious public debate of the implications for global peace and security of NATO acting without such a mandate. In 1990-1991, in response to Saddam Hussein's invasion of Kuwait, the UN had shown a unity of purpose, authorising both the operation to remove Iraqi forces from Kuwait and the subsequent peacekeeping mission in northern Iraq to protect Iraqi Kurds from further repression by Saddam's forces. At this time, Britain had been at the forefront of efforts to strengthen the effectiveness of the UN Security Council. Writing in 1991 to his Foreign Secretary Douglas Hurd, Britain's Permanent Representative to the United Nations, David Hannay, was able to report a United Nations Security Council at the height of its powers. Hannay saw a particular role for Britain, 'in ensuring that the Americans remain alive to the advantage of action through the UN, as opposed to going it alone or to bilateral dealings with the Soviet Union.' Observing the realities of the post-Cold War world, Hannay argued: 'There is a great deal to be said for thinking imaginatively about an expansion of the UN's capabilities and activities in the field of collective security.'

By 1999, then, Britain was claiming that a UN resolution was no longer necessary for the authorisation of military action in Kosovo. Yet it devoted a surprising amount of its diplomatic capital trying to secure one. This led to wildly contradictory arguments from British diplomats. On the one hand the British argued that NATO's actions in Kosovo were justified by fundamental human rights considerations that had primacy over the UN itself. At the same time, these same British diplomats were claiming a UN justification for military action under UN resolutions 1199 and 1203 (which called for an immediate cessation of security operations by Yugoslav forces). Also at the same time these diplomats argued no UN authorisation was needed anyway for this type of 'limited' military operation. If these arguments are hard to follow it's because the policy was contradictory. When Milošević agreed, somewhat unexpectedly in the face of a possible land invasion, to a ceasefire in June 1999, the arrangements were made under UN auspices – with significant concessions to the UN's role. First, the UN was given a central role in the administration of Kosovo; second, KFOR was made up of NATO and non-NATO countries including Russia, and third, an earlier proposal to give NATO personnel unimpeded access throughout former Yugoslav territory, was dropped.

Britain's contradictory behaviour at the UN was the symptom of a much bigger inconsistency at the heart of its foreign policy. The UK considers itself a pillar of the liberal international order, also known as the 'rules-based international order.' This clumsy term summarises the architecture of international institutions and customs that have preserved peace and security since the end of World War II. At its centre is the UN Security Council. By sending a message that this system of global rules could be jettisoned whenever convenient, Britain struck an early, heavy blow against that order. Through its behaviour towards Serbia, Britain treated this liberal international order sitting at the centre of the Western alliance as a flexible instrument, open to interpretation to suit its needs on any given topic at any time.

America similarly viewed the international order as valuable only when it served its wider interests. But there is an important difference: America's position as a superpower. From a viewpoint of national self-interest, global rules can only limit America's freedom of action, for example its freedom to use overwhelming force against adversaries. By contrast, global rules enhance the power and influence of a medium-sized country such as Britain. Britain's permanent membership of the UN Security Council enhances Britain's influence over global affairs. Circumventing or undermining the UN reduces British influence.

A FAILURE THAT RESEMBLED SUCCESS

Should we discuss UN mandates and woolly concepts of international law when ethnic cleansing was taking place in Kosovo in 1999? Kosovars were dying and being displaced from their homes by Milošević's security forces and NATO took action to prevent that. Was that wrong? Was the Kosovo operation a success? These feel like the more relevant questions. In reality, the Kosovo intervention was a failure that looked like a success. The Blers and Toniblers of Kosovo, carrying the name of a controversial international figure, are the living testaments to the perception of success. If we remind ourselves that the sole (and novel) justification for military action was humanitarian protection of Kosovar Albanians, the primary measure of success would have to be the impact on that group. The absence of NATO troops on the ground during the air campaign allowed Serbian forces to continue to pursue far more draconian operations in Kosovo, with the intention of causing maximum disruption to neighbouring states. The Serbians believed this would cause NATO countries to back down as they became preoccupied with maintaining order in Kosovo's neighbouring countries. NATO concluded later: 'The aggression by Serb military and police forces against Yugoslav citizens of Albanian origin in Kosovo forced more than 1.5 million Kosovars from their homes, nearly a million of whom fled or were forced out of Kosovo.'

On this point the facts are clear: while Serbian forces were already engaged in widespread attacks on Kosovar civilians in the period prior to NATO's airstrikes, this persecution actually increased when NATO's campaign began. As Adam Roberts, professor of international relations at Oxford University, observed of the military action: 'In the short term it failed to stop, and probably even exacerbated, extreme violence against Kosovars.' The reliance on air power, based on an understandable reluctance by NATO's leaders to sustain military casualties, made it very unlikely that the military action itself would limit Serbian atrocities. But it allowed the Serbs a clear window of opportunity to 'finish the job' of ethnically cleansing Kosovo's Albanians. This problem was clearly identified at the time, in the Defence Select Committee of the House of Commons. Nevertheless, the operation continued and the use of land forces was ruled out repeatedly, giving the Serbs the assurances they needed that their work in Kosovo would continue unhindered.

A detailed analysis of casualty figures by Professor Taylor Seybolt, an expert in the protection of civilians in conflict zones, shows that the Kosovo and related operations to manage refugees were, at best, neutral in effect, or possibly resulted in greater casualties overall. Once KFOR ground troops deployed, the newly emboldened KLA took the fight to Serbians and Roma living in Kosovo, with hundreds targeted and killed – most of whom appeared to have had no connection with Serbian repression. But the political success of the operation was the making of Tony Blair: it put him on the global map as a serious leader of stature and courage. The British military leadership, which had been sceptical of a Prime Minister of the left, recognised Blair's willingness to put his reputation on the line for something he believed in. 'He was robust and courageous,' said General Guthrie, chief of the British defence staff. The Kosovo operation allowed Blair and the British military and foreign policy establishment to believe that humanitarian military intervention helped the world.

HUMILIATING RUSSIA

Putting NATO troops on the ground in Kosovo would probably have prevented the massacres and displacements of Kosovars that took place during the air campaign. Blair's defenders would point to the fact that he was urging the ground option from an early stage. So perhaps the problem was not Britain's willingness to be hawkish, but the failure of the wider international community to be hawkish enough, quickly enough. This attractive argument is beset with problems. First, under the scenario of the early land forces' intervention, the KLA violence against Serbs and Roma would presumably have unfolded more intensely, if the Kosovars had felt they had the Serbs on the back foot at an earlier stage. Therefore, the casualties inflicted by the KLA on Serb and Roma civilians would have been much higher still.

A related point is the nature of Kosovo's independence movement. There is no doubt that Serbian forces were guilty of human rights violations against Kosovar civilians. But there is also credible evidence that Kosovar militants continued to kill Serbians in the aftermath of the withdrawal of Serbian forces. These actions included harvesting the organs of murdered Serbian detainees and heavy involvement in the European trade in illegal drugs and people trafficking. This involvement went all the way to the top, involving Kosovo's President Hashim Thaci, according to an investigation carried out by the Council of Europe, a human rights organisation.

More important is the wider geopolitical impact of the ground war in Kosovo. This was a moment of huge strategic tension between Russia and the West. Russia had a long-term relationship with Serbia and saw NATO action without UN support as a direct threat to its interests. At a famously delicate moment during the inception of the ground invasion of Kosovo, the American General Wesley Clark, NATO's Supreme Commander in Europe, ordered the British General Mike Jackson, commander of NATO forces in Kosovo, to seize Pristina airfield. This was under the control of a Russian military contingent that had pre-empted

NATO. General Jackson did something that isn't supposed to happen: he countermanded an order from a senior officer, with the words: 'No, I'm not going to do that. It's not worth starting World War III.' Instead of a direct confrontation with the Russians, a diplomatic solution was found in which the Russian military was technically made part of KFOR. The peacekeeping operation in a small corner of former Yugoslavia had come close to an armed confrontation between NATO and Russia.

In the run-up to NATO's action in Kosovo, Russia had made it very clear that it opposed military intervention. Russia's Foreign Minister, Igor Ivanov, made clear both in public and in private discussion with other foreign ministers that it would veto any such action. A later assessment from a former Russian foreign ministry official admitted that Russia's policy had been 'inflexible and unimaginative.' However, Russia may have been relying on a NATO commitment to abide by the determinations of a multinational forum to deal with the crisis in the former Yugoslavia, the Contact Group, of which Russia was a member. In the event, NATO consulted neither the Contact Group nor Russia prior to its air campaign – a humiliation for Russia. Indeed, the Russian Prime Minister, Yevgeny Primakov, was flying to Washington when he heard that the NATO campaign had begun. He turned his plane around and returned in fury to Moscow. While Russia's position was obstructive and indifferent to human rights, it was not irrelevant. Russia is a vast country made of up numerous semi-autonomous republics. Serbia's experience with Kosovo created a worrying precedent for any Russian separatist region. At the same time as the Kosovo conflict unfolded, Russia was facing down an armed independence movement in the breakaway region of Chechnya.

Russia's humiliation came at a time of economic and political chaos at home and was subsequently a low point in Russia's international standing. This humiliation cemented Russia's support for Serbia, rendering future co-operation over the former Yugoslavia less likely. The Russian analyst Maxim Samorukov observed in late 2019, 'Serb and Russian political elites bonded over their shared grudges against the United States and NATO. The two countries soon revived a century-old narrative of Slavic brotherhood, bringing their political relationship unprecedentedly close.' This resulted in Serbia and Russia developing very close economic relationships. Gazprom, Russia's state-owned gas giant, owns 51 per cent of Serbia's oil and gas monopoly and Moscow is viewed as a friend and a protector. As a result, Russia has no incentive to allow Serbia to normalise its relations with Kosovo or the West. If Serbia reaches agreement with Kosovo, it will be able to join the EU, permanently taking it out of Russia's sphere of influence.

Kosovo deeply affected Russia. It was the turning point in Russia's relations with the West; the moment at which Russia concluded that it would not trust the West or NATO countries, in spite of the Cold War having come to an end. Liberals in Russia were forced to defend the charge that the 1990s policy of cosying up to the West had delivered nothing but humiliation. Meanwhile, nationalist fervour swept through Russia. In August 1999, the embattled President Yeltsin appointed an unknown former KGB officer called Vladimir Putin as his Prime Minister. Putin made himself immediately popular by restarting Russia's war against the breakaway republic of Chechnya, justifying his actions on a series of apartment bombings across Russia blamed on Chechen terrorists. As the Russian-born journalist Masha Gessen wrote of Putin's move: 'Politicians formerly known as liberals praised the Russian army for its performance there; one said it was regaining its dignity.'

As we shall see in later chapters, Vladimir Putin has become a profoundly destabilising and cynical global leader. He owes much of his early success to the wave of angry nationalism created by the Kosovo operation. But Putin also bases his foreign policy thinking on the concept of grudge and vengeance, all the while generating nostalgia for the 'great' days of the Soviet Union when the country was a feared superpower. Russia's humiliation in the late 1990s must be repaid in kind. Putin spelled this out very clearly in 2014 when he annexed the Crimea, part of the sovereign territory of Ukraine. In a speech to Russia's parliament in March 2014, he stated:

It was our Western partners who created the precedent; they did it themselves, with their own hands, as it were, in a situation that was totally analogous to the Crimean situation, by recognizing Kosovo's secession from Serbia as legitimate.

Later in his speech, Putin appeared visibly angry as he said, 'They wrote it themselves. They spread this all over the world. They screwed everybody [the actual word used is closer in meaning to anal rape]—and now they are outraged!' Six years later in Syria in 2020, Russia behaves as the leading international power, coordinating between the Syrian government, Kurdish rebels, and a range of other foreign countries.

Russia justified its invasion of Ukraine in early 2022 by falsely claiming that Ukraine's leadership were 'Nazis' who threatened Russia. A desire to expand its territory and resentment at the West's growing reach in eastern Europe were almost certainly the real drivers. During its invasion, Russia massacred civilians in cities it occupied across Ukraine, including Bucha, Kharkiv and Chernihiv. Russia's war crimes are its own responsibility. But they do not absolve Britain of the need to examine its own decision-making in the Kosovo campaign.

BLAIR'S AWAKENING

For Tony Blair, a religious man with a strong sense of vocation, Kosovo was, in his own words, his 'awakening' on foreign policy. When he visited the province in July 1999 he was greeted as a hero, showered with bouquets and cheered at the airport. 'During the bombing campaign, his words were our bread, our hope,' said a tearful bystander who had survived the bombardment. Bler Thaçi himself was well aware of the significance of his name from a tender age. In 2010, he and the other young Kosovars named after Blair met the great man at a special ceremony in Pristina. 'It was the best feeling for me as a child to appear in front of all the audience so big that they had come to see Tony Blair.... It was an unforgettable feeling,' he recalled.

Both for Blair himself and for Britain's foreign and defence policy community, the false conclusion that Kosovo was a success vindicated Britain's position as an outlier for military action, even without UN authorisation. It became a pillar of Britain's interventionist approach. Had Kosovo gone badly, had there not been a generation of Blers and Toniblers growing up in Kosovo celebrating the leadership of Britain's former Prime Minister, things might have been very different in later conflicts. Because it was deemed to have gone well, Kosovo became a model to repeat, rather than being seen as a weakening of the rules-based international order.

What really happened in Kosovo? NATO's military operation failed to save Kosovar lives and came at the cost of the Serbian lives lost to Kosovar militants and the rise of a Kosovar-Albanian mafia operating across Europe. That may be a price worth paying for the ultimate freedom and independence of the Republic of Kosovo. The undermining of the rules-based international order and Russia's retreat into rejectionist bad actor on the international stage, though, feels like a very high price to pay. But the highest price of all would come next: Kosovo turned out to be a necessary preliminary for Britain's greatest intervention and its greatest act of global vandalism: the war in Iraq. Just as the Kosovo intervention could not have happened without the forceful lobbying of Tony Blair and the legal creativity of British lawyers, the Iraq war could not have happened without the contribution of the British intelligence services.

3. IRAQ, MI6 AND A BOTCHED INVASION

'How come all the good reporting I get is from SIS?'
CIA Director George Tenet to his Iraq Operations Chief,
February 2002

'I was trained by the best. British Intelligence.'
John Mason (played by Sean Connery) in the 1996 film *The Rock*

In the Iraqi man's voice was the sound of deep, existential despair. His son had been kidnapped. At the time kidnappings were rife across Baghdad. An entire industry existed to seize people, assess their value, and extract returns from desperate family members willing to pay a ransom. Outside Iraq, the complexity of its kidnap industry was little understood. Low-level criminals specialised in seizing unwary individuals and passed them on to appropriate gangs higher up the value chain, depending on the hostage's identity. Shi'a Iraqis and foreigners would tend to reach Sunni insurgent groups. High-value foreigners (Westerners and officials, with Western officials commanding the highest price) would go to the jihadist groups, such as Al-Qaeda in Iraq, who would seek millions in ransom payments from Western governments. Many countries paid these sums. In other cases, the jihadists decided to behead the hostage, posting grisly videos on the internet for maximum impact. Iraq's state security agencies, largely controlled by Shi'a politicians, took part in this lucrative trade, too. They had a record of imprisoning and torturing young Sunni Iraqis, such as Umar's son, until the family paid a sufficient bribe for their release. In sum, Iraq's kidnap industry was a microcosm of the sectarian chaos that had been created in the country since the allied invasion and occupation in 2003.

He was begging for help, believing that Allied intelligence resources would be able to locate and rescue his son. The tragic case of Kenneth Bigley, a British hostage beheaded in September 2004, showed that the UK's ability to prevent these tragedies was actually limited. In the end, as a relatively 'low-value' hostage, this family settled the case in the depressingly normal way – by selling their most treasured possessions and begging loans from a wider circle of relatives. They paid the ransom – to a militia that operated within the Iraqi Ministry of the Interior – and their son was returned, physically unharmed and mentally scarred.

In a few weeks the boy's parents aged visibly, a grey pallor etched into faces that were normally creased with smiles. In Iraq after the 2003 US-led invasion such stories were being repeated daily. Personal tragedies were further traumatising a country that had been through decades of war, insurrection and terrorism.

SHI'A AND SUNNI

In a corner of a glass cabinet in the British Museum sits an unprepossessing block of clay, about the size of a football, broken at one corner, covered in spiky inscriptions. This cuneiform tablet, the Nabonidus Chronicle, records one of the most important transitional moments in world history: the fall of Babylon and the rise of Persia. In 540 BC, Cyrus the Great, ruler of Persia, crossed the river Tigris somewhere near Irbil and began his invasion of Mesopotamia, birthplace of agriculture and settled societies: the cradle of world civilisation. Herodotus tells us that Cyrus's men diverted the course of the river Euphrates, enabling his armies to wade through the ankle-deep waters into the strategically important city of Opis. Shortly afterwards, King Nabonidus surrendered to the Persian armies. His better-known son Belshazzar is thought to have been killed during the fall of Babylon. Magnanimous in victory, Cyrus ended the Babylonian captivity of the Jews, allowing them to return to Jerusalem to begin construction of the Second Temple.

With the invasion of Babylon, which Herodotus tells us was the most fertile land in the ancient world, a contested frontier between the Persian and Semitic cultures was established. To this day, Iraq represents the frontline between the Arab and Persian worlds. It is also the frontier between the often rancorous two sides of the Muslim world – Sunni and Shi'a.

Theologically, the distinction between Sunni and Shi'a Islam – which goes back to the earliest days of Islam – is limited, technical and lies beyond the scope of this book. But it is important to know the general distribution of their followers in the Middle East and something of the differences between them.

1. Distribution of Sunni and Shi'a in Iraq

The vast majority of Muslims are Sunnis, who focus heavily on the teachings (the '*sunna*') of the Prophet Muhammad. Sunnis dominate the Middle East states of Saudi Arabia and the oil-rich Gulf emirates. Historically, Sunnis have also run Iraq. Such rulers have ranged from the Abbasid caliphate in the 8th Century to the late 20th Century dictator, Saddam Hussein.

By contrast, Shi'as, estimated at 10–13 per cent of Muslims, tend to revere their leading clerics, known as Ayatollahs. Shi'as dominate the north-eastern countries of the Middle East, most notably Ayatollah-run Iran. Shi'as also form most of the population in Iraq. Historically, however, they have been disenfranchised there and have periodically risen up against authority, such as against British rule in the 1920s.

This disgruntlement has increased in recent decades as Saudi petro-dollars have promoted a narrow version of Sunni orthodoxy that has stressed the 'heretic' nature of Shi'a Islam. In the 21st Century, then, Iraq is slap bang in the middle of a battle for power between oil-rich Sunnis to the west and Iranian Shi'a Ayatollahs to the east. While sectarian rivalry does not lie at the heart of all the country's problems, Iraq's geopolitical faultline has made it prone to invasion, instability and religious rivalry.

After 2,500 years, this faultline is still soaked in blood. Since US-led forces invaded Iraq in 2003, armed conflict has repeatedly broken out between the Sunni minority and the Shi'a majority. During his 24-year rule from 1979, Saddam Hussein cannily avoided overemphasising the differences between Sunni and Shi'a. After deposing him, the US abruptly disbanded Iraq's army and police forces without replacing them. Unsurprisingly, security collapsed and resentment of the invaders grew. Many Iraqis saw the country's new government and coalition troops as puppets of Western imperialism and, thus, legitimate targets of the resistance to occupation. Islamist jihadists were the most ruthless and effective of these insurgents. Their leader was a Jordanian Sunni, Abu Musab Al-Zarqawi, head of the Iraqi branch of Usama bin Ladin's Al-Qaeda movement. Before the invasion, the Americans had falsely claimed that Saddam's regime had been working with Zarqawi. While this was untrue, after the invasion many former senior members of Saddam's regime did begin to co-operate with the anti-American jihadists. This fuelled the growing insurgency. Within a few months of the March 2003 invasion, a massive suicide truck bomb destroyed the United Nations headquarters in Iraq. A few weeks later, the Red Cross headquarters was targeted by a suicide bomber driving a bomb-laden ambulance.

Attacks on international 'soft targets' were the first step to an even darker campaign by the jihadists to target their fellow Shi'a Muslims in Iraq in order to stoke a civil war. In a letter to Al-Qaeda's leadership in 2004, Zarqawi claimed that the Shi'a had 'augmented their atheism with political cunning... in cooperation with their hidden allies the American.' Zarqawi described Shi'a Muslims as 'the lurking snake, the crafty and malicious scorpion, the spying enemy, and the penetrating venom.' He decried their practice of religion, naming 'patent polytheism, worshipping at graves, and circumambulating shrines' as particularly outrageous activities. While these might sound uncontroversial to the uninitiated, Zarqawi was effectively accusing Shi'a of not being Muslims at all, thereby justifying their killing.

When they lived under Saddam Hussein few ordinary Sunni or Shi'a Iraqis had a deep sense of enmity to the other group. But after the invasion, Zarqawi was seeking to persuade Iraqi Sunnis that they had a duty to attack and kill Shi'a just as much they had a duty to attack the occupying Americans. In March 2004, a month after writing this letter, Zarqawi's group launched a co-ordinated series of attacks on Shi'a Muslims celebrating the Ashura holiday (specifically, a festival celebrated by Shi'a but not Sunnis) killing nearly 200 civilians.

So began a sectarian civil war between mostly Sunni insurgents and mostly Shi'a government-backed forces, some formally part of the state security apparatus, some private militias operating with covert support from Iraq's government. The Shi'a response was often unfocused, targeting Sunnis that had no connection to the terrorists beyond a distant family relationship to a known insurgent. Male Sunni Iraqis were routinely arrested, imprisoned and tortured by the forces of the Iraqi state, thereby feeding the cycle of reprisal and retribution, with violence escalating on both sides.

During my time working in Iraq in 2005-2006, this civil war was growing in intensity. A complex and opaque situation saw a range of Iraqi Shi'a politicians, many of whom had spent years in exile in Iran and maintained strong connections to the security services there, established in positions of power and authority in the new Iraqi state. Later reporting has shown that the Ministry of the Interior had plans to establish an entirely new security force, separate from the Iraqi military and law enforcement, that appeared to be a front for Iranian-controlled Shi'a militias. Rumours abounded of a secret underground torture centre full of Sunni prisoners used by Shi'a militias with the full knowledge of the Ministry of the Interior. These were mostly discounted until they proved, shockingly, to have been true. In November 2005 nearly 200 prisoners were found beaten, tortured and starving to death in an underground government bunker right in the middle of Baghdad. Most of the prisoners had nothing to do with the insurgency but had been selected for their Sunni Arab connections.

Nothing in Iraq is simple: some of the Shi'a militias, such as that led by Muqtada Al-Sadr, were fiercely nationalistic, equally opposed to intervention by Iran or by the United States. But many were (and remain) effectively controlled entities of the Iranian state, working directly to orders issued by the hardline Iranian Revolutionary Guard Corps (IRGC). So, a direct result of the 'liberation' of Iraq was that it was beset with Islamist extremist terrorism and much of its security was under the indirect control of the Islamic Republic of Iran – America's greatest antagonist in the Middle East region. If the invasion of Iraq was supposed to institute a pro-Western, democratic Iraq, it failed, totally.

THE MARCH TO WAR

Indeed, the 2003 invasion of Iraq has proved a tragedy for the Iraqi people and for the wider region, empowering malign actors from Islamic State to Iran's Revolutionary Guards Corps. Iran, the US, Saudi Arabia and Israel are on a hair-trigger for a major conflict. Iraq is riven with political division, a population increasingly at odds with the political class and facing the constant risk of the resurgence of the Islamic State. Despite American efforts, Iran remains the pre-eminent regional power, controlling much of Iraq's political class. But how did this extraordinary failure of foreign policy and strategy come about? And what was Britain's role in all of this?

Among a certain class of neo-conservative American, the removal of Saddam Hussein from power in Iraq had been a priority since the end of the first Gulf War in 1991. For adherents of this ideology, this ousting could be justified purely on the basis that Saddam was a dictator opposed to the United States' interests and, therefore, a threat to global security. With great hypocrisy, Arab dictators and absolute monarchs who supported the United States, such as the rulers of the Gulf States and much of North Africa were not regarded as being similarly destabilising, despite the fact that many of them had supported extremist Islamists over the years. Paul Wolfowitz, who held a variety of defence and diplomatic appointments under successive Republican administrations, first advocated military intervention in Iraq as early as 1992. From 1998, the Iraq Liberation Act made regime change official US policy, passing the United States Congress with overwhelming levels of support from both Republicans and Democrats and signed into law by President Clinton. This act stated: 'It should be the policy of the United States to support efforts to remove the regime headed by Saddam Hussein from power in Iraq and to promote the emergence of a democratic government to replace that regime.'

Initially, the United States showed no signs of committing serious resources to achieve this outcome. A State Department briefing in February 2000 explained: 'The United States believes that if there is to be change, it must come from within Iraq, led by Iraqis. We do not seek to impose an American solution or a foreign opposition on the people of Iraq.'

9/11 changed everything. After the 9/11 attacks, the prospect of US-led regime change in Iraq became a major preoccupation of George W Bush's administration. There was no connection whatsoever between the 9/11 attacks and Saddam's regime in Iraq. This was well-known by intelligence experts at the time and validated in subsequent research based on documents captured from Saddam's fallen regime. But the false connection was widely promoted by political leaders looking for an excuse to attack Iraq. Iraq hawks such as Wolfowitz, Vice-President Dick Cheney and (a convert to the cause) Defense Secretary Donald Rumsfeld frequently made untrue claims about Iraqi links to the 9/11 attackers. In his now famous State of the Union address in 2002, President George W Bush made a connection between terrorism, Iraq, Iran and North Korea, binding them together in an 'axis of evil.' Bush issued a clear threat:

America will do what is necessary to ensure our nation's security.... We'll be deliberate, yet time is not on our side. I will not wait on events while dangers gather. I will not stand idly by, as perils draw closer and closer. The United States of America will not permit the world's most dangerous regimes to threaten us with the world's most destructive weapons. Our war on terror is well begun, but it is only begun. This campaign may not be finished on our watch – yet it must be and it will be waged on our watch.

The threat facing the US was actually very different. While Iraq had neither the inclination nor means to attack America, Al-Qaeda had devastatingly demonstrated its intent and capability to do so. But 9/11 was an opportunity for ambitious people close to President Bush to push for regime change. Some of these, such as Paul Wolfowitz, were inspired by a naïve belief that US-style democracy could be forcibly implanted in Iraq, combining a genuine desire to increase political freedom with an assumption that doing so would help America.

The American public still needed a clear rationale for an invasion of Iraq, particularly if Congress was going to authorise the deployment of US troops into a dangerous Middle Eastern battlefield. As early as December 2001, the *Observer* was reporting a 'Secret US plan for Iraq war,' noting: 'US proponents of extending the war believe they can make the case for hitting Saddam's regime over its plan to produce weapons of mass destruction [WMD].' The need for intelligence that demonstrated the existence of Iraq's WMD programme became an overriding priority for the CIA and its allies, including Britain's MI6.

The CIA's Director George Tenet was kept in post by President George W Bush after the presidential election in November 2000, despite having been a Democrat appointee. Tenet quickly became close to the new President, the pair described by one White House official as being 'like fraternity brothers.' This relationship was strengthened in the traumatic days of the 9/11 attacks on the Twin Towers and the Pentagon and the CIA's subsequent prominent role in Afghanistan. Mere days after the attacks, officers from America's Central Intelligence Agency were in Afghanistan forming alliances with the Afghan rebels, building a coalition that could take on the Taliban. The 9/11 attacks had been a humiliation for US intelligence: coming out of a clear blue sky, unpredicted and shocking. After that failure, the CIA in Afghanistan quickly proved its relevance, capability and agility during a remarkable

60-day campaign that saw the Taliban defeated by a mixture of special forces soldiers, Afghan rebels and intelligence agents from the CIA and its allies.

In early 2002, the attention of the Bush administration turned towards Iraq. From that time, Tenet was under pressure to generate incisive intelligence on the country. However, there was a problem: for years, the CIA had regarded Iraq as an unimportant intelligence target. As a result: 'There were four [CIA sources reporting inside Iraq]. And those sources were in Iraqi ministries such as foreign affairs or oil that were on the periphery of any penetration of Saddam's inner circle.' As Tenet observed, 'all the good reporting' came from the British Secret Intelligence Service (SIS, better known as MI6).

A 'DEVELOPMENTAL CASE' FOR WAR

Writing about intelligence is not easy, for two reasons: there is a practical obstacle that intelligence agencies have good reasons to need to keep secrets in order to preserve the security of their operations (this culture also enabled them to cover up their mistakes). There is also an ethical dimension: those serving in intelligence undertake an extremely difficult task in often dangerous circumstances and do so out of a sense of public service and duty. In identifying failings of strategy and policy, I yield to no one in my respect and admiration for those that toil unsung in the shadows. With these caveats in mind, the following is based entirely on information released into the public domain by official inquiries. By definition, this is information that MI6 is content to see made public.

When Tenet expressed his frustration with the thin reports emanating from the CIA's Iraq Operations team, it was because the CIA was not providing the necessary intelligence to make the political case for war, forcing a reliance on British material to carry the argument. The CIA's relationship with Britain's MI6 has tended to involve competition as much as co-operation. So, the fact that MI6 had proved able to provide a slew of high impact intelligence on Iraq's weapons of mass destruction programmes would have been galling to Tenet. MI6's best reporting was being actively promoted by the service's Chief, Richard Dearlove, to senior officials and politicians outside the intelligence field. A report produced in early September 2002 offered, in the words of Dearlove, 'phenomenal access' to Iraq's biological and chemical weapons programme. This report was 'High Impact Intelligence.' It explained that Iraq was actively developing biological and chemical weapons and that plans existed for their use.

This was dynamite. Iraq had been the subject of extensive sanctions, United Nations weapons inspections, and repeated airstrikes by the US and UK airforces. To discover that, in spite of all this international containment activity, Saddam still had access to deadly WMD, made a powerful case for war. The intelligence was effectively saying, in an era of mass casualty terrorism, sanctions, monitoring, airstrikes and inspections could not prevent rogue states from getting hold of WMD. This added weight to the case for war as the only means of preventing Saddam from using these terrifying weapons. The report was considered to be so significant that it was briefed personally by Dearlove to Sir John Scarlett, chairman of the Joint Intelligence Committee (JIC), the British government's pre-eminent intelligence assessment body. On 12th September 2002 Dearlove briefed the contents directly to Prime Minister Tony Blair, when he 'underlined to the Prime Minister the potential importance of the new source [of the September report] and what SIS understood his access to be; but also said that the case was developmental and that *the source remained unproven* [my emphasis].'

A 'developmental' case, with 'unproven' intelligence had already been briefed directly to the Joint Intelligence Committee, the Prime Minister, the Prime Minister's Foreign Policy adviser, the Prime Minister's Chief of Staff and a range of other officials at the apex of the British national security system. At the time, MI6 did not let the report's readers know that it had no direct access to the source of the intelligence. To spell this out in layman's terms: MI6's report, which had been shown round the top of the British policy community, came from a source that it couldn't even name, still less identify.

None of the small number of officials that had been shown the 'unproven' intelligence from the 'developmental' case were expert analysts of chemical and biological weapons systems. Such experts exist in the British system, not as part of MI6 but as part of the Defence Intelligence Staff (DIS), a specialist analytical wing of the Ministry of Defence. But the report, whose distribution was approved personally by Dearlove, was not shown to the DIS experts who could have commented on the credibility and validity of the 'unproven' intelligence. As the Iraq Inquiry observed:

Sir Richard Dearlove's personal intervention, and its urgency, gave added weight to a report that had not been properly evaluated and would have coloured the perception of Ministers and senior officials. The report should have been treated with caution.

On 23rd September, MI6 had issued a second report from the same 'phenomenal' sourcing chain. That stated that the deadly nerve agents VX, Sarin and Soman had been produced at an Iraqi weapons facility and were loaded into a variety of 'containers,' including 'linked hollow glass spheres.' The report was circulated to the same group of high-level officials as the report on 11th September.

As intelligence professionals, it is reasonable to suspect that at least some of the people involved in the production of this report were fans of the work of Sean Connery. While 'linked hollow glass spheres' have not been used in any real-life deployment of chemical or biological weapons, they feature prominently in Sean Connery's 1996 action movie *The Rock*, co-starring Nicholas Cage. In a tense scene, Cage's character pulls a column of linked hollow glass spheres containing VX from a rocket intended to be fired at the unsuspecting population of San Francisco by a dastardly terrorist. Its screenwriter, David Weisberg, commented in 2016:

Anybody in the poison gas community would immediately know that this was total bullshit — such obvious bullshit.

Unfortunately, the 'poison gas community,' notably the DIS specialist analysts, were not shown this report whose distribution was limited to political decision makers and senior officials.

These reports, along with a famously inaccurate intelligence report alleging that chemical and biological weapons could be deployed on the battlefield by Iraqi units within '45 minutes,' formed the core of an intelligence dossier that was released to the public on 24th September 2002 in order to build support for a war against Iraq. This dossier also contained a significant claim that Iraq was trying to acquire uranium from Africa for its would-be nuclear programme (more on this important aspect of the intelligence case later). Given that the case for war depended so heavily on intelligence, it would be reasonable to expect that any doubts or concerns over the intelligence would be articulated at the highest levels as soon as possible. In fact, the opposite was true.

As early as October 2002, members of the British intelligence community began to raise concerns about some of the 'developmental' reporting on Iraq's biological and chemical weapons programme.

By December 2002, even MI6 was questioning internally whether the entire reporting had been invented. Nonetheless, at the same time this now-questionable source was the subject of a discussion between Dearlove and then Foreign Secretary Jack Straw about whether the source would provide 'silver bullet' intelligence to guide the UN weapons inspectors operating on the ground in Iraq. In this discussion, the source's validity was described by Dearlove as being 'still in the balance.'

THE KEY ISSUE: RELIABILITY

MI6 did not share its concerns about its 'phenomenal' source with those relying on the intelligence. As the Iraq Inquiry noted:

The Assessments Staff and most members of the JIC [Joint Intelligence Committee] were not aware at the time of the details of the sourcing chains and that little of the information provided by "reliable sources" was based on first-hand knowledge.

To explain this point, it is necessary to delve into the world of human intelligence, the business of secret agents known in the trade as HUMINT.

While fans of James Bond films will think of MI6 as an organisation focused on sabotage and military-style operations, or using ingenious gadgets that can record an opponent's words or blow up their helicopter, in reality MI6 specialises in HUMINT. At its simplest this means someone with access to sensitive information (known as an 'agent') sharing that information with a representative of an intelligence service (known as a 'case officer' or 'handler').

MI6's job is to gather information of value to the British government that is not available by other means. By necessity this means a heavy reliance on talking to people (agents) with access to secret intelligence. These might be agents with direct access, such as a government official or in the case of Iraq's purported WMD, a scientist working in a weapons programme. More often, particularly with isolated, autocratic countries such as Iraq, this comes from indirect access: an Iraqi based outside the country who regularly travels to Baghdad might be able to speak to people with knowledge of Iraq's WMD activities. These people may have no idea that the ultimate destination of their information is British intelligence. In the case of Saddam Hussein's Iraq, it would be far safer not to know.

It's clear that any use of indirect intelligence puts great weight on the reliability of the agent. If an agent claims to have access to intelligence on something as important as Iraq's WMD in the run-up to a possible invasion, the need to analyse and validate that reporting is essential. The Butler Inquiry, the first inquiry into Britain's misleading intelligence in the run-up to the Iraq war, helpfully explains the practical challenges of HUMINT. It is worth quoting at length:

> **Human intelligence reports are usually available only at second-hand (for example, when the original informant talks to a case officer who interprets – often literally – his words to construct an intelligence report), and maybe third- or fourth-hand (the original informant talks to a friend, who more or less indirectly talks to a case officer). Documentary or other physical evidence is often more compelling than the best oral report, and has the advantage of being more accessible to specialised examination, but is usually more difficult to acquire. Conventional oral reporting can be difficult enough if all in the chain understand the subject under discussion.**
>
> **When the topic is unfamiliar to one or more of the people involved, as can be the case when details of (say) nuclear weapons design are at issue, there is always the chance of misunderstanding. There is in such cases a considerable load on the case officer to be familiar with the subject-matter and sufficiently expert in explaining it. It need only be added that often those involved in providing intelligence may for one reason or another have**

**deliberately misrepresented (or at least concealed) their true
identities, their country of origin or their employment to their
interlocutors, to show how great is the need for careful evaluation
of the validity of any information which eventually arrives.**

The validation of a reporting chain requires both care and time,
and can generally only be conducted by the agency responsible for
collection. The process is informed by the operational side of the
agency, but must include a separate auditing element, which can
consider cases objectively and quite apart from their apparent
intelligence value:

- Has the informant been properly quoted, all the way along
  the chain?
- Does he have credible access to the facts he claims to know?
- Does he have the right knowledge to understand what he
  claims to be reporting?
- Could he be under opposition control – or being fed
  information?
- Is he fabricating?
- Can the bona fides, activities, movements or locations
  attributed to those involved in acquiring or transmitting
  a report be checked?
- Do we understand the motivations of those involved, their
  private agenda, and hence the way in which their reports
  may be influenced by a desire to please or impress?
- How powerful is a wish for (in particular) financial reward?
- What, if any, distorting effect might such factors exert? Is
  there – at any stage – a deliberate intention to deceive?

Generally speaking, the extent and depth of validation required will depend on the counter-intelligence sophistication of the target, although the complexity of the operational situation will affect the possibility of confusion, misrepresentation or deception.

To create a practical example, suppose an Iraqi scientist with reason to know, perhaps because he works in Saddam's WMD programme, tells an MI6 officer that Iraq's programme for chemical and biological weapons are still continuing, contrary to all of Iraq's protestations and the findings of UN inspectors. Suppose, however, that there is a longer reporting chain: someone who works in Saddam's WMD programme (a sub-source) tells someone (a source, or agent), who in turn tells the MI6 case officer. How do we validate this intelligence? Is it corroborated by any other information from another source? (Not unless the movie *The Rock* is considered a corroborating source.) Has the agent been given an incentive to fabricate information? (Yes, as Dearlove explained when asked by Tony Blair, the agent was motivated by ideology and money.) On the face of it, while Butler observed that the 'validation of a reporting chain requires both care and time' it may be that neither care nor time was taken to validate these reports before they were issued to the most senior decision-makers in Britain.

Certainly, the problems with the source of the two September reports became clear to MI6. As early as mid-February 2003 the source had been revealed to have been lying. But at that point MI6 did not tell the key decision-makers who had been briefed in September that their reports were untrue, even though a war against Iraq was looking almost certain. Instead, the reports of 11th and 23rd September were reissued to a wider readership on

3rd April 2003, after the invasion of Iraq. The fake reports were not withdrawn by MI6 until after the war, in July 2003 (although even at this point the Prime Minister's office was not informed of the fact). As the Iraq Inquiry explained:

> **SIS finally met the sub-source in June 2003. He had been involved in Iraq's CW programme before 1991 and had also been involved in Iraq's destruction [of WMD] activities. The sub-source denied that he had provided any of the material attributed to him. SIS concluded that its source was a fabricator who had lied from the outset.**

In September 2003, Dearlove gave evidence to the Hutton Inquiry into the death by suicide of the MoD weapons expert David Kelly. Intriguingly, he stated that the intelligence in the government's famous dossier was 'well-sourced' and 'sound.'

A significant proportion of the intelligence provided by MI6 to justify the war against Iraq was subsequently shown to be inaccurate. Why this happened was a central question of the 2004 Butler Inquiry into WMD intelligence. As Butler observed, 'weaknesses ... of its validation procedures' appears to be at the heart of the problem. It is worth quoting Butler's observations on validation in full:

> **[E]ven taking into account the difficulty of recruiting and running reliable agents on Iraqi issues, we conclude that part of the reason for the serious doubt being cast over a high proportion of human intelligence reports on Iraq arises from weaknesses in the effective application by SIS of its validation procedures and in their proper**

resourcing. We received evidence from two witnesses about the impact of organisational changes in parts of SIS relevant to our Review. Following reductions in SIS's budget in the mid-1990s, these were made with the goal of making overall staff savings and freeing experienced case officers for operational work. *This weakened SIS's internal processes for the quality assurance of agents.* [My emphasis] One of those witnesses also noted that the level of staff effort applied to geographical and functional tasks relevant to our Review was too thin to support SIS's responsibilities. We believe that the validation of some sources on Iraq suffered as a consequence of both problems.

...The Chief of SIS acknowledged to us that a problem had arisen. He attributed it primarily to the shortage of experienced case officers following the rundown of the size of SIS in the 1990s. Our Review has shown the vital importance of effective scrutiny and validation of human intelligence sources and of their reporting to the preparation of accurate JIC assessments and high-quality advice to Ministers. We urge the Chief of SIS to ensure that this task is properly resourced and organised to achieve that result, and we think that it would be appropriate if the Intelligence and Security Committee were to monitor this.

Other studies have been done of the role of British Intelligence in the run-up to the Iraq war. Their consensus is that source validation was inadequate and that MI6 sought to get its intelligence in front of decision makers before figuring out whether it was true. The bigger question is: did this really matter? In Britain, the public's faith in the intelligence services (and by extension the wider government) has been seriously damaged by the false claim about WMD. But of course the gravest damage has been done in Iraq and throughout the wider Middle East. The tinderbox ignited by the 2003 invasion continues to burn in that country and further afield. Terrorists have struck repeatedly in Iraq and Syria. Others inspired by their example have committed mass murder across the world. The whirlwind of destruction wrought by the 2003 war continues to this day and for the foreseeable future.

IRAQ'S CIVIL WAR

Iraq's civil war stumbles on, seemingly endless, from one dismal chapter to the next. When Sunni-Shi'a violence appeared to be escalating out of control, the US targeted Zarqawi who was killed in a missile strike in 2006. Violent attacks by minority Sunni jihadists continued and 2006 saw the formal establishment of the 'Islamic State of Iraq' group. In response to continued sectarian attacks, the US mounted a 'surge' of additional troops in 2007. This reduced sectarian killings but had the side effect of empowering majority Shi'a militias under the protection of the authoritarian pro-Iranian Prime Minister, Nouri Al-Maliki. The surge also mobilised Sunni Arab Iraqis in western Iraq who directly confronted the jihadists claiming to be fighting on their behalf. These Sunni groups, known as the Anbar Awakening, were under the direct control of the US military. In late 2008, the Shi'a Maliki persuaded the US to transfer control of the units and promptly disbanded them. By contrast, the Iranian-backed Shi'a militias have remained a significant and growing feature of Iraq's security architecture to the present day.

As Maliki tightened his grip on the country's institutions, his tendency to sectarianism paradoxically weakened his control. US forces had mostly left Iraq by 2011. He began to order arrests of senior Sunni politicians as well as ordinary citizens, usually on trumped-up charges of terrorism. Sunni Iraqis protested in their thousands and Maliki's security forces took part in increasingly savage responses. In 2013, a raid on a protest camp in a Sunni-dominated area resulted in the deaths of 44 civilians. In this toxic environment, Islamic State (IS) flourished, gaining supporters and power. Defiant support for Islamic State continued to rise in Sunni areas, culminating in major cities falling to Islamic State control. Mosul, Iraq's second city of more than a million people, fell into IS hands in June 2014. As the world looked on in horror, it seemed that all of Iraq might fall under IS control. A hastily assembled international coalition saw Iranian-backed Shi'a militiamen fighting alongside Western special forces and Kurdish separatists. In bloody street-fighting supported by Western airstrikes and shadowy special forces units, Islamic State was rooted out of Mosul and other cities in north and western Iraq.

THE PICTURE NOW

Iraq remains in chaos. Mosul, its second city, remains largely in ruins after the punishing battles of 2016 and 2017 to recover it from the Islamic State. That battle involved thousands, perhaps tens of thousands of casualties in Mosul alone. According to UNICEF, nearly seven million Iraqis are in need of humanitarian assistance and nearly two million are displaced from their homes. Iraq has seen almost 800,000 children lose one or both parents since the 2003 invasion by the US and the UK. Around 200,000 civilians have died since the allied invasion in 2003 and 288,000 when combatants are included (the majority of whom are Iraqi security forces), according to one of the most conservative tallies, which relies on cross-checked media reporting. Other estimates have suggested twice this number.

One of the problems in understanding the scale of destruction in Iraq in recent years is the lack of transparency by Western allies in reporting military actions. Thousands of airstrikes were carried out by the US, UK, French and Australian air forces, among others, against Islamic State forces. Western militaries like to boast of their ability to conduct precision strikes, minimising civilian casualties. We have all watched the silent video feeds from airborne cameras, showing target buildings quietly vapourising. But this creates a delusion. A major ground-up study of 150 airstrikes across northern Iraq identified that more than 30 times the number of civilians were killed than the official allied records claimed. As the study's authors observed: 'This may be the least transparent war in recent American history.'

The bloodletting has not ended. Iraq has never had a functioning criminal justice system. Under Saddam Hussein, Iraqis lived in constant fear of arrest, torture, imprisonment and arbitrary killing by Saddam's security agents. Since the 2003 invasion, the constant violence and unpredictability of Iraqi life has meant that an independent, fair criminal justice system has never been established. Torture is routine and suspects rarely expect adequate legal representation or anything approaching a fair trial. The defeat of Islamic State has given rise to thousands, possibly hundreds of thousands of Iraqis being wrongly accused of membership, or association with IS, often purely on the basis of a denunciation from an aggrieved neighbour or rival, or simply a case of mistaken identity in a society where millions carry the same name. With a law that makes no distinction between committing terrorist acts and support for terrorism, and conviction rates at 98%, what could have been a campaign for justice has become another cycle of vengeance by the Shi'a-dominated majority against the Sunni majority. This leads to cursory trials in which bored judges nod through death sentences in trials lasting a few minutes based on confessions extracted under torture. Over 8,000 people are believed to be on death row, according to local officials. Outside the courtroom, things are no better. In a December 2018 article, a senior Iraqi intelligence officer described 'battlefield executions, murders in detention centres, and coverups organized by the state.' This officer took the view that the court cases were a tiny minority compared to those extra-judicially killed by security forces, militias and private citizens.

THE TRAGEDY OF IRAQ

The tragedy of Iraq is measured culturally as well as in raw numbers. Saddam Hussein was a vicious and bloodthirsty dictator but in spite of this he allowed a surprising measure of religious freedom under his secular nationalist rule. In addition to its large Sunni and Shi'a populations, his Iraq had a varied mix of religious groupings, including various types of Christians, obscure monotheists and even small numbers of Baha'i. The insecurity that has been rife since 2003 has fallen particularly hard on minority groups. In a country where power is wielded by religious militias, Sunni and Shi'a extremists have targeted 'unIslamic' followers of other faiths. Sabean-Mandaeans, followers of John the Baptist, face extinction as a people, having fallen from 30,000 in the mid-1990s to less than 5,000 today. Similarly, Yazidis, a monotheistic religion focused on a peacock-angel known as Melek Taus, were targeted for genocide by the Islamic State (IS). From a population of 500,000 before 2003, at least 200,000 Yazidis fled IS, with another 10,000 killed and similar numbers enslaved by IS. Similarly, after years of persecution and emigration, Iraq's Christians, who numbered around one million in 2003, are now at least half that number. Ancient religious communities that have survived for thousands of years are rapidly disappearing.

Iraq's physical heritage has also been decimated in the years since 2003. In the immediate aftermath of the US-led invasion in 2003, mass looting occurred at the Iraqi national museum in Baghdad. Allied troops ignored pleas from museum staff to intervene, standing aside as 15,000 priceless antiquities were seized from the building, more than half of which have never been recovered. Across Iraq, archaeological and historic sites have been destroyed, sometimes by warfare or terrorist violence, sometimes by allied troops siting their bases inside ancient fortifications. IS's obsessive hatred of any cultural heritage that does not conform to the strictest tenets of Islam has fuelled the vandalism. Much of this has been targeted at Muslim sites: IS supporters believe that shrines to revered figures in Islamic history are idolatrous. But among other targets, possible tombs of the biblical prophets Jonah and Daniel were ruined by IS in 2014, as well as numerous historic mosques. Ancient churches and monasteries across northern Iraq, some predating Islam itself, were bulldozed or blown up.

IS's destructive instincts were not absolute – they made an exception for the sorts of antiquities that could be smuggled out of their territory and sold on the international black market. According to a report in the *Wall Street Journal* in 2017, a French security official judged that IS was making $100 million annually from trafficking looted antiquities from Iraq and Syria. According to a US Department of Justice filing, the Christian fundamentalist Green family in America, billionaires thanks to their ownership of the craft chain Hobby Lobby, paid $1.6 million to a middleman in the United Arab Emirates for thousands of ancient clay artefacts looted from Iraq, despite warnings from an expert adviser retained by the firm. These were destined for a museum in Washington DC that purports to retell history from a biblical perspective. In July 2021, Hobby Lobby agreed to forfeit 5,500 smuggled artefacts.

Political chaos is the analogue of Iraq's chronic violence. In January 2020, a US airstrike killed Iran's Major-General Qassim Soleimani, a man who had done more than anyone alive to increase the power and influence of Iraq's Shi'a militias. Soleimani was a pivotal figure in the fight against the Sunni Islamic State, both in Iraq and Syria. While it is true that IS's defeat could not have been achieved without Western military intervention, it is equally true that the role played by Soleimani and the Iranian-backed Iraqi and Syrian militias was vital. Soleimani's assassination reflected the ongoing political chaos in Iraq.

Protesters objecting both to Iranian interference in the country and to the incompetence and corruption of Iraq's political class took to the streets in cities across the country from October 2019. In November 2019, a remarkable leak of Iranian intelligence files outlined indisputably the degree to which senior Iraqi politicians, from Prime Minister Adel Abdul-Mahdi down, were working to an Iranian agenda, sometimes as recruited agents of the Iranian intelligence services. In late November, protesters set fire to the Iranian consulate in Najaf, objecting to Iran's meddling, an extraordinary act of defiance toward the regional powerhouse. This was particularly notable because it was an act largely undertaken by Shi'a Iraqis, ostensibly the Iraqi community that Iran seeks to protect (and control).

Iraq's authorities responded to these protests with brutality. From October 2019 to January 2020, Iraqi security forces shot dead more than 500 unarmed protesters. Many of the victims were shot by snipers, but other prominent activists were killed in targeted assassinations.

WOULD THE US HAVE INVADED ANYWAY?

The ongoing impact of the Iraq war is not in doubt. The important question is whether it would have happened anyway. Perhaps the United States would have invaded Iraq whatever the MI6 reports said, whatever the strength of the intelligence. We can never know the answer: the small number of those that know the truth are probably not inclined to be honest about it. But there are some useful points of evidence.

On 12th March 2003, only eight days before the start of military action against Iraq, the US Defense Secretary, Donald Rumsfeld, was asked in a press conference: 'Would the United States go to war without Great Britain?' His answer did not rule it out, explaining 'there are workarounds' if the UK did not participate. What looked like a reasonable answer to an important question caused a flurry of British media speculation and howls of anguish from the British military who were deployed in the Gulf and ready to proceed, desperate to be involved. As Tony Blair recalled later: 'By then the military were absolutely determined, rightly, that they would be part of the action from the outset, and took amiss any sense that we might be in the second rank.' Within hours, Rumsfeld had issued a clarification: 'I have no doubt of the full support of the United Kingdom for the international community's efforts to disarm Iraq.' Might the Americans have gone alone without the British? Perhaps, but, at least publically, that could not be countenanced.

A more important and even trickier question is whether there could have been an Iraq war without the input of British intelligence. The evidence suggests that British input was central to the US case justifying the war. We know that 'all the good reporting' that Tenet was seeing in early 2002 was from MI6. Recruiting new agents takes time, particularly if new sources are carefully validated. So it is likely that the problems the CIA had in early 2002 were still affecting them in some way later that year. At the time that MI6's 'phenomenal' reporting was being issued in

September 2002, it is reasonable to assume that the CIA was still heavily reliant on their British counterparts for Iraq reporting.

We also have two further indicators of the importance placed by the Americans on intelligence reporting from the British. The first came in 16 words in George W Bush's 2003 State of the Union Speech. Bush said:

The British government has learned that Saddam Hussein recently sought significant quantities of uranium from Africa.

This was the significant claim, included in the dodgy British intelligence dossier mentioned earlier, that Iraq had attempted to purchase hundreds of tonnes of uranium powder, known as yellowcake, from the African nation of Niger. A President's State of the Union address is not off-the-cuff. It is probably the most carefully written, extensively planned, heavily discussed and debated piece of oratory in the modern world. Michael Waldman, president of the Brennan Center for Justice, spoke of his experience writing the State of the Union for Clinton:

It's not just a speech, it's not just to get applause. It's really a state paper. You start weeks or even months in advance. Every word matters.

In a speech where every word matters, President Bush was telling the world that the story about uranium from Niger had to be true because it had been confirmed by the British.

Like so many other claims made in intelligence relating to

Iraqi WMD, this claim proved to be entirely inaccurate. The Niger yellowcake tale revolved around a single piece of circumstantial evidence. In February 1999 an Iraqi official visited various African countries including Niger, whose very limited exports included uranium. This visit has been confirmed. But in the febrile world of suspicion surrounding Iraq's activities, the allegation grew that Iraq had attempted to purchase uranium from Niger to use in a nuclear weapons programme. That idea has never been confirmed in any intelligence or other evidence and has been repeatedly dismissed by various investigations. The Niger yellowcake allegation was clearly one of the worst-kept secrets in international espionage. A wide range of intelligence agencies acquired knowledge of the Iraqi visit to Niger and drew a range of conclusions, usually far-fetched suggestions that Iraq was buying uranium in huge quantities from Niger for its nuclear weapons programme. These included MI6, GCHQ (Britain's signals-intelligence service), the CIA, the Italian intelligence service, Israeli intelligence and at least one other undisclosed agency. A set of documents which purported to demonstrate contracts between the Iraqi government and Niger were quickly exposed as fake by the UN's nuclear experts, the International Atomic Energy Agency (IAEA). As Hans Blix, the UN's chief weapons inspector observed:

The Niger document was scandalous. If IAEA could conclude in a day's time that this was a forgery and this document had been dancing between the Italians and to British and the Americans and to the French and they all relied upon it and Bush alluded to it and

**mentioned it in the State of the Union message in 2003, I think that
was the most scandalous part.**

But it was not just the IAEA that had concluded this claim was
untrue. About a year earlier, in early 2002, a former United States
Ambassador, Joseph Wilson, travelled to Niger to investigate
these claims on behalf of the CIA and concluded that there was
no truth to them. Wilson described how he had met officials at the
US embassy in Niger as well as a wide range of officials, former
officials and nuclear industry figures. He found no evidence
that Niger had sold uranium and reached a clear conclusion: 'In
short,' Wilson wrote, 'there's simply too much oversight over too
small an industry for a sale [of uranium] to have transpired.' On
Wilson's return to the US he briefed the State Department and
the CIA on his findings and assumed that this issue had been put
to bed. But in September 2002 MI6 repeated the claim, and it was
this that enabled Bush's speechwriters to include it in the State of
the Union.

There is a prima facie reason to dismiss the Niger story based
on a basic understanding of Iraq's access to uranium and Niger's
uranium exports. As the US think-tank the Carnegie Endowment
for International Peace found in research published in 2004:

**Iraq purchased uranium from Niger, Portugal and Brazil during the
early stages of its nuclear program in the 1970s, but by the next
decade halted these imports because it became self-sufficient in
uranium production. In March 2003, Iraq had an inventory of over
500 tons of natural uranium and almost two tons of low-enriched**

uranium. This uranium was kept under IAEA seal and checked annually by the nuclear agency – theoretically unavailable to the Iraqi regime for use in a nuclear program.

It's worth reiterating one point. Since the 1980s Iraq has been self-sufficient in uranium production, with significant uranium reserves on its own territory.

A brief study of Niger's uranium industry further underlines the improbability of these claims: there are two uranium mines in Niger, both owned by a French-led consortium (this has changed its name over the years but is currently called Orano Mining). Orano has traditionally supplied European and Japanese operators of civil nuclear reactors and produces over 2000 tonnes per year. To obtain 500 tonnes of yellowcake from Niger, Iraq would have been acquiring close to a quarter of the annual production and would have had to hide those imports from the consortium that controlled the mines and supplies countries reliant on uranium for their national electricity generation. It is not credible to claim that Iraq could have acquired such quantities of uranium without France and Japan noticing an interruption to their supply. On this basis, the CIA determined that the President should not publicly make this claim.

The ability of Bush's speechwriters to include the claim which had already been so thoroughly discredited by US intelligence required them to rely on the apparently lower verification standards of British intelligence. In his evidence to the Iraq Inquiry, MI6's Dearlove clung doggedly to the idea that British intelligence had a separate, credible line of reporting on the Niger yellowcake story, unaffected by the slew of forgeries and investigations: 'There's no question in my mind that the intelligence is correct,' said Dearlove, apparently oblivious to the basic implausibility of the story. Dearlove was apparently unable to entertain the idea that his 'original intelligence' was, like the forged documents, also fake, not supported or corroborated by any independent evidence. Had anyone attempted to validate MI6's separate intelligence on Niger? Given that all of Joseph Wilson, the International Atomic Energy Agency and the Carnegie Endowment were easily able to demonstrate the impossibility of Niger exporting significant quantities to uranium to Iraq, the only conclusion must be that, yet again, the intelligence was issued by MI6 without any serious analytical attempt to check its truthfulness.

When President Bush specifically and publicly attributed the Niger yellowcake story to Britain, he was doing so for two reasons: the first was that no US intelligence agency would credit the demonstrably false story; the second was that, in spite of this, 'the British government' was (at the time) a credible brand, likely to be taken seriously by his audience. But here lay a paradox: it was only because British intelligence had failed to validate its flaky reporting that the report existed at all. The story was an indication of a lack of professionalism in the British government, not of British credibility.

The reliance by the US on British intelligence to make the case for war when America's own intelligence services had rejected a source reached a high-point with Secretary of State Colin Powell's presentation to the UN Security Council on 5th February 2003. In a wide-ranging speech that was watched all over the world, Powell spoke chillingly of 'the existence of mobile production facilities used to make biological agents,' information which had been received from an eyewitness defector 'hiding in another country with the certain knowledge that Saddam Hussein will kill him if he finds him.' This defector has become one of the most notorious cases of fabricated intelligence in history. His name was Rafid Ahmed Alwan Al-Janabi, but he has become widely known by the codename assigned to him by his handlers, Curveball. In 1999, Curveball left Iraq and claimed asylum in Germany, where he lives to this day. Shortly after his arrival in Germany he began to fabricate intelligence about Iraq's biological weapons programme and especially its mobile production facilities, alleging that the Iraqis had developed trucks that could churn out terrifying weapons from mobile units that could evade capture or discovery by weapons inspectors.

Curveball has been disarmingly straightforward about the untruth of his claims and his motivation for doing so. In a 2011 interview, he stated:

I had the chance to fabricate something to topple the regime. I and my sons are proud of that and we are proud that we were the reason to give Iraq the margin of democracy.

There is also ample evidence that both the CIA and MI6 were doubtful of Curveball long before the rush to war in 2003. A senior MI6 officer told the Iraq Inquiry:

The fact that Curveball was controversial was known right from the beginning.

How Curveball's claims found their way into Powell's crucial speech to the UN remains less clear. According to former senior CIA officer Tyler Drumheller, CIA Director George Tenet called Dearlove at home to negotiate inclusion of some of the latest MI6-issued reports that were ultimately sourced to Curveball. If Dearlove was aware of his service's concerns over Curveball, this was not sufficient to prevent his intelligence forming the centrepiece of Powell's showdown at the United Nations. The subsequent revelation that Curveball had been a fabricator led to the major protagonists, including Tenet and Powell, vigorously defending their roles in books and interviews. As Colin Powell argued:

> **It has been known for several years that the source called Curveball was totally unreliable. The question should be put to the CIA and the DIA as to why this wasn't known before the false information was put into the NIE sent to Congress, the President's State of the Union address and my 5 February presentation to the UN.**

The question might also be put to MI6 – why did you brief Tenet on Curveball's material, knowing it to be unreliable?

POOR INTELLIGENCE

The decision to launch the war on the basis of intelligence required there to be intelligence that made the case for war. MI6 was asked to produce the intelligence and it duly did so. The fabrications and inaccuracies were not, of course, produced in-house by British intelligence. There is no evidence that British intelligence officers knowingly made up stories about Iraq's WMD to satisfy their political masters. But there is ample evidence that British intelligence took insufficient measures to verify the stories they were being told about WMD, promoted these stories ('intelligence') to senior politicians including the Prime Minister, and prevented expert analysts from seeing the same reports. When these reports were proved to have been fake, MI6 didn't tell the people responsible for making the decision to go to war, burying this bad news until months after the conflict. Tony Blair has widely been accused of lying to the country and the world about Iraq's WMD. However, the major source of information available to him was his own, much-vaunted Secret Intelligence Service, MI6. As much as Blair can be accused of poor decision making, he appears to have accurately reflected what he was being told about the 'phenomenal' intelligence being presented to him. It doesn't seem reasonable to expect Blair to have contradicted the advice he was receiving from his world-famous intelligence agency on Iraq's weapons.

Would the Iraq war have happened without the input of MI6 to America's policy community and the executive branch? There are strong indications that it would not: Tenet's complaint in 2002 that 'all the good reporting' was coming from MI6; President Bush name checking 'the British government' in his 2003 State of the Union; George Tenet calling Dearlove at home to get inputs for Powell's speech; Colin Powell relying on British intelligence at key points in his speech to the United Nations; Donald Rumsfeld hastily correcting the idea that the British might not take part. Rather than the 2003 invasion of Iraq being an idea cooked up by neo-conservatives and justified by faulty intelligence, the evidence points to the invasion being an idea made possible by British intelligence. Without it, the war, and the chaos that continues to destroy the wider region, might not have happened at all.

To take this point further, if British intelligence had applied appropriate validation and analytical resources to the issue of Iraq's WMD, it's possible that it would have found the opposite – that Iraq, in fact, did not have these weapons. That the reports to the contrary were, in fact, untrue. If that had happened, would Britain have stood up to America, urging a focus on the existing operations in Afghanistan and cautioning against a costly and unnecessary distraction in Iraq? Could Britain have prevented a war in Iraq with the same power and influence of its intelligence agencies as it was able to bring to bear to cause a war? We shall never know.

POSTSCRIPT

A strange postscript to the inaccuracies of MI6's Iraqi intelligence appears in the foreword to MI6's annual report for 2003, written by Dearlove. This came at a time when the realisation was sinking in that Iraq didn't in fact have WMD and the war had been based on a false premise. 'We risk damage to the credibility of the intelligence community,' Dearlove wrote, 'if the public perception remains that our intelligence may have been wrong. If we can persuade Iraqi scientists involved in the programme to go public, then we may be able to turn the media debate more in our favour and reduce our dependence on the eventual outcome of the physical search.' By this stage, Dearlove was clearly worried about 'public perception' and 'media debate' in the light of the continuing failure to find tangible evidence of Iraq's purported WMD programme on the ground.

In 1968 the doyen of spy writers John Le Carré, himself a former employee of MI6, noted that: 'The British secret services are microcosms of the British condition, of our social attitudes and vanities.' This idea that a country's intelligence services are the truest expression of a nation's character is much quoted, including in my direct experience by British intelligence officers. Applied to the case for war against Iraq, it suggests that Britain is, at the very least, desperate to please, delusional, self-important, and slapdash.

4. AFGHANISTAN: 'GOVERNMENT IN A BOX'

'Time will, doubtless, reveal the true History of all that took place at Cabool at present, we, at least, know, for certain, that, a most blind confidence, totally unwarranted, brought about the danger, and, that, imbecility, unprecedented, completed the catastrophe.'
From the journal of Captain Julius Brockman Backhouse, Bengal Artillery, 1842

I'm in a Merlin helicopter hurtling over rocky ground. The landscape is arid, almost lunar. Deep ravines alternate with gravelly hillsides, 50 shades of brown. Except for the odd flash of brilliant green where the opium poppies grow – Helmand's only successful economic activity. The helicopter is hugging the hills to make it harder to shoot down. This is no idle threat. It is only a week since an American Black Hawk, sent in to evacuate some wounded Royal Marines, was shot down within view of the Forward Operating Base, killing the medical crew onboard. The enemy are the Taliban, a radical Islamist movement that has controlled most of Afghanistan since 1996.

'The most dangerous place in the world' is something people say to make the place they're talking about sound interesting. But Sangin in 2010 was almost certainly the most dangerous place in the world to work for the British state. At a time when Helmand province was seeing the most sustained violence in all of Afghanistan, Sangin was the most violent place in Helmand. Of the 457 British lives lost in the Afghan conflict, more than 100 of those were in Sangin, a remote town with a population of 20,000.

Once we had landed and made our way into the base, I walked up onto the roof of the building that had been a drug baron's palace, commanding a hilltop vantage point. As I made to look out over the parapet to take in the view of the Helmand river valley running northwards, my colleague cautioned me back: the Taliban positions were well within view. Throughout the day, our discussions would be interrupted by sporadic gunfire.

Why was Sangin so dangerous? There are many reasons why, within a larger conflict, a particular place might be especially prone to violence. But much of what happened in Sangin was because it lay at the heart of Afghanistan's opium-poppy country, an important nodal point between producers and processors. And NATO forces, in this case Britain's Royal Marines, were stuck in the middle of a drugs war between people we labelled as Taliban and others we called Afghan police. They were, in fact, both tribal militias protecting their livelihoods in a drugs trade the West had made illegal.

AL-QAEDA VANQUISHED

After the 9/11 attacks in 2001, the world quite reasonably asked why Afghanistan had been allowed to become a failed state. From this lawless swathe of territory, larger than France, Osama bin Ladin's associates had been able to plan and execute the greatest terrorist outrage in history. Bin Ladin's Al-Qaeda operated in Afghanistan as paying guests of the Taliban. The Taliban was not anything approaching a conventional government. It was obsessed with applying ultra-conservative cultural and religious practices, famously banning girls from schools and destroying cultural artefacts such as the gigantic Buddha statues of Bamiyan. But the Taliban had hardly any understanding of geopolitical affairs, relying on its paymasters and patrons in Pakistan's intelligence agencies to manage its external relations. Indeed, the Taliban were so naïve about international affairs that in the desperate days prior to the US intervention in 2001, they resorted to calling the White House switchboard in an attempt to reach President Bush, having no other means of contacting him.

Within a very short period after the attacks on the 11th September 2001, special operations teams from a range of Western countries, led by the US and with the UK in a prominent role, were on the ground working with Afghanistan's anti-Taliban forces. In two short months, the Taliban government was toppled and Al-Qaeda driven from its network of bases and training grounds. While bin Ladin was not captured, other senior members of his network were. A larger number dispersed across the world, some with Al-Qaeda money and ambition to carry out more attacks. But the ability of Al-Qaeda to plan and execute complex operations against Western targets from its secure Afghan base had ended by mid-December 2001. No senior Al-Qaeda figure was apprehended on Afghan soil after this date.

This did not mean that Al-Qaeda was no longer a threat. In April 2002 Al-Qaeda proved it could continue external operations, with an attack in Tunisia that targeted Western tourists (although this attack was planned prior to September 2001). In October 2002 more than 200 were killed in bombings at Bali nightclubs. Terror attacks would continue throughout the decade, some linked back to bin Ladin's networks. But the specific circumstances that had spurred the ambition and sophistication of the 9/11 attacks had ceased to be. The US had completed its initial objectives in Afghanistan by the end of 2001. Twenty years and more than $2 trillion later, that initial success remains intact. Al-Qaeda was never again able to establish a safe haven in Afghanistan and the evidence suggests that from 2001 no terrorist action targeting the West has been successfully planned from Afghan soil. However, the wider ambition to reshape Afghanistan into a stable democracy has failed – with the Taliban in complete control of the country by 31st August 2021.

WEAKNESS OF AFGHAN GOVERNMENTS

Clichés abound to describe the essential difficulty of military operations in Afghanistan. The 'graveyard of empires' where Alexander the Great, the Victorian Britons and Soviet Russia all met their match. Writing his diary in 1842, Captain Backhouse was reflecting on the catastrophic retreat from 'Cabool' (now normally rendered as Kabul) in which a British imperial army and its camp followers of roughly 20,000 were destroyed by Afghan tribal militias. A single British officer rode his wounded horse into the British fortress at Jalalabad, memorably depicted in an 1879 painting by Elizabeth Thompson, all Victorian pathos and heroic failure. This lone survivor, William Brydon, was asked where the army was. He replied, 'I am the army,' sending shockwaves across the British Empire. Afghanistan was a rugged, inhospitable land, peopled with rugged, warlike people. In the West in the 1980s, we were taught to think of the Afghan Mujahidin, portrayed in films such as *The Living Daylights* and *Rambo III*, as heroic warriors combating an evil Soviet empire. Few people took much interest in the fundamental weakness of every Afghan state that has ever existed – whether as an independent monarchy, a Soviet-occupied communist republic, a Taliban Islamic emirate, or a supposedly democratic state supported by Western militaries and development aid. No central government has ever achieved full control over all of Afghanistan's 421 districts.

To illustrate this, some districts of central Helmand were so ferociously fought over by British troops and the Taliban, Musa Qala, Sangin, Nad-e-Ali, that they almost became household names. But there remained a whole district of the province, Baghran, which never came under full NATO control and which was never seriously contested by foreign forces. This same district had been the location of sustained fighting against the Russian occupation. Afghanistan has many Baghrans: places that are always beyond the reach of the supposed power in the land. Afghan governments face the physical challenge of high mountains, deserts and limited infrastructure. They also face the cultural challenge of governing a patchwork of ethnic groups, including Pashtun, Tajik, Uzbek and Hazara. All these have numerous tribal and geographic subdivisions, speak different languages, practise their faith in different ways and, perhaps most importantly, have a range of relationships with neighbouring and regional powers, all of whom pursue different agendas. Afghanistan is a ferociously difficult country to govern, as its turbulent history shows.

BRITAIN'S HISTORY IN AFGHANISTAN

Somewhat confusingly, Britain's part of the modern Afghan story begins in Iraq. Knowing what happened during British military rule in southern Iraq is crucial to understanding what led senior military officers and planners to decide to deploy to Helmand in Afghanistan. The behaviour of the British military in Iraq, and subsequently in Afghanistan, also shares many parallels, which illustrate a wider point about Britain's modern effectiveness during interventions in other countries. So, to Iraq for a short while, before returning to Afghanistan.

From the 2003 invasion of Iraq onwards, the British army was responsible for the occupation and ongoing security of Basra, the country's second city. At this time, the British felt they had a lot to teach the world about military operations in culturally-sensitive environments. Much was made of the fact that Basra was peaceful, that the British forces could patrol with minimal weaponry wearing their berets rather than their helmets. They could do this, it was suggested, because the British Army was more intelligent, experienced and able to conduct 'hearts and minds' operations.

The idea was reported uncritically throughout the early period of the occupation that Britain's long history of soldering in imperial deployments gave it an edge over the Americans in dealing with civilians. In particular, we were told that the 'success' of Northern Ireland meant that the British Army was able to work with, rather than against, the local population.

While their US counterparts may have been better kitted out, a British officer, Lord Attlee, said they had a long way to go to achieve the success of the British in winning over the 'hearts and minds' of Iraqi people. 'The Americans are very, very good at providing overwhelming military force, and now post 9/11, they are prepared to use it – but they are not so good at peace support operations,' Lord Attlee told BBC News Online in June 2003.

At a time when I was walking around with a floppy hat on, no body armour and just a Browning 9mm pistol, the Americans were running around with full body armour, helmets - a very aggressive posture. They seem to find it very hard to establish a relationship with the local population. If you have that relationship and the confidence of the locals, they will help you finger the bad guys. If you are trying to chase the bad guys and they run into a house and you have their confidence, the locals will point and say: 'He's in there.' In principle we carry our body armour, but when you have established a safe and secure environment, you don't have to wear it all the time, because it intimidates the locals. It's our experience of Northern Ireland that makes us so good.

Even the most experienced British reporters appeared to buy into this story. The veteran BBC journalist John Simpson said: 'If they[the Americans]took a leaf or two out of the British handbook they would do themselves and everyone else a favour.' One aspect of this superiority complex was the belief that Britain's previous colonial occupation of Iraq in the 20th Century meant that it had a superior understanding of the country in the 21st. In my experience, Iraqis would often tell British interlocutors 'you know our country, not like the Americans.' It was the sort of harmless compliment that anyone might pay, but was taken seriously by the British who started to believe they had an inherent ability to understand 'the Arab.'

Of course, sometimes we didn't get the joke. The British called one of their main military bases 'Camp Abu Naji' because many Iraqis used this name to refer to the British. It was not widely understood in British circles that this name came from a belief that we were cynical manipulators, working in the shadows to destabilise Iraq. Abu Naji had been the name of the former King Ghazi's driver, who was suspected of assassinating him on British orders in 1939.

Britain was not able to buck the trend facing the rest of the country. During 2005-2006, when Baghdad and Iraq's major northern cities were collapsing into a Sunni-Shi'a civil war, a related dynamic was unfolding in Iraq's deep south around Basra. Militias, some of them with close links to Iran's intelligence services, began to escalate their attacks on British troops, at the same time as sending out death squads against perceived elements of the former Saddam regime. Many of these targets did not have any serious connection to the Ba'athists and were killed merely for representing an alternative to the militias' vision of a Shi'a theocracy. As the occupying forces began to retreat into better protected vehicles, the militias switched to sophisticated roadside bombs that could penetrate armour plating. These so-called EFPs (explosively formed projectiles) were made in Iran and were widely used by Iran-backed militias in Lebanon. They were clear evidence of external support for the insurgents. Meanwhile, ordinary Iraqi citizens were acutely aware that the British occupiers had brought neither peace nor security, and still less a functioning justice system.

By 2006, British troops in Basra devoted most of their resources to guarding their own heavily-fortified bases. The actual centres of population were increasingly abandoned to Iraqi militia control. After making a deal with Shi'a militia leader Ahmad Al-Fartusi, who could accurately be described as a radical terrorist, British forces were withdrawn from urban centres and redeployed to Basra airfield. Future British patrols in Basra city could only be undertaken with permission from the Jaish Al-Mahdi, one of the most violent militias. David Kilcullen, the pre-eminent counter-insurgency expert who at the time was advising the American General David Petraeus, judged that the British had been 'beaten in the field.' Petraeus himself observed: 'The short version is that the Brits have lost Basra, if indeed they ever had it.' Basra, Iraq's gateway to the Persian Gulf and one of the largest cities in the Arab world, had been turned over to a bewildering array of criminal gangs and radical militias.

But Britain's final humiliation in Basra would come in March 2008. Security in Basra had completely collapsed and Iraq's Prime Minister Jawad Al-Maliki had had enough. But it was also the Easter holidays and British General Barney White-Spunner, a product of Eton, Sandhurst and the Household Cavalry, had gone skiing in Austria. Al-Maliki took matters into his own hands and deployed the Iraqi army to retake the city, without any reference to the British forces on the ground, supposedly responsible for the security of that part of Iraq. The US army sent its advisers to work with the Iraqis; the British were completely sidelined, holed up in their base at Basra airport. As former intelligence officer and historian Frank Ledwidge recorded: 'When the commander of the British brigade visited [Al-Maliki] at his operational headquarters during the battle, the officer was left waiting outside. Maliki never trusted the British again.' Meanwhile, the American troops deployed on the ground alongside the Iraqi army were cheered by a population that was desperate for a credible force to take back control from the militias. Numerous ordinary Basrawis interviewed at the time by reporters covering the military operation expressed their disdain for the British failure to tackle the militias. A year later the last UK troops left Basra airfield, handing over to an American force.

The failed Iraq operation had cost the lives of nearly two hundred British troops with several hundred injured. In the same period, around 10,000 Iraqis living in the British zone of operations lost their lives. Britain's reputation for military prowess and counter-insurgency expertise, particularly with its American partners, was in ruins. This strategic failure is no reflection on the individual bravery and professionalism of the British armed forces and their civilian partners. During Al-Maliki's Operation Charge of the Knights to retake Basra, many British soldiers were desperately unhappy that their role was nugatory: their instinct being to head towards the sound of gunfire but their orders were to stay put. But there can be no avoiding the fact that an army that celebrated its centuries of knowledge of counter-insurgency operations and particularly its knowledge of Iraq, had been comprehensively defeated.

TO HELMAND

Afghanistan's attraction to Britain's military top brass was partly that it wasn't Iraq: it allowed the British a fresh stage on which to demonstrate their military capabilities to their American allies. As a senior British officer observed: 'Basra was a political and military defeat. But at least it allowed us, in very senior military eyes, a "better go" at Afghanistan, in a rural province – Helmand – where the conventional strengths of UK forces, including its air power, could be brought to bear clear of the urban mire.'

Although it is a very poor country, Afghanistan has a sophisticated agri-business sector that produces a high-value crop for processing and export worldwide. Unfortunately, the crop in question is the opium poppy and the product is an illegal drug, heroin. Most of Afghanistan's opium is produced in Helmand, the country's largest and most important agricultural territory. While Western countries have an insatiable demand for Afghanistan's high-value export, they also have an unappeasable desire for it to be criminalised. Ironically, Helmand owes its agricultural prowess to a huge US-financed Cold War-era scheme, the Helmand Valley Project, that dug hundreds of irrigation canals across the province. While Helmand stayed a governance desert it became an oasis of agricultural wealth. This brought with it economic change and some instability as newly settled farmers struggled to interact with the indigenous population and disputes flared up over now-valuable land. Inhabitants who did not benefit from these new canals became marginal and resentful. This complex, multifaceted society was riven by deep internal conflict.

Since the British decision to go into Helmand was largely to deflect attention from the failure in Basra, very little attention was paid to these realities on the ground. When the first troops arrived in April 2006, they failed to take account of their history there. In the 1840s, the British had mounted punitive expeditions into Helmand that left the Alizai tribe feeling they had been victimised to the detriment of their historic rivals the Barakzai. At the Battle of Maiwand in present-day Helmand in 1880, the Alizai and Barakzai briefly united with other tribes to defeat the British-Indian imperial army. While this engagement might not have been remembered in Britain, it has assumed a totemic significance in Afghan national consciousness as a triumph against colonial oppression. Maiwand features in songs, in legendary tales told to children and in the imaginations of many Afghans, particularly Helmandis, and the victorious Afghan commander, Ayub Khan, is a national hero. Almost certainly, a British force would arrive in Helmand with a worse reputation than in any other Afghan province. Famously, Ashraf Ghani, President of Afghanistan until he fled from the country in August 2021, said: 'If there's one country that should not be involved in southern Afghanistan, it is the United Kingdom.'

As the Helmand scholar Dr Mike Martin found when he looked up the historic records of these engagements, the British had taken little or no interest in its own history in Helmand. According to the British Library, the official records of Britain's 19th Century escapades had not been accessed at any point during Britain's Helmand campaign. Helmand's more recent history also appeared to have been missed by the British. They failed to understand that they were walking into a flashpoint region. From the communist coup to the Russian invasion and the mujahidin resistance, particularly complex fighting took place in Helmand. There, pre-existing local inter-tribal struggles over land and access to resources, rather than high-flown ideological factors, dominated factions and conflicts. As Martin found, the Western narrative of a war fought by religiously-motivated mujahidin against Soviet Russia and Afghan communists was not what ordinary Helmandis experienced. For example, the Akhundzada family, prominent in the Alizai tribe, portrayed themselves as key figures in the mujahidin, but also collaborated with the Afghan communist government's security service (and later collaborated both with the Taliban and with US forces).

By the time of the British intervention in 2006, Helmand had returned to its traditional position as the world-leading opium-growing territory. In the eyes of Western military planners, the challenge could be framed simply: the corrupt provincial leadership, entwined with the opium trade, was causing the

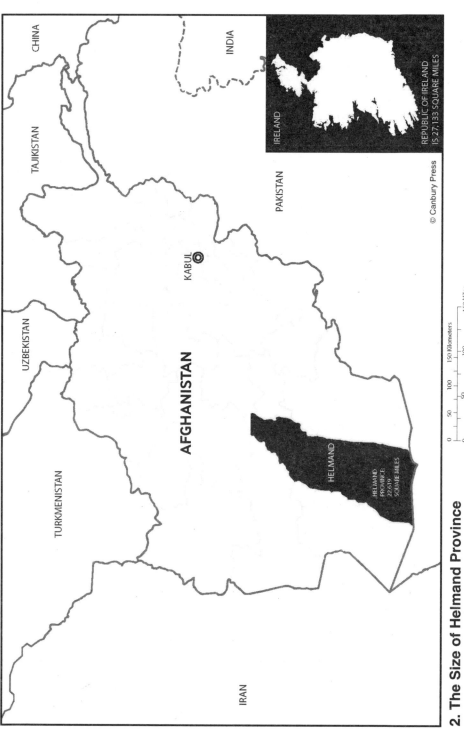

CHINA

INDIA

IRELAND

REPUBLIC OF IRELAND
IS 27,133 SQUARE MILES

TAJIKISTAN

PAKISTAN

© Canbury Press

UZBEKISTAN

KABUL

AFGHANISTAN

TURKMENISTAN

HELMAND

HELMAND
PROVINCE:
22,619
SQUARE MILES

IRAN

0   50   100   150 Kilometers

0   50   100   150 Miles

Scale 1:6,900,000

2. The Size of Helmand Province

population to side with the Taliban. The British, with their self-designated historic expertise in counter-insurgency, would be able to establish a more responsive administration that would encourage the population to turn their back on the Taliban, while reducing the main source of income, poppy farming.

The focus of senior British military officials planning the Helmand intervention was on ensuring that the army had the opportunity to do 'some real soldiering' after the Basra humiliation. As Matt Cavanagh, a former Special Adviser to Gordon Brown has written of the recommendations of the military chiefs of staff to the Cabinet at the time:

> the Chiefs advised that a stint at the overall ISAF [the NATO force] command in Kabul together with taking on the largest and potentially most difficult province, Helmand, as part of ISAF's move into the south was an appropriate level of ambition for a country with the UK's military capabilities and its place in NATO and the world. Indeed, the Chiefs came close to arguing that only Britain could play this role, rescuing the campaign and prompting the Americans as well as other allies to redouble their efforts and fully commit to the ISAF plan rather than their narrower counter-terrorist objectives.

According to written evidence to a parliamentary inquiry by former British Ambassador to Afghanistan Sir Sherard Cowper-Coles: 'The then Chief of the General Staff, Sir Richard Dannatt, told me in the summer of 2007 that, if he didn't use in Afghanistan the battle groups then starting to come free from

Iraq, he would lose them in a future defence review. "It's use them or lose them". Dannatt has denied saying these specific words. But there is plenty of evidence that the British military was thinking in these terms. Dannatt himself declared in a lecture to Chatham House in 2009:

> **There is recognition that our national and military reputation and credibility, unfairly or not, have been called into question at several levels in the eyes of our most important ally as a result of some aspects of the Iraq campaign. Taking steps to restore this credibility will be pivotal – and Afghanistan provides an opportunity.**

At the same time, British ministers tried to avoid this intention of doing 'real soldiering' from leaking out: the public emphasis of the deployment was on counter-insurgency and reconstruction. As Secretary of State John Reid famously remarked: 'We would be perfectly happy to leave in three years time without firing one shot.' He was roundly pilloried for this statement, mostly by his political opponents, particularly once it emerged that the British ended up firing 4 million rounds in their first year and 46 million during their entire time in Helmand. But Reid's statement was reasonable: he had been briefed to expect a mission focused on developing infrastructure and providing farmers with profitable alternatives to growing poppy.

The problem was that, as a condition of their deployment, the British insisted that Sher Mohammad Akhundzada, the opium kingpin of Helmand, be removed from his post as the provincial governor. By his own admission, Akhundzada 'sent 3,000 of [his henchmen] off to the Taliban.' He later denied having done this. But it is clear that Akhundzada gave drugs money to Taliban commanders, both to protect his narcotics operations and to keep the British pinned down by fighters. Akhundzada had also previously managed Helmandi conflicts by judicious use of drugs money and targeted violence, which had allowed a measure of stability, albeit limited, in a complex situation that the British little understood. The British were unable to replace Akhundzada and his people with a capable, uncorrupt, and responsive provincial administration.

So the British became partisan players in a decades-old power struggle, infused with drugs money and meddling from the Pakistani leadership of the Taliban, known as the Quetta Shura.

Britain began to embrace its counter-narcotic mission with alacrity, partnering with Afghan security forces to destroy opium crops. In doing so they were destroying the livelihoods of many Helmandi farmers, while hoping that these people would instead grow alternative crops, such as wheat, which offered less than a tenth of the potential income. All the while, the Helmandi poppy growers were well aware of some key facts. Afghanistan had its own epidemic of opium addiction, but its crop was largely being grown to satisfy demand in the West. Not all farmers had their crop destroyed – appropriate payments to the Afghan police could ensure that you would be excepted. And the CIA were known to be working with people alleged to be some of the most powerful drugs lords in the land, including Ahmed Wali Karzai, brother of the President Hamid Karzai. Similarly incomprehensible was the failure of the British or American governments to do anything to prevent Pakistan from supporting the Taliban. Indeed, far from sanctioning Pakistan, they showered it with aid and attention. Understandably, many ordinary Afghans concluded that NATO's campaign was insincere and a front for the pursuit of sinister, conspiratorial and imperialist interests, such as an unholy alliance between Western powers and the Taliban.

Unsurprisingly, a wide range of Helmandis found themselves in conflict with Western forces. In an environment where no foreign unit in Helmand had detailed knowledge of the underlying tribal and district level dynamics, Afghans became adept at using the accusation of 'Taliban' to enlist British forces on their side in long-running disputes. The British were aware of this risk but had little means to mitigate it. As the academic Mike Martin reports of a typical incident in the early days of the British deployment:

When they arrived in Sangin, for example, they were immediately told where the 'Taliban' were by the 'government,' but luckily the local ANA [Afghan National Army] commander warned the British platoon commander that they were being used to settle a private feud.

Increasingly, the term 'Taliban' became meaningless, and was applied to anyone pointing a weapon at NATO soldiers, even as many of those doing so had little to do with radical Islam.

This counter-insurgency narrative supposedly justified the overall NATO mission. The idea was that there was a legitimate Government of the Islamic Republic of Afghanistan that was in opposition to a radical Islamist movement called the Taliban. It was the duty of Western forces to fight this movement in order to stabilise Afghanistan and to defeat Islamism worldwide. This insurgency narrative guided all of the Western planning and operations, even if it didn't conform to the situation on the ground.

The original British plan for Helmand was to focus a zone of security around the provincial capital Lashkar Gah and the neighbouring town of Gereshk, with the aim of gradually moving this perimeter outwards. This was a classic counter-insurgency model, sometimes known as the 'ink-spot' strategy: the idea being to create a zone of control by the Government of the Islamic Republic of Afghanistan and NATO – which would contrast positively with the areas under 'Taliban' control, driving support away from the Taliban and towards the 'legitimate' government. But such a plan did not find favour, either with Afghan politicians or with their British counterparts who wanted to see more 'real soldiering.' Instead, it was decided that the British must take the towns of northern Helmand, such as Sangin, Musa Qala and Now Zad, to prove that the Afghan government controlled the whole province, not just its central belt. The problem with this was that the British force in the field was tiny. Its total number was said to be 3,500, but in practical terms, this meant only a few hundred fighting men able to combat the enemy. While these numbers seem counterintuitive, they are perfectly normal: modern armies, particularly those of sophisticated NATO militaries, require huge 'back office' teams to sustain small numbers of frontline troops.

This was the period of 'platoon houses' – tiny, fortified positions – pinned down against incredible concentrations of insurgent firepower in places such as Musa Qala and Sangin. Backed by air power, the British infantry fought with intense professionalism, bravery and tenacity and inflicted major casualties. But the collateral damage was considerable: thousands of people died. Some were Taliban militants, including recruits from Pakistan, but others were Afghan civilians who lost homes, livelihoods and lives. And, amid the fighting, there was no question of the British being able to engage in reconstruction or development. The centres of Sangin, Musa Qala and Now Zad were reduced to rubble. The British were again conforming to their reputation as colonial oppressors, allying with unpopular local tyrants and carrying out punitive raids.

In an echo of similar deals in Basra, the British agreed to withdraw from the centre of Musa Qala on the understanding that local elders would keep the Taliban away. The deal failed to hold and the fighters were back a few months later. As in Basra, the Americans were unimpressed with this apparent lack of fighting spirit on the part of the British. The war that had been undertaken to reassure the Americans of British martial qualities was rapidly having the opposite effect. The British way of doing war in Afghanistan was also undermining its effectiveness. Every six months, a new British brigade would rotate in, bringing in new commanders, new headquarters and new troops on the ground. And a new set of objectives. For the brigade commander, Helmand was the most significant command in the British Army. The new brigadier would be expected to carry out a signature operation, reported in breathless detail by the embedded media. Whether such an operation had any inherent strategic value was far harder to determine.

One notable example was the operation to move a huge electricity turbine and associated equipment right through Helmand as far as the Kajaki dam in the north of the province. On this occasion the British media outdid itself, with a banner headline in *The Times* proclaiming 'Triumph for British forces in Boy's Own-style Kajaki mission.' As ever, the focus of this media coverage was on the heroism and professionalism of the fighting troops. But boring details were missed: the Kajaki dam provided no electricity to the people of Helmand – the power lines led to the major city of Kandahar. This was in spite of the Ministry of Defence announcing that 18.5MW of 'economically viable, renewable energy' would now be provided to Helmand to 'light up classrooms, allowing Afghans across southern Afghanistan to learn to read and write in evening classes; farmers to store their produce in chilled storage... and clinics to offer improved health services.' For all these grand claims, the operation was pointless: not even the people of Kandahar benefited from the increased electricity, as the turbine was never installed. It remains there to this day, slowly gathering dust in the harsh climate of southern Afghanistan.

Again, the bravery and professionalism of the British military was never in doubt, but it obscured the fact that the battle for Helmand's hearts and minds was being lost. The Taliban were winning that battle. This was despite the fact that the Taliban were not especially popular in Helmand. While Helmand is a very conservative province with a largely Pashtun population, some of its people did not share the extreme cultural positions of the Taliban. But, the presence of hated British troops gave Taliban propaganda there a boost. The Taliban commander in Helmand, Mullah Dadullah, had recruited fighters in Pakistan and Pakistani identity documents were sometimes found on the bodies of killed Taliban fighters. In Helmand, the British had taken a quiet backwater and created a major new Taliban front.

Given how little the British knew of Helmand before their arrival, was it excusable that such a major conflict erupted? No. Ahead of the main British deployment, a secret SAS mission was undertaken in mid-2005 to assess the situation on the ground and make recommendations for the subsequent British deployment. As military expert Frank Ledwidge reported having spoken to officers involved:

This SAS report expressed concern about the UK's ability to carry on the effective work... without a significant uplift in the amount of civil aid money being made available... The report also recommended that the Provincial Governor... be allowed to remain in power given his influence over all the factions in the province.

A special forces officer interviewed by Ledwidge observed of the situation in Helmand: 'There's no insurgency now, but you can have one if you want one.' This was a crisis foretold.

As in Basra, the Americans had to come to the rescue. In February 2009, President Obama sent an additional 17,000 US troops to Afghanistan, rising to a peak of over 100,000 in 2011.

Around 20,000 went to Helmand. British military losses had become politically embarrassing, as an increasingly unpopular Gordon Brown tried to defend himself against allegations that the army was under-equipped. For David Cameron, the new Leader of the Opposition, this was a tempting target. Afghanistan allowed his Conservatives to reclaim the national security agenda after years in which Tony Blair prominently stood shoulder to shoulder with President George W Bush.

At the same time, the British public started to see the plight of the British military in Afghanistan as a tragedy. From my experience working in Helmand in 2010 at the time of the highest casualty numbers, the near-daily death toll was taken by the professional military as part of the remorseless grind of doing 'real soldiering.' The deaths were honoured solemnly, but they were not an existential threat to the mission. But in the UK, the mounting death toll became a subject of public fascination and alarm, with increasing attention paid to the large repatriation ceremonies held in Wootton Bassett where the coffins of fallen service personnel were driven through the Wiltshire town after landing at a nearby RAF base. The deaths in action of a notable bomb disposal expert and of the commander of the 1st Battalion of the Welsh Guards, the most senior officer to die in combat since the Falklands War, played into a politically convenient allegation that Brown's Labour government had broken the military 'covenant' – the understanding that members of the armed forces could trust the government to protect them in return for their unstinting service. After years when military matters were above party politics, the opposition began to turn this to its advantage. The former chief of the army, Richard Dannatt, took the unusual step of becoming a Conservative political adviser, breaking a long tradition that senior British military officers stayed aloof from party politics. This was described as a 'major error of judgement' by a former head of the civil service, but it allowed Cameron to make a strongly pro-military statement in his 2009 party conference speech, generating wild applause from the membership.

'GOVERNMENT IN A BOX'

Back in Helmand the new American forces were making their presence felt. Priding themselves on being austere, remorseless warriors, the US Marine Corps were culturally miles from the British, 'soft' approach to counter-insurgency. Pinned down in their platoon houses, the British had reached an uneasy stalemate with the Taliban in parts of Helmand. As the *Washington Post* writer Rajiv Chandrasekaran noted:

The Brits lived according to what they regarded as a gentleman's agreement: You have your side, I have mine. But the Talibs rarely kept their part of the bargain.... The British called the perimeters FLETs – the forward line of enemy troops. The first time [US Marine General] Larry Nicholson heard the term, he shot a look of disgust at his staff. 'We don't do FLETs,' he said. 'We're Marines. There's no place we won't go.

The Marines' approach was to destroy their opponents with devastating force and then flood that zone with government services. Stanley McChrystal, the ambitious new NATO commander who had made his name pursuing terrorists in Iraq, spoke of 'government in a box' that would be dropped into areas of Helmand newly-liberated from the Taliban. The problem was, government services don't come in boxes. Civilian government relies on a set of relationships between its representatives and the population. These are based on trust and security. A school teacher, administrator or judge will not be able to function if the local people do not trust them. The population of areas of Helmand such as Marja that had, only weeks before, been firmly Taliban territory had no reason to believe that the new overlords (the US military) would be there for the long-haul. On the other hand, the Taliban, in the form of individual commanders with local relationships, were a feature of Marja society and were still a presence there, even if they were not out in force as they had been prior to the Marines' operation. Local contractors who had been paid to build small-scale infrastructure had been attacked and, in some cases, killed by Taliban enforcers. Shopkeepers were threatened against reopening the bazaar. Helmandis knew that the Taliban would be there long after the Americans had left. In desperation the Marines did something they had only recently criticised the Brits for: they ceded outlying areas to the Taliban in order to focus their efforts on population centres.

In May 2010, when McChrystal arrived in Helmand to assess progress of NATO's key frontline operation in Afghanistan, I was in a small leadership group that flew into Marja itself to get the latest from the Marine commanders. McChrystal was the world's most famous military commander and he moved with a huge team of bag-carriers and advisers. Like the people whose job it is to keep you away from a Hollywood movie star, his entourage was aloof and unapproachable. The status of its members depended solely on their closeness to the General and they could conceive of no reason for listening to those of us working on the ground. Their job was not to find out what we thought. Their job was to tell us what to do.

Inside a briefing tent at Marine Forward Operating Base, the atmosphere was tense. Gunfire sounded in the background. Despite its undeniable energy, the US military had not restored stable civil government to Marja. The Marines felt that the civilian team I represented was responsible for this failure. We countered that as long as Taliban could maintain even a tenuous presence in Marja, the civilian administration of the Afghan Government would be a magnet for attacks. But this debate was undercut with other disputes: the Marines' view that the British military had let things get out of control. A British general, nominally in command of all forces in southern Afghanistan, who had flown in from Kandahar to meet McChrystal, was clearly nervous. Within the civilian team, we had our own dynamics: Britain had been steadfastly supported in Helmand by Danish and Estonian teams, both of which were keen to ensure that their own hard work was noticed. And McChrystal had his own challenges – the White House had given him until July 2011 to demonstrate progress in Afghanistan. The General wanted to know why things were still unstable. The Marine commander counselled patience. McChrystal, by now clearly agitated, said: 'We don't have as much time as we'd like.'

Later, back at our office in the Reconstruction Team, the

British General, Nick Carter, argued that time was needed for the population to adjust to a post-Taliban reality. McChrystal was unimpressed. As far as Washington and European capitals were concerned, 'it's a bleeding ulcer,' he said.

There was a silence in the room. The Brits, unused to this sort of direct language, shifted uncomfortably in their seats. But we had been unaware of another factor: this was the age of the celebrity general and such people often travelled with an embedded reporter. Throughout the day, as we had discussed sensitive operational matters, unknown to the Helmand team, one of the people in McChrystal's entourage was Dion Nissenbaum, a highly effective reporter for the McClatchy news company. He filed a lengthy story on the day's visit that drew attention all over the world. The Marines' plan to clean up the Brits' mess in Helmand wasn't going as smoothly as everyone expected, and this was news.

MISTAKES ON THE GROUND

In the same month, David Cameron had been elected Prime Minister. His attacks on Brown's record on the military had contributed to a wider sense that Tony Blair's New Labour government, once the most dynamic force in British politics and the originator of an 'ethical' foreign policy, was drifting and failing after 13 years in power. Like every senior British politician, Cameron duly made his pilgrimage to Helmand, to see 'our boys' in action. But his visit had a second agenda, one that we discussed quietly, behind closed doors and without committing anything to email. Cameron had decided that the Royal Marines needed to get out of Sangin and the British needed to get out of Helmand.

The mission that Britain had picked to prove to the Americans and the world that it could still do 'real soldiering' was coming to a largely unsuccessful close.

In Sangin, the US Marines were raring to go. Spoiling for a fight with 'Taliban' in the upper Sangin valley, they began major airborne operations into areas the British had been unable to reach. Quickly they abandoned any pretence of 'population-centred' operations, or 'hearts and minds.' Within days, the Americans were facing major casualties. 'After losing ten Marines within a week of their arrival, [Marine Lieutenant Colonel Jason Morris] realized that much of the battalion's predeployment training, which had focused on the soft side of COIN – engaging with tribal elders and rebuilding infrastructure – didn't apply... "We threw out the COIN playbook and treated this like a conventional battlefield".'

Around the same time, reports had reached us in the civilian reconstruction office that an airstrike in Sangin had killed scores of civilians. The death toll was as high as 50, none of them insurgents. Dispiritingly, NATO's initial response was denial, followed by obfuscation. But the Afghan government dug in its heels, insisting that over 50 civilians had died. This came just as President Karzai had been ratcheting up rhetoric against air-strikes targeting Afghan civilians, and the incident became a national political issue, causing riots on the streets of Kabul. Eventually, it was acknowledged by NATO that 36 women and children had died in the strike. Sangin elders demanded compensation and President Karzai sent his emissary to negotiate a truce. The identity of this person summed up the limits and failings of Britain's approach in

Helmand: Sher Mohammad Akhundzada, senator, drugs king-pin and ousted governor, was sent by Karzai as his trusted envoy on Helmand matters to negotiate a settlement. As the British began to withdraw from the fight in Helmand, the man they had defined as their key adversary turned out to be the person the rest of the country saw as the key power-broker in the province. Underlining British impotence, it later emerged that the Americans had a regular dialogue with Akhundzada, noting that 'he was a really useful guy, and seemed to know loads of people.'

UK LEAVES HELMAND

The British pulled out of Helmand altogether in 2014, having suffered more than 450 deaths. Many more servicemen were left with permanent, life-changing injuries. It is impossible to know the level of Afghan casualties in the same period, although they will have been far higher. The Sangin airstrike was a widely analysed confirmed incident – but there were hundreds, perhaps thousands of others that would pass unnoticed. The death toll on ordinary Helmandis, particularly in those areas of heavy fighting such as Sangin, Marja or Musa Qala, may be incalculable, but it was considerable. A great number of these killings will have been at the hands of the foreign military or its Afghan partners. A journalist, Anand Gopal, found that every single family in Sangin had lost at least ten of its members to what is bloodlessly termed by Western militaries as 'collateral damage' – non-combatants killed by poor targeting or pure error. Regardless of whether the responsibility lay with Western or Afghan forces, it is not difficult to understand the hatred such indiscriminate killing stoked.

Absurdly, David Cameron claimed that by the time they left the British had 'accomplished' their mission. The attempt to stabilise Helmand had, in fact, been a total failure. The British had started a counter-insurgency mission and swollen the ranks of an armed resistance movement. In its first days the American surge appeared to be more successful, but it had little lasting impact. The dynamic was the same for the US as it was for the UK: a military not able to understand the locale, falling into a pattern of receiving denunciations of certain individuals as 'Taliban,' and working to uphold a concept (the Government of the Islamic Republic of Afghanistan) that was irrelevant to many Helmandis who had little regard for central government, or for its security forces that were merely another armed group in an ongoing conflict for control of resources.

By appearing to take sides with a group of corrupt and violent local warlords, Western forces strengthened a resistance movement. The Taliban were in no way morally superior to the Afghan government, far from it. But it was not possible for the counter-insurgency narrative to hold in the minds of most Afghans, since the Government of the Islamic Republic of Afghanistan had so little validity and Helmandis' lived experience of their government was rarely, if ever, satisfactory. Whereas, the evidence of the destructive power of the British Army or the US Marine Corps was witnessed daily.

Whether anything changed fundamentally in the way the people of Helmand carried on their lives can be assessed by the underlying economy. Throughout this period, opium production in the province, the main economic activity, held steady, reaching peaks in 2014 and 2017, according to the United Nations. Meanwhile, by 2017, the Taliban had retaken large parts of Sangin, a prelude to the entire province falling to the Taliban in 2021.

THE TALIBAN TRUMP THE TALKS

The beginning of the end of the NATO mission in Afghanistan was Donald Trump's deal with the Taliban, agreed in February 2020. A 'peace at any costs' arrangement, it provided for the release from captivity of 5,000 Taliban prisoners held in Afghan detention (including senior leaders), a promise that foreign forces would leave the country by May 2021 and, perhaps most devastatingly, an end to military or contractor support to the Afghan security forces (which would have the practical effect of grounding the Afghan airforce). The Taliban made no promises to stop its campaign of violence, merely promising not to target Western forces and not to harbour terrorists. But the deal contained no verification or enforcement measures, so any undertakings were questionable. It was, in the words of Trump's former National Security Adviser HR McMaster, a 'surrender agreement.' This was a deal over which the Government of Afghanistan, which Western nations had pumped $2 trillion into in the preceding 20 years, not the mention the lives of thousands of troops, had no influence or control.

The most surprising thing about Trump's deal is not how bad it was (as we have seen elsewhere, he has mastered the bad deal), but how readily his successor Joe Biden stuck to it. The only change Biden made to the overall terms was to shift the departure date for foreign troops from May to August. This gave the Taliban the green light they needed and, equally importantly, signalled to others around the country that Government of the Islamic Republic of Afghanistan was finished. The Taliban's surge through the country in the summer of 2021 involved little fighting and many commanders switching sides. Very few people expected the Taliban to be able to take Kabul as quickly as they did, by mid-August. But most people also had little idea of the continued campaigns of violence carried out against Afghan civilians by forces belonging to the Government of the Islamic Republic of Afghanistan. In 2021, the Afghan state had little more to offer to the people of places such as Helmand than it had in 2006.

As the downfall of the unwieldy Afghan state seemed imminent, British politicians started to ask how America, Britain's supposed inseparable ally, had become so clearly indifferent to its priorities and campaigns that it had agreed such a 'surrender deal.' What was the meaning of NATO if its key member was willing simply to walk away from its biggest commitment? Some on the right in British politics sought to blame Biden, alluding to his age and mental faculties. One Conservative MP, Bob Seely, went on the record, saying:

You have got to address Biden's intellectual fitness and health fitness for the role... I'm sorry, he is just gaga... he doesn't have a grip. How many slip ups before people think, yep, he can't do the job?

Even Britain's Defence Secretary Ben Wallace claimed that Britain was willing to continue the Afghan mission without the US involvement, but had been let down by other Europeans. This was a well-judged message for a British public infantilised by tales of European military incompetence, but it was pure fantasy. Without the Americans' logistical underpinnings, there was no chance that Britain could have sustained a mission in Afghanistan and it was deliberately misleading to claim otherwise.

The urge to blame Biden showed how little British politicians had been aware of their own actions. America's retreat from global entanglements did not begin under Biden or even Trump. It began, at least partly, with the realisation that European partners, even the so-called stalwarts such as the UK, could not be relied upon. Nowhere was this seen more starkly than in the bungled intervention in Colonel Qadhafi's Libya.

5. LIBYA: CREATING A POWER VACUUM

'A shit show'

President Obama on the Western intervention in Libya

In this account of Britain's foreign policy missteps, certain patterns emerge. Hubristic belief in military prowess led to Britain losing control of Basra, which led to it engaging militarily in Helmand in an attempt at redemption. Where it lost control again. By a similar token, the justification for an earlier invasion, of Kosovo, was built purely on a human rights basis. There was no suggestion that the persecution of ethnic Albanians in the Balkans was a threat to the people of Britain. In this respect, Kosovo shares similarities with an intervention after Iraq and Afghanistan, one that shows Britain's resolute failure to learn from its own history, even when that history is less than 10 years old. This was the intervention in Libya in 2011.

To understand this disaster, we must delve into Libya's turbulent past. Like Iraq, Libya was a state hollowed out by years of authoritarian rule. The institutions of the Libyan state barely existed after decades of dictatorship under its volatile leader, Muammar Qadhafi. The unique political philosophy of Qadhafi, a charismatic autodidact whose Green Book was supposed to chart a new path between capitalism and communism, was ultimately a crude form of autocracy in which rule by 'people's committees' was, according to the BBC's Libya specialist Martin Asser, in practice 'an ultra-hierarchical pyramid – with the Qadhafi family and close allies at the top wielding power unchecked, protected by a brutal security apparatus.' Any alternative political or social expression, such as political parties or religious groupings, were banned and mass executions took place. As Qadhafi himself warned would-be opponents in a speech on 9th November 1974: 'I could at any moment send them to the People's Court ... and the People's Court will issue a sentence of death based on this law, because execution is the fate of anyone who forms a political party.'

Under Qadhafi, any Libyan suspected of opposition to the 'brotherly leader' was at risk of arbitrary arrest, torture, and execution. Show trials were televised live, followed immediately by public hangings of the 'guilty parties.' There is no way of knowing the number of Qadhafi's victims in Libya. But evidence abounds of horrific massacres, such as one in 1996 at the notorious Abu Salim jail that may have involved 1,200 victims. In one particularly bizarre incident Qadhafi is alleged to have ordered the shooting down of one of Libya's own civilian aircraft full of passengers with the aim of demonstrating to the West that sanctions were rendering Libya's airliners unsafe. Libyans who fled overseas were often no safer. Qadhafi's assassins tracked them down abroad and killed them, or at least made attempts on their lives. In one case, Nuri Al-Mismari, a former minister under Qadhafi, had to be placed in protective custody in France until the assassination squad had given up on its mission and returned to Libya.

Qadhafi's bloodlust was not limited to his own people. Notoriously, he became a supporter of any terror organisation that might strike a blow against Western capitalism, even when these terrorists had ideologies and aims completely at odds with his own. At various points, Qadhafi supplied weapons and support to Irish republicans, European Red Army factions, Palestinian extremists and even Trinidadian Islamists. In 1988, a Pan-Am airliner was destroyed over Lockerbie in Scotland by a bomb hidden inside luggage, killing all 259 onboard as well as 11 residents on the ground. There is strong evidence that some of the bomb components had been supplied to the Libyan government. In 2001, Abdelbaset Al-Megrahi, a Libyan intelligence officer, was convicted of the bombing and, in 2003, Qadhafi accepted responsibility for the attack, although debate rages to this day over the exact nature of Libya's involvement.

Qadhafi's acceptance of responsibility for Lockerbie was a key milestone in the rehabilitation of his regime by the West. Despite his extreme brutality and support to terrorists who killed Western citizens including Britons, Qadhafi was, by the mid-2000s, enjoying support from Western leaders. This was largely thanks to a successful intelligence operation in 2003 that had been spearheaded by MI6 in the preceding two years. Just a few weeks after the 9/11 attacks on the United States, a delegation of Libyans, including its intelligence chief Moussa Koussa, attended a secret meeting with MI6 officers in a quiet corner of the Travellers Club on London's Pall Mall. The Libyans had realised that the game of supporting terrorism was up. In the aftermath of 9/11 it was clear that the US and its allies were prepared to take aggressive military action against any state that supported or harboured terrorists, and Libya was in the firing line. In a series of secret negotiations between the Libyans and MI6, the West agreed to lift Libyan sanctions in return for Libya ceasing support for terrorism and renouncing its own chaotic and ineffectual programmes for weapons of mass destruction. In December 2003, the Libyans publicly ended these programmes and promised to adhere to a range of international non-proliferation treaties.

In March 2004, Tony Blair made a historic visit to Libya, cementing Qadhafi's rehabilitation and opening the way for British oil companies such as Shell and BP to agree lucrative contracts to extract oil. There was no expectation that Qadhafi would change all of his ways. He remained firmly in power as an autocrat meting out severe punishment to his enemies. Although it was not reported at the time, Britain had also done a deal to kidnap a Libyan Islamist and ship him, illegally, back to Libya. Abdel-Hakim Belhaj and his wife were seized in southeast Asia after the local authorities there were tipped off by MI6. Belhaj was flown in a CIA jet to Libya where he was tortured and imprisoned. According to a contemporary letter from a senior

British intelligence officer to the Libyan intelligence chief Moussa Koussa discovered years later in Tripoli, 'this was the least we [Britain] could do for you and for Libya to demonstrate the remarkable relationship we have built over the years.' The Belhaj case became a source of considerable embarrassment to the British government and resulted in a public apology from Prime Minister Theresa May in 2018 to Belhaj and his wife, in which she stated: 'On behalf of Her Majesty's government I apologise unreservedly. We are profoundly sorry for the ordeal that you both suffered and our role in it. The UK government has learned many lessons from this period.'

Qadhafi evolved from Western pariah to a mercurial Western ally and in the years from 2004 to 2011, Libya began to share some features of the wealthy states of the Arabian Gulf: a small population and increasingly generous national welfare systems supported by a burgeoning oil and gas sector. Expatriates and tourists started to become a common feature of life. As with Gulf countries, Libya remained undemocratic, but well-targeted public relations and widespread opportunities for Western businesses maintained its place as a Western ally. There were gestures towards political openness, particularly in the person of Saif al-Islam Qadhafi – Qadhafi's son – who made numerous speeches about Libya's potential transition to democracy. The London School of Economics, a world-renowned university, happily took funding from Qadhafi and awarded Saif a doctorate, while making plans to educate Libya's elite. These associations allowed Libya to approach 'respectable' status at the start of the second decade of the 21st Century. In June 2010, the *Financial Times* reported that Libya had allocated US$66 billion to infrastructure projects that were eagerly being managed by Western consultants. Despite an absence of any regulatory framework or even a banking sector, the prospect of transformational finance flooding in to support improbable vanity projects such as Qadhafi's 'Great Man-Made River' was described with breathless enthusiasm in the Western press.

THE ARAB SPRING

With economic growth and the beginnings of political openness, Libya in 2011 may not have seemed a likely territory for revolution. But the Arab Spring of 2011 confounded the forecasters. Things began with a desperate young man. Muhammad Bouazizi grew up in Tunisia, where your chances of getting anywhere depended largely on your connections. He didn't have any connections. When he tried to provide for his family by selling fruit in the street of Sidi Bouzid, a poor town in central Tunisia, he was constantly harassed by the authorities demanding bribes. On 17th December 2010, they pushed him too far: his wares were thrown into the street and his weighing scales seized. Enraged, Bouazizi went to the Governor's office to demand the return of his property. The Governor refused to see him, no doubt for the same reasons that had dogged Bouazizi from the start – he had no money for bribes. So Bouazizi gave an ultimatum, declaring: 'If you don't see me, I'll burn myself.' This was not youthful bravado: he meant it. He took a can of gasoline and set fire to himself in a busy street.

It took Bouazizi three weeks to die from his burns, but within hours of the incident, protests against the authorities had erupted in Sidi Bouzid. His funeral was attended by thousands. Demonstrations extended across the country and into the capital city. Ten days after Bouazizi's death, President Zine El-Abidine Ben Ali, Tunisia's dictator for a quarter of a century, fled to Saudi Arabia. Bouazizi had started a firestorm that spread across the region. Within a month, Hosni Mubarak, Egypt's longest-serving ruler in 200 years, had resigned after similar mass protests in Cairo. The same month, Yemen's President Saleh, in office since 1978, announced he would not seek re-election. Sustained demonstrations took place in Lebanon, Jordan, Morocco, Iraq, Algeria, Sudan, Bahrain and Oman, among other places. Peaceful protests in Syria were crushed by the paranoid government of Bashar Al-Assad. In Saudi Arabia, the oil-rich state offered subsidies, free housing and public-sector jobs in a successful effort to stave off widespread unrest.

In Libya, the regime's history of violent repression might have deterred the protests. But it didn't. By early February sustained unrest had broken out in cities such as Zintan and Benghazi that had traditionally seen a lack of investment from Qadhafi's regime despite the recent influx of Western money. While being the source of much of Libya's energy wealth, Benghazi, in the east of the country, had seen little development in a period when those closest to Qadhafi had become fabulously wealthy through corruption. The initial protests in Benghazi were about inadequate public housing. But they quickly morphed into wider and more violent clashes, with police firing live ammunition into crowds.

On 18th February 2011, troops shot dead at least 200 civilians in a funeral procession in Benghazi, according to local doctors. Angry protesters seized a barracks in the city. Within a week, Benghazi was being described as the 'nerve centre of Libya's revolution,' with reports of other towns falling into rebel hands.

By the end of February, Qadhafi's forces had lost control of a significant proportion of the country, and the leader had seen defections of his top associates to the rebels. Qadhafi counter-attacked in March, with his forces threatening to retake Benghazi and dark talk of a possible massacre of rebels. In the midst of this uncertainty, Britain launched a secret operation. A Chinook helicopter adapted for special operations flew in the dead of night to a few miles outside Benghazi. On landing it disgorged two vehicles and seven men not in uniform. They were heavily armed and equipped with explosives, communications equipment and detailed maps. Their objective was to make contact with rebel leaders in Benghazi.

If the intention had been to operate under the radar, the mission had been a failure from the start. Within hours of arrival, the six SAS operatives and an MI6 officer were surrounded as they tried to organise their equipment in a farmer's compound on the outskirts of Benghazi. A group of local farmers, armed with AK47s, fired into the air. The undercover unit accepted the inevitable and surrendered to a large group of heavily-armed militiamen, turning over their sophisticated weaponry and comms equipment as they did so. Over a tense 72 hours, delicate negotiations eventually led to the release of the group, which sheepishly retreated on a Royal Navy frigate that briefly docked in Benghazi port. They had been well-treated and came to regard the whole escapade as a professionally enriching experience.

The wider world regarded the episode as something from a *Carry on Spying* movie. At one point, Libyan rebels released an excruciating recording of a British diplomat floundering as he tried to explain what the group of armed men had been doing in Benghazi. Ambassador Richard Northern sounded as though he was describing a tourist group, rather than a heavily-armed special operations unit: 'We sent a small group just to find if there was a hotel, if everything was working, if there was somewhere they could stay and work.' His Libyan interlocutor observed: 'Actually they made a big mistake coming in a helicopter, I think, actually – coming in an open area.' A wide array of media outlets observed that international journalists had managed to report from the centre of Benghazi without needing to arrive heavily armed in the dead of night by helicopter. A more serious problem was the impression that the rebels were merely the tools of Western governments, rather than being a genuine popular uprising. A well-informed analysis written in early 2012 concluded: 'As a result of what happened with [the secret Benghazi mission], those who would advocate using special forces to help topple the regime were sidelined for months. It also caused great difficulties for MI6, which had plans to turn some key figures in Qadhafi's inner circle.'

In spite of this misstep, by the middle of March 2011, United Nations Security Council had agreed a new resolution, 1973. This demanded a ceasefire, imposed a no-fly zone and agreed 'to take all necessary measures to protect civilians under threat of attack in the country, including Benghazi.' A day after the passing of resolution 1973, Qadhafi's government announced 'an immediate ceasefire and stoppage of all military operations.' However, there was little evidence of any let-up in military activities and within a day, British, French and American forces were in action, bombing Qadhafi's forces as they approached Benghazi. This international coalition quickly became enmeshed in complex disputes about objectives, leadership and mandate. The US President, Barack Obama, was doveish. Some of Obama's electoral appeal had come from his record of having opposed the invasion of Iraq and his clear desire to take a cautious, consensual approach to foreign policy. His approach to Libya demonstrated this. As British Prime Minister David Cameron and his French counterpart Nicolas Sarkozy urged intervention, Obama had insisted on a UNSCR backing action and building a broad base of support from Arab allies – not too difficult, as Qadhafi had made a point of alienating most of the rulers in the Arab world. After an initial strike to defend Benghazi from Qadhafi's advance, Cameron and Sarkozy pushed to provide extensive support to the rebels and topple Qadhafi's regime, far beyond the intention of resolution 1973, once again undermining the authority of the United Nations. This was a long way from Obama's original intention just to prevent a massacre of rebels. It pushed the intervention into something that Obama wanted to avoid from the outset: regime change. As Cameron explained in his autobiography, '[Obama] was unenthusiastic and matter-of-fact.... He said he felt forced into it.'

On 31st March 2011, NATO took command of the intervention and the UK and France joined Qatar and the United Arab Emirates in supporting the rebels' advance on the capital. Tripoli finally fell in August. In September 2011, Sarkozy and Cameron visited liberated Benghazi. 'It's great to be in free Libya,' declared Cameron – 'as he strained, rock-star hoarse, above the chants in televised scenes both men will hope play well back home' as Reuters put it. Back in London, Cameron had been buffeted by a scandal over the continued use of phone hacking by elements of the British media, including newspapers close to Cameron and his project. So he probably appreciated the distraction of an overseas victory. In a speech to the UN soon after, Cameron declared: 'The Arab Spring is a massive opportunity to spread peace, prosperity, democracy and vitally security but only if we really seize it.' In October 2011, Qadhafi himself, who had been hiding in a large drainage pipe with bodyguards, was captured and killed. The ogre-turned-ally-turned-ogre had been slain. In early 2012, the two most senior US officials in NATO, Ambassador Ivo Daalder and Admiral James Stavrides, published a paper entitled 'NATO's Victory in Libya – The Right Way to Run an Intervention.' In it, the authors declared: 'NATO's operation in Libya has rightly been hailed as a model intervention' which 'demonstrated that the alliance remains an essential source of stability.'

WHERE IS THE GOVERNMENT?

The residents of Libya in the 2020s might be hard-pressed to find this 'stability.' At the time of writing in 2022, Libya is now a failed state. A UN-recognised government rules Tripoli and some nearby areas, with support from Turkish and Qatari troops who identify with the government's Islamist tendencies. The oil-rich east of the country (including Benghazi) is under the control of a powerful warlord, Khalifa Haftar, who is backed by various Arab states considered to be against Islamists, notably the UAE, Saudi Arabia and Egypt. Apart from Turkey, NATO members such as the UK and France have at different times given low-key support to Haftar, but this has come under strain as his militias have launched indiscriminate attacks on Tripoli. Russia has also supported Haftar, deploying both mercenaries from Wagner Group, a private military company linked to the Kremlin, and fighter jets from its own air force. With major powers ranged on all sides of the conflict, there is no reason to believe that any resolution will be found in the short to medium term. Libya's chaos has destabilised the wider region. Arms looted from Libya and fighters of sub-Saharan African heritage have washed into neighbouring countries throughout the Sahel, increasing instability in a swathe of countries including Mali, Burkina Faso, Niger and Chad. Migration from across the Sahara seeps into Europe, fuelling alarmist claims by rightwing, nativist politicians. A noted Libya scholar, Jason Pack, observed:

Libya's implosion post-2011, combined with Syria's civil war, led to these two countries becoming prime movers of the migration crisis that has in turn moved previously marginal neo-populist politics into the mainstream centre-right and allowed anti-globalist and pro-Russian sentiment to gain ground throughout Europe.

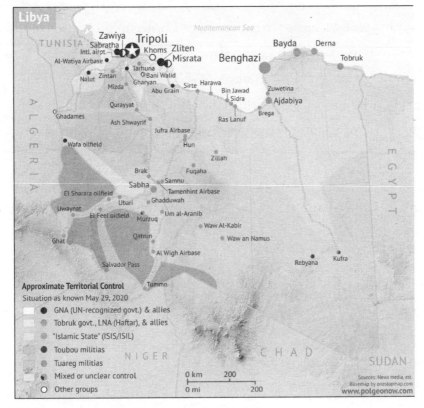

3. Control of Libya by armed groups

Obama himself said that his 'worst mistake,' was 'probably failing to plan for the day after what I think was the right thing to do in intervening in Libya.' In another lengthy interview with *The Atlantic* magazine, Obama described the Libya intervention as a 'shit-show' and remarked:

'When I go back and I ask myself what went wrong there's room for criticism, because I had more faith in the Europeans, given Libya's proximity, being invested in the follow-up,' he said. He noted that Nicolas Sarkozy, the French president, lost his job the following year. And he said that British Prime Minister David Cameron soon stopped paying attention, becoming 'distracted by a range of other things.'

This diagnosis is borne out by Cameron's own account of his activities relating to Libya. He devotes 12 pages of his autobiography to the account of his 'victory' over Qadhafi, explaining how as Prime Minister he was forced to get into the minutiae of the unfolding campaign. 'I spent vast amounts of time on the situation,' he said. He deals with Libya's descent into anarchy in less than a page and blames the UN. Perhaps he no longer had vast amounts of time to devote to the issue. Maintaining and building peace is just not as interesting as fighting a war, particularly if you are the leader of a medium-sized country that is desperate to show the world that it is still militarily virile. Whilst the casualties from Libya's Civil War now stand at over 5,000 dead inside the country, according to the NGO Action on Armed Violence, it is worth considering the counter-factual. Had Western nations not intervened and had Qadhafi been left to quell the rebellion, what might have been the outcome? It seems likely that a low-level insurgency might have persisted, perhaps propped up by Gulf Arab support, particularly around Benghazi. Would Qadhafi have returned to pariah status, like Assad propped up by Russia and Iran? This is very possible, although Libya's vast reserves of the highest quality crude oil close to European buyers might have pushed a faster normalisation of relations. In any case, the wider effects of the Libyan war, including a migration crisis and destabilisation of the Sahel region, affecting tens of millions of people, would almost certainly not have occurred.

UK'S PAST FAILURES IGNORED

It is hard to understand the headlong rush to war in Libya. In 2011, Britain was well-aware of its failures in Iraq and its continued challenges in Afghanistan, where Cameron had made it a clear objective to withdraw British troops, especially from the highly dangerous district of Sangin. A British parliamentary inquiry in 2016 attempted to unpick the reasons for the failure. One of these was a simple lack of knowledge of the country. A noted Libya expert expressed shock at the lack of awareness in Whitehall of the 'history and regional complexities' of Libya. It was also acknowledged that, 'with the benefit of hindsight' it proved to be wishful thinking that Libya's rebels would exclude radical Islamists. A key early moment in the war was the escalation by Britain and France, with the reluctant involvement of the United States, to 'prevent a massacre' of Libyan rebels in Benghazi by Qadhafi's forces. Cameron's account is unequivocal. As a result of allied airstrikes, 'Benghazi was saved, and a Srebenica-style slaughter was averted. I've never known a relief like it.' This 'Srebenica-style slaughter' was, however, never a real risk. As the parliamentary inquiry heard, Qadhafi's forces had not massacred civilians on their advance through rebel-held towns towards Benghazi. Libya experts concluded that there was little evidence for the likelihood of such bloodshed, save for Qadhafi's violent rhetoric, which, in the absence of serious intelligence, seemed to have been taken at face value. The inquiry concluded: 'We have seen no evidence that the UK government carried out a proper analysis of the nature of the rebellion in Libya.'

I saw at first hand some of the reasons for this lack of analysis.

At a high-level Whitehall meeting during the early stages of the conflict, an external Libya expert made a presentation on the tribal dynamics in the country. This was listened to with moderate inattention, possibly boredom. Shortly afterwards a military commander spoke of options available for special forces operations on the ground in Libya. The excitement and energy in the room was palpable. Sending in guys with guns was more interesting than trying to understand the territory. But Libya was about more than just military machismo. By 2011, Britain was facing a crisis of foreign policy expertise.

And here we must take a step back and, with the experience of Libya in mind, look at what has happened to Britain's Foreign and Commonwealth Office over the past few decades. Essentially, the budget, manpower and influence of British diplomacy has been cut back year after year. In June 2019, a report identified that the Foreign Office's budget has received a progressively lower proportion of government expenditure almost every year since the 1970s. Possibly more damaging is the proportion of that budget that now goes into cross-government programmes. This tendency has only increased with the merger of the Foreign Office and the aid ministry, the Department for International Development, in September 2020. While that has artificially inflated the top-line budget of the combined department, there is still less money in real terms to spend on the Foreign Office's core objective: having experts with deep understanding of foreign countries and devising policies that incorporate that understanding. The number of diplomatic staff posted overseas where they can become Britain's eyes and ears in their host country has been reduced significantly. While exact figures can be hard to acquire due to security classification issues, the overall trend is unambiguous. In the mid-1980s the UK had around 3,000 diplomats posted around the world. By the mid-1990s this figure had fallen to 2,500. By 2018 this number was around 1,700, the lowest in modern British history. In the same period, France has posted roughly twice as many diplomats abroad.

Diplomats do not make straightforward cases for generous public funding. In the popular imagination, a diplomat attends glamorous parties ('Ambassador, you are spoiling us,' says the beautiful woman as she helps herself to a Ferrero Rocher chocolate), lives in a palatial residence in the smartest part of town, and could easily be replaced by email and video-conferencing in the information age. They do not have the voter appeal of poorly-paid nurses working night shifts, or army recruits risking their lives for the nation's security. The case for spending more money on British diplomats is undermined by their privileged backgrounds. On average they are posher, older and whiter than other civil servants. Many avail themselves of a lucrative perk to educate their children at exclusive private schools for free while they serve abroad. Diplomats can claim more than £10,000 per term at taxpayer's expense to pay boarding school fees for an unlimited number of their children. In 2018, this bonus cost taxpayers nearly £11 million and paid for the children of senior diplomats, many on six-figure salaries, to attend such elite schools as Eton, Harrow and Winchester. During a cost of living crisis, the diplomat doesn't cut a very sympathetic figure.

Nevertheless, the Foreign Office faced repeated budget cuts and the practical impact of these cuts was often well-masked by the willingness of British diplomats to go the extra mile, to paper over the cracks. Sometimes this was literally the case: as a British High Commissioner (Ambassador equivalent) in the 2010s I would climb ladders to fix the roof of my official residence myself (because there was no budget to do so). I also paid for cultural engagement activities from my own pocket (again, because I had no discretion to promote and project British culture with government funds) and bought a British-made car with my own money (a Mini, manufactured in England by BMW). I don't resent doing any of this during a fascinating and memorable career. But throughout the period in question I would receive exhortations from the Foreign Secretary to do 'more with less,' including pressure to rent out my home as a venue for commercial events, which was possibly against international laws governing diplomatic premises. It was definitely a hostage to fortune, as some of my colleagues discovered when the commercial client for their events proved an unseemly associate of British diplomacy.

All of this was happening at a time when the autonomy of a British Ambassador was being reduced to a minimum. In common with my colleagues, I had no discretion over any immigration matter, meaning that I was unable to rectify the situation when the Home Office made flagrantly incorrect and unfair decisions (which it often did – while a British High Commissioner even my own son was denied a British passport on his first attempt). I had no authority to issue birth certificates, British passports or in general to offer services to British citizens in need, which is of course the thing that most people regard as the primary duty of an Embassy. And in common with most public service managers, it was almost impossible for me to deal with poor performance except by foisting the problematic individual onto some other manager within the civil service.

In spite of all this penny-pinching, diplomats represented excellent value for money. The Foreign Office's core annual budget has been roughly £1 billion in recent years (excluding development aid). This makes it one of the smallest government departments. To put this into context, former Foreign Secretary David Miliband recently pointed out that the Foreign Office's annual costs equated roughly to one day of NHS spending or the annual budget of Kent County Council. The international aid budget dwarfs the Foreign Office's. To some extent this is obvious: development means running and funding international programmes that reduce global poverty; diplomacy is rarely about programmes and always about having good people able to build effective relationships. But in developing country contexts, it is well-known that the British diplomats aren't the ones with access to resources. On the contrary, this sits with the development workers. As a result, diplomats lose their authority and influence. Whether or not the merger of DFID with the FCO, undertaken in late 2020, will make much of a difference remains to be seen. I have been told by current Foreign Office officials that there is little or no integration between the two institutions, beyond the new letterhead. It may be that the development workers continue to be the ones who matter in the countries where British aid makes a difference.

But diplomacy can still be effective. As Harold Macmillan famously said in 1958, 'jaw, jaw is better than war, war.' Even the smallest military engagements are ruinously expensive, destructive, and likely to lead to widespread loss of life compared to a diplomatic engagement that averts conflict. Britain's Foreign Office has in the past played a role as a behind-the-scenes peacebroker, for example in Mozambique in the early 1990s or in South Sudan as recently as March 2020. But for all these isolated examples, the Foreign Office has seen a steady degradation of its influence, quality of staff, and insight, all to generate cost savings that are nugatory in the wider context of overall government spending. This decline is so widely noted that it is almost taken for granted.

In December 2019, John Casson, who acted as David Cameron's most senior foreign policy adviser from 2010 to 2014, observed: 'There has been an absence of any depth of strategic thinking not just at political level but also confidence amongst officials not just in the Foreign Office but across Whitehall to think clearly about what is the nature of the power that we hold.' Casson's views have been echoed by a stream of former senior diplomats. Sir Simon Fraser, who headed up the Foreign Office until 2015 wrote: 'It is now painfully clear to our allies and adversaries alike that the FCO is way beyond any ability to do "more with less" and is now drawing ever deeper on irreplaceable reserves of long nurtured capital – whether that be the sale of high status property around the world or simply the goodwill of our friends, and of course staff.' In the same report, Tom Tugendhat, chair of the House of Commons' Foreign Affairs Committee, observed:

'[the Foreign Office] is now a shadow of its former self. Once one of the great offices of state, its role directing foreign policy has been gradually hollowed out, as new government departments responsible for aid and trade have been created, and it has faced a tug-of-war over key aspects of policy with the Cabinet Office. The FCO's entire budget now amounts to a rounding error — at barely 0.1% of Government spending.' Again, Sir William Patey, a recently retired senior diplomat, formerly Ambassador to Iraq, Saudi Arabia and Afghanistan, said: there simply is 'not time anymore' for diplomatic staff to travel the country and engage at length with the local populace. This has limited the 'time to reflect' which reveals, 'a depth of knowledge being lost in each and every campaign undertaken, with no meaningful alternative to replace it.'

Alongside funding cuts runs the issue of losing the 'depth of knowledge.' Britain's Foreign Office has a strange indifference to expertise. The British civil service lays much weight on the value of a high-calibre generalist demonstrating corporate 'competencies,' rather than a specialist with expert knowledge or experience of a certain subject. Unlike many foreign ministries in comparable countries, the Foreign Office does not recruit or promote experts into its senior management roles, even where there are complex cultural and linguistic barriers to understanding the underlying issues, such as when working overseas. Indeed, the Foreign Office appears actively hostile to recognising and promoting such experience. I made a Freedom of Information request to know what proportion of the senior management of the Foreign Office had doctorates in any field relevant to their work (such as international relations, area studies or modern history). The reply was curt: 'we have no legal reason to hold this information.' One rather obvious reason would be that it's advantageous for an organisation to know which of its staff has advanced knowledge of their work.

By contrast, under President Obama several US deputy- and under-Secretaries of State held doctorates in relevant fields, as did many senior officials. All of the official biographies of senior Foreign Service staff in the Obama administration contained information on their higher education, as you would expect for a job where understanding complex and unfamiliar issues represents the core task. This is not the case with the British Foreign Office.

It may be reasonable for the Foreign Office to have generalist managers and rely on specialist advisers to give insight on complex questions of international relations. The Foreign Office has a cadre of Research Analysts, many of them academic experts in their field and all of them tasked with focusing on research and analysis of a specific geographical area or subject, such as counter-terrorism or multilateral policy. The standard Foreign Office team dealing with a country such as Libya or Syria would be staffed with generalists, few of whom can be expected to have any detailed knowledge of the country. But this team could draw on the knowledge of a specialist Research Analyst to answer specific questions, analyse a particular policy proposal or provide background detail on persons of interest. However, the standard Foreign Office procedure was that the Research Analysts responded only when commissioned, rather than as a matter of course. The analyst might be asked to produce research explaining why a certain policy had merit, or to demonstrate the effectiveness of dealing with a particular group or faction. Effectively, the analyst is invited to provide research that supports the policy, rather than assessing the policy on its merits. This analyst input, if it is invited, occurred only at policy level. The Research Analysts are not represented at senior levels. As a result, as Greg Shapland, former head of Foreign Office Research Analysts, explained to me: 'What would often happen, if the Research Analyst was producing analysis that didn't suit the policy line, then the political department would just ignore it and it wouldn't go any further up the chain.' As a result, a policy decision might get taken with no expert input whatsoever. This was particularly the case with fast-moving situations such as those around the interventions in Libya.

In addition, like much else in the Foreign Office, Research Analysts faced chronic under-resourcing and years of falling budgets undermining the efficacy of the institution. During the Arab Spring, the head of the Research Analysts cadre was supposed to manage the entire Foreign Office team of analysts as well as being responsible for analysis of a particular country, while at the same time trying to get the department through a very threatening review process that dominated his time and attention. The idea of an expert cadre, considering policy against a wider evidence base and advising ministers on the best path to take, or offering an informed critique of a proposed policy, simply does not exist in the British system. As a result, momentum could easily build around an exciting idea such as the defenestration of the Qadhafi regime, with little or no input, let alone pushback, from experts.

Diplomacy is not an activity whose outputs are easily assessed or measured. The narrow, arithmetic mentality of consultant-politicians (William Hague was proud of his background with McKinsey) does not easily translate into the intangible effect of national influence. But, at its best, as well as preventing wars and creating economic opportunity, diplomacy can open up trade markets and remove national borders. The European Union is a good example. After centuries of conflict in Europe, the European Union, above all a diplomatic endeavour, has succeeded in bringing peace, economic development and cultural harmony to a disparate continent. It would be hard to assess the value of this if the unit of measurement is the cost savings to European Embassies. But the value to humanity is incalculable.

While cuts to the Foreign Office may have amounted to a rounding error in overall government spending terms, they have devastated Britain's diplomatic efficacy. The real-world impact of these cuts can be seen in Libya and in Syria, which we visit next.

6. SYRIA: A CONFLICT WITHOUT END

'Assad is finished. What seems left to discover is how much time will be required before he is either killed or flees.'
Steve Coll, writing in the *New Yorker*, July 2012

AT HOME WITH THE AL-ASSADS

'ASMA AL-ASSAD empties a box of fondue mix into a saucepan for lunch. The household is run on wildly democratic principles. "We all vote on what we want, and where," she says.' Readers of March 2011's edition of *Vogue* magazine glided through a glossy account of Syria's glamorous, British-born First Lady. At length, it extolled Asma Al-Assad's good looks and fashion sense, her modern, 'democratic' approach to parenting and her humanitarian work with Syria's children. In a heartwarming finale, Syria's bloodstained dictator Bashar Al-Assad rings a handbell at a charming Christmas concert, exclaiming: 'This is the diversity you want to see in the

Middle East. This is how you can have peace!' As *Vogue* published its cosy feature, Al-Assad was facing the first wave of Arab Spring protests. In the week the edition popped through letterboxes, Syrian troops opened fire on peaceful protesters in several cities, killing around 70 civilians. While his troops crushed dissent within his own borders, Bashar Al-Assad was paying a US lobbyist $5,000 a month to generate fawning coverage about his family.

The Arab Spring threatened the Al-Assads more deeply than some other rulers in the Middle East. The reason was – is – partly religious.

Like his father, Hafiz Al-Assad, from whom he inherited Syria, Bashar Al-Assad is an Alawi. The Alawis of Syria represent around 1.3 million people and 13 per cent of the pre-war Syrian population. Despite their relatively small numbers, the Alawis 'hold in their hands the crucial threads of power' in Syria and have done so since Hafiz Al-Assad took power in 1966. However, such dominance is a relatively recent phenomenon. For many years the Alawis were regarded as the poorest, least politically influential group in Syria. As recently as the 1950s:

It was common for upper-class Syrian families, mostly urban Sunnis, to have Alawi maidservants. The practice was indicative of the extreme poverty and low status of the Alawis, whose most needy families indentured their daughters to domestic servitude.

Historically, economically marginal Alawis were used as agricultural labourers for the wealthy Christian and Sunni landowners. The Alawis' low status and poverty was in part a reflection of their unorthodox religious views. While the modern Alawi state in Syria has sought to emphasise its connection to Shi'a Islam, Alawi beliefs are at the fringes of mainstream Muslim ideology. Alawi doctrines date from the ninth century and have their roots in Shi'a Islam but are largely distinct from mainstream Shi'ism. Alawi beliefs and practices appear to have drawn from Christianity and other traditions and involve un-Islamic practices such as drinking wine. Alawis celebrate certain Christian festivals, including Christmas, Easter, Pentecost and Palm Sunday. They honour many Christian saints: St. Catherine, St. Barbara, St. George, St. John the Baptist, St. John Chrysostom, and St. Mary Magdalen.

Some aspects of Alawism are particularly challenging to mainstream Sunni Islam: Alawis revere an early figure in Islam, Ali Ibn Abi Talib, who is viewed as an exemplar by Shi'a Muslims. But the superficial similarity to Shi'ism ends here: Alawis consider Ali to be a divinity (analogous to the Christian belief regarding Jesus). This is considered in orthodox Islam to be the sin of 'shirk' (literally, 'sharing' one's devotion with more than one deity). According to the Qu'ran, shirk is an unforgivable sin: 'God does not forgive the joining of partners with Him: anything less than that He forgives to whoever He will, but anyone who joins partners with God has concocted a tremendous sin.'

Sunni Muslims, who are in the majority in Syria, have specific authorities that condemn Alawi beliefs. For example Ibn Taymiyya, a 14th Century Islamic scholar who is one of the most important figures in orthodox Sunni Islamic thought, wrote three fatwas condemning Alawis. The fiercest of these fatwas stated:

They [the Alawis] are heretic apostates whose repentance is not accepted, and they must be killed wherever found, and to be cursed as described ... their scholars and [notables] must be killed so that they would not lead others astray.

Ibn Taymiyya is a core authority to modern Sunni Muslims of the Wahhabi-Salafi tradition practised in Saudi Arabia and by adherents of the Islamic State. For this reason, modern fatwas against Alawis make reference to Ibn Taymiyya's views, such as one given by Saudi cleric Hamoud bin 'Aqla' Al-Shu'eibi in 2000 and cited on a contemporary jihadist website.

When Syria gained its independence from France in 1946, the Alawis were living in grinding poverty. Ambitious Alawis had an incentive to gravitate towards two relatively classless institutions in post-Independence Syria. One was the Arab-nationalist socialist Ba'th Party (Iraq's Saddam Hussein was also a secular Ba'athist). The other was the army. As the number of Alawis in senior positions in both entities increased, so did the attractiveness of these institutions to greater numbers of Alawis, thereby creating a self-reinforcing tendency. Military coups beset Syria in the late 1960s, and by 1966 the Alawis had taken control of Syria, a position they still hold nearly 50 years later. From the start the Al-Assads had a strong incentive to shore up their power-base through inter-marriage, self-enrichment and repression of the majority. A Syrian researcher, Karam Shaar, has demonstrated the extent to which the Assad family dominates both the formal structures of the security state and a network of commercial interests and violent militias. As Shaar explained, in times of peace 'a good family member is one who can do the regime's day-to-day work or turn a financial profit.' When times get tough, the Al-Assads are ruthless at holding onto their hard won power.

In 1979, for instance, Alawi cadets were murdered in Aleppo by Sunni militants. The Al-Assads banned the Muslim Brotherhood (a Sunni Islamist movement) and made membership a capital offence. In 1982 Hafiz Al-Assad brutally suppressed a Muslim Brotherhood uprising in Hama, killing more than 25,000, including civilians, according to Amnesty International. This was an avowedly sectarian act of repression; the forces sent to retake Hama were largely Alawi.

BASHAR THE REFORMER

Despite this viciousness, in its early days Bashar Al-Assad's regime was relatively normal by Arab world standards: a corrupt hereditary ruler (albeit called a 'President' rather than 'king' or 'emir') presided over a brutal, kleptocratic state that offered little economic opportunity to those outside the charmed circle around the ruling family. However, while Syria was reputed to have the highest level of state surveillance in the Middle East, Bashar was seen as a pragmatic reformer of the second generation, in contrast to his father. Indeed, on coming to power after the death of his father in June 2000, Bashar had allowed a period of intense political activism to occur, which became known as the Damascus Spring. While this period ultimately ended in a return to authoritarianism, some tentative reforms were enacted, including releases of political prisoners and a brief period in which human rights organisations were allowed to exist. By 2005, most of these minor reforms had been withdrawn, in part in response to the security threat felt by Bashar because of the invasion in 2003 of next-door Ba'athist Iraq by the US-led coalition. But the Damascus Spring at least showed the possibility that Bashar might allow pragmatic reform.

His potential ability to work through the 2011 crisis appeared to be on display in April, when he rescinded a state of emergency that had absurdly been in place for 50 years and had allowed the Syrian state to carry out arbitrary arrests and detentions throughout that period. At the same time, he announced a range of reforms, including releasing political prisoners, cutting taxes and raising wages. But these gestures were insufficient alongside numerous incidents of excessive brutality by Syria's military and security forces. As with Tunisia, a single event ignited a raging fire. As protests swept through the wider Middle East and presidents fell in Tunisia and Egypt, a group of schoolboys in the unremarkable Syrian town of Dara'a, close to the border with Jordan, graffitied on a wall the fateful words: 'It's your turn, doctor.' The 'doctor' in question was Bashar, a British-trained ophthalmologist. The local security agents arrested a group of teenage boys. The boys were held for weeks and hideously tortured. Parents pleaded for their release, to no avail. After a month they were released, but protests continued. On 25th April, Syrian security forces responded with military force, sending tanks into Dara'a. Demonstrations spread to other towns, growing all the time. By July, the Free Syrian Army had been formed and Syria's uprising had become a civil war.

By mid-2012, repeated massacres had been carried out by Syrian government forces and attempted ceasefires mediated by outsiders such as the UN and Arab League had failed. In July 2012, the rebels made a major push on Damascus. On 18th July, the collapse of the Al-Assad regime appeared imminent after the President's defence minister and brother-in-law were among those killed by a devastating suicide bombing of the national security council headquarters. This attack also pointed to another development: the increasing radicalisation of the uprising, with Islamist suicide bombers taking the place of conventionally-armed rebel fighters.

With the President's most senior officials not safe from the rebels, many expected the rapid fall of the Al-Assad regime in July 2012. However, Bashar Al-Assad has been rescued twice by external powers: once by Iran's foreign legions from 2012 to 2013 and a second time from 2015 onwards, by Russia. In Syria, many different conflicts happened at the same time. It was both a civil war for political control, as well as a regional conflict between the Gulf States and Iran. It was a religious war between Sunni and Shi'a Muslims from all over the world and, finally, a war between Western states and their allies, such as the United States and United Kingdom, and their opponents led by Russia. As a consequence, Syria's war has become one of the bloodiest and longest conflicts in the Middle East. In 2022, it is still raging. More than any other conflict associated with the Arab Spring, Syria has become a battlefield for regional and global powers to play out their rivalries. At different times, fighters from Afghanistan, the Arab Gulf, Australia, Iran, North Africa, Pakistan, Russia,

Turkey, the United States and a range of European powers have been engaged in the conflict. The original cause of the war, the prospect of greater freedom for ordinary Syrians, has long since disappeared into the bitter realities of regional and sectarian conflict.

By March 2020, the Syrian Observatory for Human Rights estimated the death toll to be close to 600,000. Two million have been injured and 12 million (more than half the pre-war population) displaced from their homes. Of these, around 6 million are estimated to have left the country as refugees. Why has the Syrian civil war been so long and so bloody? It's worth looking in more detail at its religious and geopolitical facets before turning to Britain's role.

RELIGIOUS WAR

From the outset, the sectarian character of the Syrian war has been evident. In April 2011, a Sunni resident of Jabla, a coastal city populated by both Sunnis and Alawites, said: 'There's strife between us now, it's been planted, and the problem is going to exist forever in Jabla.' As the Syria expert Joshua Landis noted: '[t]he Syrian regime – the Baathist Alawite-dominated regime of Assad – is the last minoritarian regime in the Levant.' Before Syria, the Christians of Lebanon and the Sunni of Iraq had both fought civil wars to prevent power falling into the hands of the Shi'a majority. An authoritarian, minoritarian regime cannot assume there will be an uncontested transition to another ruler from its clique. By definition, upheaval represents an existential threat to Syria's Alawis. Within living memory, Alawis know what it is like to be at the bottom of the social order and have no desire to return there.

Meanwhile, as we have seen, their religious practices are abhorred by many other Muslims. Orthodox Sunni Muslim states in the Gulf, notably Saudi Arabia, the United Arab Emirates and Qatar, threw their weight behind Syria's predominantly Sunni rebel groups. From a theological perspective although not in their practices, these Gulf states, especially Saudi Arabia, have little in their beliefs that separate them from ISIS: a literalist interpretation of Islam that is intolerant of religious diversity and focused on trying to replicate the example set by the prophet Muhammad and his earliest followers. This is not to suggest that any Gulf state has offered official support to ISIS. In spite of numerous attempts to prove a funding link from Gulf countries to ISIS, the conclusion of a wide range of analysts and experts is that support has come from wealthy individuals, rather than any official body. Gulf states' governments have, however, offered extensive support to other jihadist groups in Syria that can still be defined as Islamist terrorists. For example, there is evidence that Qatar supported Hay'at Tahrir Al-Sham, an Al-Qaeda affiliate. Similarly, Saudi Arabia provided extensive support to another Islamist terror group opposed to Assad called the Nur al-Din al-Zinki brigade, which at one point reportedly beheaded a captured child. While not sharing the religious conservatism of the Gulf states, Turkey, ruled by a strongman Islamist in Recep Tayyip Erdogan, has channelled support to Sunni Islamist militants in Syria and even to ISIS.

Bashar Al-Assad learned important lessons from the 2003 invasion of Ba'athist Iraq. As largely Sunni Arab Iraqis turned to insurgency activity against the US-backed governments of Iraq, many former Ba'athist leaders found refuge in Syria's capital, Damascus. Al-Assad allowed key border posts to become highly porous and expressed his public support for the principle and practice of 'resistance,' as did his senior ministers. Key financiers of the Iraqi insurgency such as Muhammad Yunis Ahmad operated from Damascus largely unmolested by the Syrian authorities. At the same time, Syria thickened its relations with Iran, both in operational co-ordination between security units and underlying religious connections between Iran's Shi'a Ayatollahs and Syria's ruling Alawite sect. The Iraq crisis empowered Iran and created an 'axis of resistance' between Iran and Syria. Unsurprisingly, when the Arab Spring mutated into a full-scale civil war in Syria, Iran threw its support behind Syria's ruling regime. With its expeditionary military, capable special forces and range of proxies from Lebanon's Hezbollah to the Iraqi Hashd Al-Sha'bi militias, Iran could offer up well-trained, experienced fighters. By contrast, the Gulf and Western countries that supported the Syrian rebels had little to offer beyond cash, sprayed out among a range of groups accurately described by Joshua Landis as 'incompetent and unpopular.'

Iran, and a wide range of Iranian-controlled Shi'a militias, have become a buttress holding up the Assad regime. These Shi'a militias, notably Lebanese Hezbollah and the Afghan Fatemiyoun Division, operate in Syria in close coordination with, and sometimes under the command of Iran's 'Qods' special forces. Iran's Shi'a 'Foreign Legions' have become a crucial aspect of the

Islamic Republic's ability to project its power overseas. In Syria in 2012 and 2013, these groups, especially Hezbollah, saved Assad's regime from collapse by participating in operations to secure crucial territory around Damascus. This intervention, publicly acknowledged by Hezbollah's leader, Hassan Nasrallah, in April 2013, proved a crucial turning point in the early stages of the war. Unlike Syria's corrupt and incompetent army, Hezbollah fighters had frontline experience against Israel, the pre-eminent military power in the region. They made an immediate impact in Syria's civil war.

ENTER PUTIN'S RUSSIA

It is possible to make the case for a religious-cultural basis to Russia's military involvement in Syria. Syria has a significant Orthodox Christian minority, similar to the main religious grouping in Russia. Further, Russia fears Islamist terrorism, including from its own Muslim minority populations. President Putin has often characterised his country's actions in Syria as being a defence against terrorism. However, pure realpolitik clearly guides Russia's actions. For Russia, Syria represents its most significant and longest-standing ally in the Middle East. During the Cold War, the supposedly socialist Assad regime made common cause with the USSR, signing a military agreement in 1971 that gave Russia a naval base in Tartus, its only military presence in the Mediterranean. For Russia, the decision to support Syria is based on the historical relationship to the country and its strategic interests there. But alongside the historical factors was a reason grounded in current affairs.

As we have already seen, in 2011 Russia (and China) perceived that a peacekeeping mission in Libya had morphed into unauthorised regime change implemented by Western nations, led by the United Kingdom and France. This undermined already low trust at the United Nations Security Council, making it all the more likely that Russia would block any form of restrictive action against the Syrian regime. As demonstration of this, Russia's first veto on United Nations action in Syria came in October 2011, just two weeks before the capture and killing of Qadhafi, after his regime had fallen to Western-backed rebels. Russia's Ambassador to the United Nations, Vitaly Churkin, spelled out Russia's view:

'The situation in Syria cannot be considered in the Council separately from the Libyan experience. The international community is alarmed by statements that compliance with Security Council resolutions on Libya in the NATO interpretation is a model for the future actions of NATO in implementing the responsibility to protect. It is easy to see that today's "Unified Protector" model could happen in Syria. All present should understand that the Russian position regarding the conflict in Libya is in no way based on any kind of special ties with the Al-Qadhafi regime, especially since a number of States represented at this table had warmer relations with the Libyan Arab Jamahiriya.'

Russia and China made it very clear that their veto was a response to Western powers having exploited ambiguities in the Libya resolutions. As we have seen, these ambiguities had allowed a regime-change operation initially justified on the grounds of a relatively novel concept in international practice, Responsibility to Protect, that proposes a framework for intervention to prevent massacres. For authoritarian regimes such as Russia and China, UN-mandated regime change justified on human rights grounds represents an existential threat. This is the case even if there is no foreseeable possibility of any UN-approved operation against Russia or China. As early as June 2011, the British Foreign Secretary, William Hague, said that Assad, 'needs to reform, or step aside.' This was by no means a considered British position – as a senior adviser told me: 'He said it off the cuff, publicly, and then he was tied to that policy. He didn't, as far as I know, ask, do we have a viable alternative that can take over the country?' This is a classic example of British foreign policy. Even momentous decisions on regime change arise as a result of immediate domestic political opportunism, rather than any considered policy process.

At the time of Russia's first veto in October 2011, few would have predicted that Russia (with China as its enabler) would veto attempts by the UN Security Council to take action on Syria a total of 16 times up to June 2021. In 2011, the prospect of Syria's civil war continuing for another eleven years would have seemed an extreme, worst-case scenario. Sadly, in Syria, the worst case has become the base case.

It is important to be clear-eyed about Russia and China's behaviour at the UN. It is not contradictory to state that Russia and China allowed themselves to be heavily influenced by a sense of betrayal over Libya while also seeing a cynical, zero-sum calculation based on Russia's long-term interests in Syria, with complete indifference to human suffering that characterises both of these authoritarian states. These are mutually supporting, rather than mutually exclusive factors. The idea that Russia or China cares at all about international human rights concepts is not supported by any recent evidence. It is possible that Russia would have vetoed UN action in Syria regardless of the situation in Libya. But the NATO operation in Libya made a veto inevitable.

USE OF CHEMICAL WEAPONS

To a significant extent, Russia's later vetoes have been an irrelevance. It was clear from early 2013 onwards that no substantive UN resolution on Syria would pass, however complex and extenuated the mitigations offered to placate Russia's intransigent negotiators. Action at the UN became a sideshow. The main event was the question of direct military intervention in the conflict by outsiders. In August 2012, President Obama was asked what would lead him to take military action against the Assad regime. His answer seemed unambiguous: 'We have been very clear to the Assad regime that a red line for us is we start seeing a whole bunch of chemical weapons moving around or being utilized. That would change my calculus.' As Obama's former deputy national security adviser Ben Rhodes explained, in July 2012 the Obama administration became aware that Syria was considering using chemical weapons. Syria's government itself had already confirmed at that time that it possessed these banned arms. According to Rhodes's description, the Obama administration privately warned Syria, as well as its allies Russia and Iran, that Assad 'would be held accountable,' if it used chemical weapons.

Perhaps in response to these warnings, Syria's government does not appear to have used chemical weapons until later in 2012, although it had already deployed cluster munitions and helicopter gunships against unarmed civilians as well as against armed opponents. This changed in December 2012. As Charles Lister, the leading scholar of Syria's insurgency, wrote in his comprehensive history of the Syrian jihad: 'Activists reported an alleged chemical attack by regime forces on the FSA-controlled al-Bayadah district of Homs city on 23 December. At least six people were killed.... This marked the regime's first alleged chemical attack of the conflict. More were to follow.' This attack was subsequently reported by French intelligence and verified by the US State Department.

The fog of war, as well as mustard gas, which surrounds this first attack, began to dissipate during early 2013. In March, 26 civilians died in Khan al-Assal, a suburb of Aleppo. Improbably, the Syrian government claimed that rebels had managed to acquire and weaponise delivery systems for Sarin, a nerve agent, and launch it against their own side. As this debate raged, events took over: a series of increasingly serious and deadly chemical attacks occurred, some clearly deployed from helicopters (none of the rebels had helicopters) and some using 'Volcano' rockets that were known to be part of Syria's arsenal. Chemical attacks against Syrian civilians only occurred in areas under rebel control, even as the Syrian government, which had publicly acknowledged its chemical weapons arsenal, insisted that these attacks were 'false flag' operations carried out by rebels. By August 2013 UN investigators were on the ground in Syria trying to get to the bottom of the Khan al-Assal attack. Their arrival coincided with a devastating, overwhelming chemical attack on Eastern Ghouta, a rebel-held suburb of Damascus. In the early hours of 21 August, Volcano rockets containing Sarin were fired into the crowded streets of Ghouta.

In the initial hours following the attack, there was room for doubt and misunderstanding over what had happened. Wildly varying casualty figures allowed Syria's allies to question the reality of eyewitness reports. Russian media outlets, including English-language channels such as *Russia Today* (RT), tried to sow confusion and falsehood. But as the hours ticked by on 21st August 2013, it became increasingly clear that a horrific massacre had occurred. Eyewitnesses, professional journalists, and media organisations posted images and videos that were impossible to ignore. Piles of dead bodies with no visible signs of injury, harrowing videos of convulsing children foaming at the mouth, rows of dead bodies, the sheer variety of images posted on a single day from a range of unrelated social media accounts, made it impossible for the incident to be dismissed out of hand. The scale of the attack and its target pointed directly to the Syrian government. The Sarin used was later shown to be from the same stocks as that used in Khan al-Assal. This did not prevent sceptics in the West from doing their best to sow doubt in the days that followed. A singular example of this came from Seumas Milne, who would later work as Director of Strategy to Jeremy Corbyn as Leader of the Opposition. He wrote in the *Guardian* on 27th August 2013 that, although the Ghouta atrocity 'appears to have been a chemical weapons attack', 'no reliable evidence' had 'been produced to confirm even what chemical might have been used, let alone who delivered it,' adding that 'it's hard to see a rational motivation' for the Assad regime to have deployed the weapons – beyond, presumably, the rational motivation of killing hundreds of your opponents and generally striking terror into them.

Dan Kaszeta, a veteran of chemical and biological weapons response in both the US army and the US Secret Service, explained the developing pattern of chemical attacks in Syria:

> **All the way back to the seventies, the Syrians had an offensive programme which they likely inherited via the Egyptians from the time of the United Arab Republic [when Syria and Egypt were united as a single national state]. The whole Syrian setup was based on it being a poor-man's nuclear bomb deterrent against Israel. It was classic Soviet chemical warfare doctrine, deploying large scale mustard gas attacks against airfields or cities to prevent the Israelis from being able to launch a nuclear attack on Syria. So the Syrians had delivery systems that weren't suitable for close quarter fighting of the kind they had in the civil war. At the early stage of the conflict there was improvisation to see what worked in field conditions. You want Sarin, rather than mustard gas, for precision attacks on places that you plan to re-enter and they had to develop new capability, starting with small attacks like the December 2012 one. The Ghouta attack represented the full development of that chemical weapons capability.**

Obama's 'red line' had very clearly been crossed in the Ghouta attack. But the UN investigators were still on the ground, meaning that military action could not happen instantly. In the days that followed, according to an insider account, Obama's administration debated its next steps, struggling with the legacy of the fiasco of the war in Iraq and a hostile, Republican-controlled Congress. It was increasingly clear that Obama, himself an 'anti-war' politician, would struggle to convince his own Democratic party, let alone the opposition Republicans, to support his plan for military action against Syria. But the fatal blow to Obama's hopes came not from Capitol Hill but from the Houses of Parliament in London.

OPPOSITION TO INTERVENTION

Britain was having its own version of the 'red line' crisis. At the beginning of the conflict, the particular circumstances of Syria's Alawite rulers and their willingness to fight a seemingly endless civil war does not appear to have been taken seriously by British policy makers. By then, as explained in the preceding chapter on Libya, the Foreign Office was an increasingly weak institution, lacking expertise or impact among Britain's government departments. William Hague had already decided that 'Assad must go,' even if there was no clear idea how this outcome would be achieved. However, there is little evidence that the Foreign Office considered the possibility that, unlike in Egypt and Tunisia, the Assad regime would fight to the last bullet. Britain was pushing for intervention, regardless of any evidence that it would work.

Domestic politics are also relevant here. In response to the increasing unpopularity of 'Tony Blair's wars' in Iraq and

Afghanistan, a rare cross-party convention had emerged in Britain that Parliament should be consulted prior to the country engaging in military action. As a 2007 resolution passed by the House of Commons stated: 'This House welcomes the precedents set by the Government in 2002 and 2003 in seeking and obtaining the approval of the House for its decisions in respect of military action against Iraq; is of the view that it is inconceivable that any Government would in practice depart from this precedent.' This resolution did not have the full force of law but it was an important signpost of both government and opposition intent. When Parliament debated the deployment of forces in Libya in March 2011, the Foreign Secretary William Hague promised that the government would, 'enshrine in law for the future the necessity of consulting Parliament on military action.' While this promise was not in fact enacted (because it comes with all kinds of operational problems, such as how to respond in an emergency?) it illustrated an increasingly well-established consensus that Parliament should be at the heart of any decision to initiate military action.

In the absence of such a law to require parliamentary approval for their deployment, Britain's armed forces are nominally under the control of the Crown, and practically under the control of the government of the day. Therefore, although David Cameron did not need parliamentary authorisation to respond militarily to Assad's use of chemical weapons, he had made it abundantly clear that he would follow recent precedent and seek approval from parliament in the summer of 2013. Cameron needed to manage the parliamentary process. While he faced a measure of opposition from his own party and his coalition partners, the Liberal Democrats, he needed to find a way to work with the opposition Labour party, led by Ed Miliband.

In response to Cameron's overtures, Miliband tabled an amendment that was functionally nearly identical to the government's proposal, save an additional vote on the timing of a military response to Syria. But the government opposed it and accused Miliband of giving 'succour' to Bashar Al-Assad. The fault does not solely lie with Cameron. Miliband was also pursuing his own political interests. The Labour Party was trying to correct the reputation for war-mongering that it had garnered under the Blair years. Miliband himself had worked hard to differentiate his style and practices from those of his former boss. His amendment was a way of signalling Labour's more cautious approach to military action without actually making any significant change to the proposed approach.

On this topic, as with so many others, Labour continued to be in Tony Blair's shadow. Ten years on, the fake intelligence on Iraq's WMD was on everyone's mind. Also, the efforts of Labour's far left anti-war faction, Russian state media and others had an impact.

Cameron clearly does not regret his decision to brand Miliband's proposals, broadly similar to his own, as in some way supportive of Syria's murderous regime. In his autobiography he quotes himself as telling Miliband: 'you've got to understand you're putting yourself on the side of Vladimir Putin and Bashar Al-Assad by not standing up to this.' But Cameron also describes being blindsided by Miliband's amendment after extensive efforts on his part to respond to Miliband's core concerns. As the debate ahead of the vote unfolded, some of Parliament's most distinguished members observed that there was little difference between the government's proposal and Labour's amendment. The veteran Liberal Democrat MP Menzies Campbell, a barrister, admitted he could discern no important distinction between the two texts, saying:

> **I have read the motion and Opposition amendment and I believe that both are motivated by the same determination to do what is right and to see that the House endorses everything that is right. However, I have to confess that, even following the most narrow textual analysis, I can find no difference of substance or principle anywhere in the two offerings.**

In spite of this observation, Campbell voted for the government text and against Labour's.

The government narrowly lost its vote, by 285 to 272. Thirty Conservative MPs failed to back the government, as well as nine Liberal Democrat coalition partners. The Labour amendment failed by a larger margin, reflecting the smaller numbers of Labour MPs in the House of Commons. However, given that the two texts were largely the same, 492 of Parliament's 650 MPs, a majority, voted for taking military action. But neither motion passed, even though they were essentially the same. In both cases most MPs divided along party lines rather than on the substance of the issue. Tories voted against Labour's amendment and Labour MPs voted against the Tory position. It was unthinking party politics, rather than any substantial issue of principle, that led to the first British government defeat in Parliament on a matter of war since 1782 and the American War of Independence.

What makes this peculiarly ironic is the comparison with Libya. There, the British government took military action, without the authorisation of the House of Commons, in order to prevent a 'Srebenica-style' massacre in Benghazi. As we have seen, no such massacre was on the cards in Libya. In Syria, the massacres were, in fact, taking place. But Parliament chose not to act on the basis of narrow party politics.

For all the high-flown rhetoric of Britain's 'role in the world' that dominated the parliamentary debate ahead of the vote, the result came down to tribal politics. But the outcome was a bitter reminder of Britain's ability to have impact on the world stage, albeit probably not in the manner most MPs had hoped. The British votes not to back military force acted like a catastrophic breach in the hull of a stricken ship: the craft had been taking on water, but now it was sinking fast. Quickly, Obama's efforts to persuade Congress to authorise military action were washed away as America's key ally proved to be unreliable (again). Even Obama's Democratic allies in the Senate started to peel away. Accepting the inevitable, Obama eventually shelved a planned vote in Congress. Britain's refusal had killed the plan. Attention turned to France, the only other Western nation that had a meaningfully effective air force. Within a few days of Britain's vote, John Kerry, Obama's Secretary of State (the Americans' grand name for their foreign minister) publicly praised France as the United States' 'oldest ally,' not mentioning Britain. Obama observed, again without naming Britain, that, 'a lot of people think something should be done, but nobody wants to do it.' While these comments might appear minor rebukes, to much of Britain's security and military community, whose raison d'être is largely defined as maintaining a close relationship with the Americans, these slights were devastating. Lord Ashdown, the former Liberal Democrat leader who had served in Britain's special forces and intelligence services, said: 'In more than 50 years of trying to serve my country in one form or another, I don't think I've ever felt more depressed this morning or, indeed, more ashamed.' The Defence Secretary, Philip Hammond, said: 'I am disappointed and I am slightly apprehensive. We have a very close working relationship with the Americans. It is a difficult time for our armed forces, having prepared to go into this action, to then be stood down and have to watch while the US acts alone or perhaps the US acts with France.' Asked about the renewed Franco-American alliance, Hammond said: 'It's certainly a reversal of the usual position and it will be an uncomfortable place for many people in the British armed forces who are used to working alongside the Americans as an everyday, normal course of business.'

Speaking four years later, John Kerry spelled out exactly how Britain's vote had torpedoed Obama's plans:

The President of the United States of America, Barack Obama, did decide to use force [against Syria]. And he announced his decision publicly and said, we're going to act. We're going to do what we need to do to respond to this blatant violation of international law. End of warnings, end of the red line he had chosen.

Now, we were marching towards that time when, lo and behold, on a Thursday of a week before the Friday decision, Prime Minister David Cameron went to Parliament... He went to the Parliament and he sought a vote of approval for him to join in the action that we were going to engage in. And guess what? The Parliament voted no. They shot him down. So, as we were briefing Congress – and I was on one of those briefing calls with maybe 100 members of Congress on the call – many of them were saying: 'Well you got to come to us. You got to, you know, go through the constitutional process and get permission from us to do something.

And the president decided – I got a call on Friday night, we met Saturday morning – and the president had decided that he needed to go to Congress because of what had happened in Great Britain and because he needed the approval and that was the way we do something like that.

As the world's democratic leaders appeared increasingly unable to manage their own legislatures, matters took an unexpected turn. Seeing an opportunity in the deadlock, Russia persuaded Syria to submit to international inspections and destruction of its chemical weapons stocks. In an environment where most of the West's leading military powers appeared unwilling to take action, it was impossible not to accept Syria's surprising offer, a diplomatic triumph for Russia. While Syria did indeed hand over many of its chemical weapons for destruction by international specialists, intelligence agencies suspected that only a proportion of its sites had been opened to inspection. Chemical weapons attacks, clearly delivered by the Syrian government, have continued to take place in Syria. As late as May 2019, the Syrian government appeared to be continuing to use chemical weapons such as chlorine against the rebels. The red line has been crossed, and re-crossed, many times.

At the same time, the West did not ignore Syria. In spite of the unenforced 'red line,' the decision was made by Western countries to continue to support rebel groups. The problem was that a significant quantity of the rebels were either hopelessly incompetent or ideologically distasteful as partners for a Western democracy. While Russia and Iran were content to partner with the chemical-weapons-using, mass-murdering Syrian regime, Western powers sought to ally themselves with so-called 'moderate' rebels, leaving the hardline Islamists (who in other circumstances would be accurately described as terrorists) to the Gulf countries, notably Qatar, Saudi Arabia and the UAE. Often this distinction was artificial at best. In Jordan at a special operations centre, Saudi Arabia and other Gulf states supported hardline Islamists. US, British and French forces working out of the same base channelled their support to moderates. But, overall, with no ability to control the constant airstrikes against them, and a tendency for the Islamist rebels to kill their moderate brothers in arms with almost more enthusiasm than they killed Assad's forces, the Syrian opposition proved itself incapable of defeating Assad. Foreign support trickled in at a level sufficient to keep it alive, but functionally pointless. It was like leaving a patient in a persistent vegetative state.

The British parliament's decision to block decisive intervention while maintaining a policy that 'Assad must go' condemned the Syrian rebels to a Catch-22 situation: they would receive nominal support, enough to keep them in existence, while never seriously threatening the Syrian regime. But because the policy was fixated on the removal of Assad rather than the overall interests of the Syrian people, no diplomatic efforts to end the conflict could be contemplated.

For the UK, this policy doom loop was further complicated by the legacy of the Iraq conflict. The Iraq Inquiry, also named the 'Chilcot' inquiry for its eponymous chairman, had been rumbling on from 2009. It only published its conclusions in 2016. The inquiry took so long that one of its key members, the noted historian Sir Martin Gilbert, died. The questions that Chilcot examined, on issues such as chemical weapons intelligence, foreign intervention in the Middle East, the response to Islamist terrorism and forcible regime change, were all directly and urgently relevant to the situation in Syria. But there was a widespread disinclination to take lessons from the Iraq conflict until the Chilcot team had published its final report. As a Foreign Office research analyst, Greg Shapland, observed:

Chilcot had not reported on Iraq and that was a real block to the discussion of possibilities in Libya and Syria.... We all wanted to talk about the lessons from Iraq and we were not allowed to. I think at the more senior levels of the [Foreign] Office they almost certainly were talking about the lessons of Iraq but actually if the whole system had been able to discuss the lessons from Iraq as relayed by Chilcot ... some mistakes could have been avoided.

Absurdly, officials weren't allowed to have better policies on Syria until the official account of their bad policies in Iraq had been published.

THE ISIS CALIPHATE

The black flag flutters in the desert wind as a bulldozer sweeps away the border between Iraq and Syria. In other images, hundreds of fighters fire their Kalashnikovs in the air, amid a sea of black banners depicting the seal of the prophet Muhammad. The great city of Mosul has fallen and Baghdad is threatened.

We are in June 2014, and ISIS has declared a caliphate, a historic term to describe a state ruled by a Muslim 'Caliph,' in its territories in Iraq and Syria. The borders drawn up in the 1916 Sykes-Picot agreement, a byword for a colonial carve-up, have been redrawn by the jihadist tsunami.

At this time, ISIS held a territory similar in size and population to its neighbour Jordan. A would-be country had emerged almost overnight with nearly eight million inhabitants. A veteran counter-insurgency expert, David Kilcullen, starkly summarised the crisis in his 2016 book, *Blood Year*:

> In the northern summer of 2014, in less than a hundred days, ISIS launched its blitzkrieg in Iraq, Libya's government collapsed, civil war engulfed Yemen, a sometime small-town Iraqi preacher named Abu Bakr Al-Baghdadi declared himself caliph, the latest Israeli-Palestine peace initiative failed in a welter of violence that left more than 2,200 people (mostly Palestinian civilians) dead, and the United states and its allies, including the United Kingdom

and Australia, sent troops and planes back to Iraq.... Iran continued its push to become a nuclear threshold power, supported Assad in Syria, and yet became a de facto ally of the United States in Iraq as Tehran and Washington sought, each for different reasons, to bolster the Baghdad government.

Amid this tumult, supporting Syria's rag-tag rebel groups was no longer an end in itself. As both the British Parliament and the US Congress had demonstrated, the debate over whether it was in the interests of Western countries to oust the regime in Syria was vexed. On the other hand, there was a consensus on the urgent need to stop a rampant terrorist state from carrying out beheadings, mass rape, attempted genocide, destruction of historic sites, and from launching attacks in Europe. The urgency was deepened by a rapidly increasing migrant crisis in European countries as millions of Syrian refugees sought refuge in Europe. The tragic images of Aylan Kurdi, a three-year old Kurdish Syrian refugee from ISIS, drowned on a Turkish beach, strengthened the argument that doing nothing was not an option. In this rapidly evolving situation, Syria's rebels only had value to the coalition if they undertook to join the fight against ISIS. From a purely pragmatic perspective, some rebels were willing to sign up to the war against ISIS if it meant they received better weapons and more support. But, as those who worked alongside these rebels have explained, these fighters never had any serious intention of taking the fight to ISIS. Their priority was toppling Assad. ISIS was not their problem.

In early 2015, the interests of Western countries diverged from the interests of the majority of the Syrian rebels. This became a turning point in the civil war. From the start, foreign powers had sought to use rebel groups to further their own interests and agenda in Syria. Countries supported groups that shared their own cultures and prejudices, as we have seen. When the priority became the fight against ISIS, these groups were, mostly, woefully ill-equipped to face a highly motivated force of religious fanatics. Perhaps more importantly, they were disinclined to do so.

This phenomenon reached its apogee with the Pentagon's $500 million 'Train and Equip' programme: an ambitious attempt by the Americans to create a force of thousands of highly trained anti-ISIS Syrian warriors. It was excitedly described as a 'silver bullet inside of Syria' in press briefings. The reality proved to be very different. From the start, the Syrian uprising had been a series of local movements, often tied together by bonds of extended family and tribal connections. The rebellion in Daraa had nothing to do with the rebellion in Aleppo or Idlib, except for having a common goal of getting rid of the Assad regime. When Pentagon trainers took fighters from all over Syria to train them in Turkey and Jordan, they found a dysfunctional force, lacking in cohesion and spirit. This sour atmosphere worsened as it became clear that the US trainers insisted that the fighters must defeat ISIS first, before turning their attention to Assad. As one of the nominated commanders observed: 'Every day I had a meeting with them. I told them the whole idea is wrong. I said: "We are Syrians. Our problem is with the regime. Help us to get rid of the regime." The response was: 'You should not shoot a bullet against the regime".'

This improbable coalition was beset with security breaches and desertions. It was also targeted by the Nusra Front rebel group, an

Al-Qaeda offshoot. Many fighters and their weapons were seized and some executed as they entered Syria to begin operations. One former fighter told me that the Nusra Front had been tipped off by Turkish intelligence, some of whose officers had worked as trainers on the programme. Others have pointed the finger at Qatar: both Turkey and Qatar had close relations with the Nusra Front and appeared to have some channels to ISIS itself.

In a memorable congressional hearing in September 2015, the US commander General Lloyd Austin (who became US Defense Secretary in 2021) was asked how many fighters from this programme were active in the field. Looking excruciatingly uncomfortable, he replied: 'It's a small number. And, er, the ones that are in the fight, is, we're talking four or five.' Calmly, Senator Deb Fischer asked whether the goal for training remained 12,000 fighters. 'At the rate we're going we won't reach the goal we initially established for ourselves,' replied the general. At that rate of progress, it would have taken the Pentagon 600 years to reach that initial goal.

Not all of the Syrian units associated with the fight against ISIS were hopeless. Notably, the Kurdish-led People's Protection Units, known as the YPG, proved an effective and mostly reliable partner to the international coalition. This co-operation was made easier by the fact that the Kurdish fighters at the core of the YPG came from a largely secular, leftist tradition that included female fighters and was open to incorporating international volunteers. In addition, the YPG was not fixated on the removal of Assad, focusing instead on the creation of a secure Kurdish zone in north Syria, known as Rojava. Unlike other Syrian rebels, the YPG took the fight to ISIS willingly as its desired territory had been overrun by ISIS, who had massacred Kurdish civilians. As a result, the force that dislodged ISIS was mostly YPG units, supported by Western special forces, with heavy air support from NATO and allied fighter jets. This combination proved effective in 2015 and 2016 in dislodging ISIS from its stranglehold in Syria. At the same time, the operation to recover Mosul and north Iraq was also taking place.

The successful co-operation with the YPG was in some senses ironic. The YPG was closely linked to the Turkish PKK, otherwise known as the Kurdistan Workers Party. This militant group had been fighting the Turkish state for decades, pushing a Kurdish separatist agenda. The PKK has targeted Turkish interests all over the world, often killing civilians, sometimes foreign tourists. Britain, the US, the EU and Australia were among the many countries to brand the PKK a terrorist organisation. Its leader, Abdullah Ocalan, was abducted from Nairobi by Turkish intelligence agents in 1999, with the assistance of the CIA. The alliance between the YPG and Western allies was therefore viewed by the Turkish government as a direct threat to Turkey's territorial security. In the midst of a campaign against ISIS, Turkey, the most important NATO member in the region, turned its attention to attacking the Kurdish allies of the coalition, rather than throwing its weight behind the attack against ISIS.

As someone who worked on the ground with Syrian rebel groups explained to me, Turkey allowed thousands of foreign fighters into ISIS-controlled regions of Syria. Turkey also moved the rebels it backed from the frontline of the fight against

ISIS to focus on attacking Kurdish groups. Rumours of direct support from elements of Turkish intelligence to ISIS have been confirmed by operatives working on the ground in north Syria. Led by an Islamist autocrat, Turkey, a key NATO ally and staunch opponent of Assad, was not a reliable partner in the war against the Islamic State.

RUSSIA'S AIRSTRIKES BACK BASHAR

As the conflict against ISIS unfolded, Russia was stepping up its own involvement in Syria. The international community's inability to respond in 2013 had sent an important signal to Russia: it could afford to become more directly involved in Syria without risking serious consequences. We have already noted Russia's historic relations with Syria, and its naval base at Tartus. Russian advisers were probably present inside Syria's air defence units in 2013 helping the Syrians operate the Russian-made S-300 missile system. Also, in 2013, Russian mercenaries, including senior reserve officers in Russian's Federal Security Bureau (FSB, successor to the KGB) were active in combat on behalf of the Syrian government. But the major Russian intervention did not occur until 2015. In that year, Putin and Assad signed an agreement that gave Russia an airbase at Hmeimim, near Latakia in the Alawite heartland of northwest Syria. This treaty allowed Russia diplomatic immunity for its personnel and no time limit on its period of occupation. Quickly, Russia established fighter jets, air defences and signals intelligence installations.

Russia portrayed its intervention as a counter-terrorism operation, conducted entirely legally at the request of its ally, the

Syrian government. To the gullible and the cynical, Russia was merely helping the international coalition against ISIS. But Russia's real target was the Syrian opposition. On the first night, Russia's airstrikes struck opposition groups in areas where there was little or no ISIS presence. There was no doubt about the nature of the Russians' targets. Two separate sources with direct knowledge of the incident have confirmed to me that the communications networks used by Western countries to co-ordinate with Syria's rebels were taken out by Russia's airstrikes on 30th September 2015. This would suggest that Russia saw its action as more than merely shoring up the embattled President Assad, but sending a clear message to Western players in Syria's war: we will destroy your allies and networks in the Syrian uprising.

The most significant direct result of the British parliamentary vote in 2013 was giving a free hand to Russian and Syrian airforces to bombard rebels and civilians in rebel-held areas. In the years since 2013, with the exception of the Kurdish zone, the Syrian uprising has collapsed into a few small pockets around Idlib and along the borders with Turkey. The fall of Aleppo, Syria's largest city and the most important rebel stronghold, was a civilian tragedy, with Russian and Syrian forces targeting hospitals and residential areas. Cluster munitions and incendiary bombs were deliberately deployed to cause excessive civilian casualties. According to the independent Violations Documentation Center in Syria, more than 31,000 civilians were killed in Aleppo during the period from July 2012 to the fall of the city to the Assad regime in December 2016. Russia's willingness to raise the stakes paid off. Russia won Syria's war for Assad.

DISHONOURABLE VICTORY

In the early 2020s, it is clear that the Syrian rebellion has failed, even though fighting continues, particularly around the rebels' stronghold in Idlib. There is no foreseeable prospect of the rebels ejecting the Syrian regime, or that Bashar Al-Assad will feel the pressure to accede to the original, seemingly long-forgotten demands for freedom and democracy. Syria's decade-long war has butchered hundreds of thousands of people and displaced 10 million. Syria is less free, more brutal, poorer, more corrupt and devastated by years of intense fighting. Assad's victory is one that guarantees further conflict. The Sunni majority in Syria, many suspicious of the Alawi sect, are now even more downtrodden and oppressed. They will be a source of future opposition. The desperate circumstances that led to Assad relying on Iran and Russia to prop him up has further complicated the politics of a volatile region. Russia has a permanent foothold in Syria and Iranian-backed militias control portions of the territory, meaning that it is unlikely that Assad himself will ever actually control much of the territory once known as Syria. Iran's influence stretches through Iraq and into Syria and Lebanon, and Tehran has achieved its long-held ambitions of establishing a land bridge from its territory to the Mediterranean. This huge expansion of Iran's power – resulting from failed international policies first in Iraq and then in Syria – has greatly inflamed tensions between Iran and Israel. It has also increased tensions between Iran and Gulf countries, notably the UAE and Saudi Arabia, which has become more aggressive in the region.

It would be ridiculous to claim that this is all the result of Britain's 2013 vote against military action, or its and Washington's policy of supporting hapless rebel groups without giving them the resources to achieve victory. It's embarrassing that Britain chose its approach on the basis of party advantage rather than deep principles of foreign affairs. It's also disappointing that the UK let the Americans down again. Nonetheless, because of the trauma and humiliation of failed interventions in Iraq and Afghanistan, Britain's decision not to intervene in Syria was understandable. Based on three major case studies (Iraq, Afghanistan and Libya) it is fairly clear that military intervention with the lofty goal of establishing democratic institutions doesn't deliver the desired outcome, but does deliver a lot of undesired outcomes. That said, Syria was different in one key respect. The Syrian regime was actively carrying out war crimes against its own people. Nerve gas attacks, massacres, industrial-scale torture of prisoners. In 2013, in Syria, unlike the case in Iraq, Afghanistan and Libya, when Western powers marched in, a humanitarian catastrophe was unfolding.

The decision not to take the fight to Assad in 2013 did not come with the readiness to follow through with that choice. The UK was not willing to take the necessary steps to remove Assad and his murderous regime, and its decision meant that France and the US also did not act. But the UK was also unwilling to accept the unwelcome implication that the Assad regime would continue to exist in Syria and attempt to make peace with that. The decision to continue to supply a hopeless rebel army prolonged the war:

the suffering, the torture, the deaths, the displacements, the refugees, the chemical weapons attacks and the drownings of desperate migrant children on Turkish beaches. Britain repeated the hollow mantra 'Assad must go,' while leaving the Syrian opposition with no chance of bringing that about.

It was, in short, an expression of arrogant privilege – a country that could posture on the world stage as a great power, without living with the consequences of its actions. When speaking of an earlier British misadventure in the Middle East, the 1956 Suez Crisis, Winston Churchill said of Britain's secret plan with France and Israel to invade Egypt: 'I would never have dared; and if I had dared, I would certainly never have dared stop.' Of Britain's Syria policy 55 years later, he might have observed that he would never have dared calling for Assad to go, but if he had dared, he would certainly never have dared to proceed without a plan for Assad's departure.

In August 2013, readers of the *Financial Times* were treated to a succinct letter describing the madness of Middle Eastern politics. In less than 100 words, KN Al-Sabah depicted the bizarre contradictions that appeared to be swirling around that region. Unsurprisingly, the letter became an internet sensation.

> **Iran is backing Assad. Gulf states are against Assad! Assad is against Muslim Brotherhood. Muslim Brotherhood and Obama are against General Sisi. But Gulf states are pro-Sisi! Which means they are against Muslim Brotherhood! Iran is pro-Hamas, but Hamas is backing Muslim Brotherhood! Obama is backing Muslim Brotherhood, yet Hamas is against the US! Gulf states are pro-US.**

But Turkey is with Gulf states against Assad; yet Turkey is pro-Muslim Brotherhood against General Sisi. And General Sisi is being backed by the Gulf states! Welcome to the Middle East and have a nice day.

Understandably, the usual reader's response was to throw up their hands in despair. Now, in the early 2020s, things are even worse. If he were writing now, Al-Sabah would need additional lines on Russia, Ukraine, Qatar, Yemen, Israel, Libya, Sudan, Lebanon and Afghanistan.

7. RUSSIA AND THE LONDON LAUNDROMAT

'Finishing schools for the children of oligarchs.'
Headmaster Andrew Halls, describing Britain's private schools

'Uprooting Kremlin-linked oligarchs will be a challenge given the close ties between Russian money and the United Kingdom's ruling Conservative Party, the press, and its real estate and financial industry.'
Max Bergmann, former senior official in Obama's State Department

COURTED

In a palatial mansion overlooking Regent's Park, guests sipped Ruinart champagne and tucked into plates of caviar. All of high society was there, from showbusiness stars to minor royalty, to newspaper editors and former Prime Ministers. But the guest who attracted the most attention was the serving Prime Minister, Boris

Johnson, accompanied by his partner, Carrie Symonds. The hosts, a former KGB officer, Alexander Lebedev, and his son Evgeny had good reason to celebrate: only hours earlier, Johnson's landslide election victory had been confirmed, one that the Lebedevs had urged through their media platform the *Evening Standard*, edited by another influential Conservative politician, the former Chancellor George Osborne. Perhaps unsurprisingly, Johnson's vanquished opponent, the Labour leader Jeremy Corbyn, did not take up his invitation and guests had to make do with an impersonator.

The Prime Minister's connections with the Lebedevs ran deep. As London Mayor, Johnson had enjoyed the support of the *Evening Standard*, and socialised extensively with Evgeny. The two joined forces for a publicity stunt in 2015 when they slept outside on the streets of London to draw attention to homelessness. In 2016, Johnson, now Foreign Secretary, attended a party at the Lebedevs' palace in the hills of Umbria. One report of the event suggested that a soft-porn model bared her breasts at the dinner table. Evgeny Lebedev's office told OpenDemocracy.net: 'This is wrong,' but declined to elaborate. However lively the event, for Britain's chief diplomat to find himself at the foreign family home of a former KGB agent was what civil servants would call a 'brave decision.' Johnson attended another of these parties, travelling alone and without his security detail, in April 2018, two days after attending a high-level NATO summit on Russia. Details of this later occasion are scant, save for the fact that he was spotted afterwards, 'wandering around an Italian airport, quite alone, seemingly wearing the clothes he had slept in and looking very much worse for wear.'

Whether or not Lebedev senior, the former KGB officer turned banker, is a pro-Putin figure, remains a subject of debate. He is a minority shareholder in *Novaya Gazeta*, one of the few largely independent newspapers left in Russia. But he also reportedly has been connected with Putin for decades. An article little-noticed outside Russia by Yuri Shchekochikhin, a renowned journalist, explains that a secret society of former intelligence officers calling itself 'Patriots of State Security' sought in the early 1990s to bring back discipline and fierce Russian nationalism, and that among its members were Vladimir Putin and Alexander Lebedev. This is not corroborated. It is the case, however, that in May 2022 Alexander Lebedev was sanctioned by Canada having 'directly enabled Vladimir Putin's senseless war in Ukraine and bear[ing] responsibility for the pain and suffering of the people of Ukraine.' Lebedev, who remains unsanctioned in Britain, responded: 'I have been an opposition figure for a decade...'

In 2020, Johnson overrode the House of Lords Appointments Commission and, according to widespread reports, the advice of Britain's security services, to give Evgeny Lebedev a peerage, making him a lifelong, unelected legislator. Most peers choose to locate their title at a single location in Britain. Lebedev, who has a manorial home in the grounds of Hampton Court Palace, wanted to name-check Russia. He took the title of Baron Lebedev, of Hampton in the London Borough of Richmond upon Thames and of Siberia in the Russian Federation.

In recent years, the Lebedevs are by no means the only Russians to have developed links with the Conservative Party. A series of Russian donors have generously supported the Tories with substantial donations. Lubov Chernukhin, the wife of a former Russian finance minister, gave more than £1.6 million to the Tories over a seven-year period, making her one of the biggest female donors in British political history. She was keen on tennis. In February 2020, she paid £45,000 to the Conservatives for a game with Boris Johnson, then Prime Minister, and the Conservatives' co-chairman Ben Elliot (whose uncle is the Prince of Wales). In 2014, the donation was steeper – £160,000 for tennis with David Cameron, then Prime Minister, and Johnson, Mayor of London. She also paid £35,000 to have dinner with Gavin Williamson, the former Defence Secretary, in the claustrophobic bunker of Winston Churchill's old Cabinet War Rooms.

Another prominent donor is Alexander Temerko, a Russian-Ukrainian former arms dealer. Based in London, Temerko portrays himself as a dissident opposed to President Putin. He is now the owner of a company seeking to build a high-capacity energy link between Britain and France, part of Britain's critical national infrastructure. Temerko is close to Boris Johnson, whom he calls by the diminutive 'Sasha' (Johnson's first name is Alexander) and with whom he boasts of putting the world to rights over a bottle of wine at Johnson's parliamentary office. Since relocating to the UK in 2005, Temerko has given £1.3 million to the Conservatives. At a fundraising auction in 2013, Temerko reportedly paid £90,000 for a bronze bust of Cameron, which is now on show at the Carlton private members club in London.

I make no suggestion that by donating money or meeting politicians, the Lebedevs, Chernukhin or Temerko have broken any laws or indeed done anything wrong at all. But the size of their donations and the existence of their personal meetings with politicians go some way to illustrating the access that Russian oligarchs have acquired in London.

In general, it is the case that Russia's rich have been given a warm welcome by the British establishment and by Britain's service industries, which have been pleased to get their hands on billions of pounds. Britain has specialised in helping wealthy Russians bank, invest and spend their wealth while living in London, and London is sometimes described as 'Moscow-on-Thames' or 'Londongrad.'

For the wealthy Russian, Londongrad is a splendid place. Prime central London property is not cheap, but once acquired it tends to go up in value. Perhaps more importantly, property rights are rigorously enforced, unlike in their home country. According to the London estate agent Aston Chase, 150,000 Russians live in Londongrad properties worth a total of £8 billion. In 2014, even after Vladimir Putin's first invasion of Ukraine when sanctions had been imposed, wealthy Russians were the largest international group of buyers of London's 'super-prime' properties (priced at over £10 million). An extraordinary number of London's most prestigious properties are owned by Russians, many of them close to Putin and the Kremlin. This includes Witanhurst, the largest private house in London, four central London properties worth over £250 million owned by Andrey Goncharenko – a key investment manager in the Russian state's strategic asset, Gazprom – and a vast penthouse overlooking the UK Ministry of Defence owned by the deputy Prime Minister Igor Shuvalov.

London has many advantages for Russia's oligarchs. Compared to Moscow, the city has little crime and a professional police force for when things do go wrong. The children of the wealthy Russian can be educated in a range of excellent private schools and if they study hard, they may be able to attend one of Britain's many great universities. London is full of highly capable professional services firms. If a pesky journalist writes something unwelcome about a Russian oligarch, he can hire investigators to look into that person, as was the case when a well-regarded private intelligence bureau identified the home address of a journalist for their Russian oligarch client. If the oligarch doesn't like what has been written, Britain's famously harsh libel laws can be brought to bear. Many stories that would have been printed have been conveniently buried by swift legal action. Particularly for smaller publications and local media, the costs of defending a libel case are simply not bearable, as the north London newspaper the *Ham & High* discovered when it reported a major oligarch on its doorstep and then had to delete the report after legal threats.

Russia's riches create ripples of opportunity for many businesses, particularly in the professional services sector. Lawyers, accountants, bankers, consultants, and public relations advisers all benefit from fat fees. For example, Linklaters, a leading City law firm, acted as adviser on several major transactions involving Russian businesses and, until February 2022, it boasted of its 'deep understanding of what our [Russian] clients want.' Linklaters refused an invitation by Britain's Parliament to discuss its work in Russia, leaving the Foreign Affairs Committee to conclude:

We regret their unwillingness to engage with our inquiry and must leave others to judge whether their work at 'the forefront of financial, corporate and commercial developments in Russia' has left them so entwined in the corruption of the Kremlin and its supporters that they are no longer able to meet the standards expected of a UK-regulated law firm.

In March 2022, Linklaters sprinted to the moral high ground and announced it would sever its links with Russian business, saying: 'Russia's invasion of Ukraine is reprehensible and it is right that we stand together in condemning it.'

TREASURE ISLANDS

Another attraction of Britain for shady Russians is the ability to use the UK's offshore territories to conceal property ownership. A British-ruled tax haven such as the British Virgin Islands is perfect for people who don't like their affairs scrutinised, unlike the direct ownership of property, which is listed publicly with the UK Land Registry. A BVI shell company with a completely generic name, such as Good Works Ventures Limited (at the time of writing, this very company was available for purchase online for US $1,500) offers no information as to the identity of its ultimate owner. Since 2016, UK companies and limited liability partnerships have been required to declare, in a public and searchable register, the names of any individuals controlling more than a 25% stake in them. While this is a positive step, there is no enforcement of incorrect entries on this register. Those that are inclined to be truthful will have listed their names and interests accurately. Those that are not, such as money launderers seeking to hide their wealth, face no sanction for providing misleading or incomplete information. Therefore, this transparency measure does not deter the corrupt.

In 2016, then-Prime Minister David Cameron announced plans to introduce a register for owners of overseas companies that own or purchase UK property or are involved in Government contracts. In early 2022, this register still does not exist, confirming this is not a government priority. There is a draft Registration of Overseas Entities Bill, but according to London lawyers active in this field, there are no current plans to give additional verification resources to Companies House. The significant risk is that, if the legislation ever comes into force, there will be nothing to compel an overseas entity, such as a Russian oligarch, to give an honest account of their ownership of a London property, and no investigative powers granted to the body that is supposed to hold this information.

Britain's overseas territories are the world's leading centres for money laundering and tax avoidance. They enable taxes that are levied to pay for essential public services to be hoovered out of corrupt countries such as Russia and deposited safely abroad. Of Britain's offshore territories, almost all are active in offshore finance, and most offer particular advantages to different activities in the lives of the super-rich. You use the Isle of Man to create an ownership vehicle for your private jet that ensures that you can get a full VAT refund, usually worth millions of dollars, when you bring your plane into Europe. As we've seen, you use the British Virgin Islands to register the shell company that will own your property. And the Cayman Islands are perfect for the notional headquarters of multinational companies whose activities are actually carried out elsewhere.

The British government hides behind the plausible deniability of autonomy. Britain's overseas territories are self-governing democracies, responsible for their own affairs, reliant upon the UK solely for defence and foreign relations. According to this argument, if the people of the British Virgin Islands choose to make managing complex financial planning their national industry, it would be neo-colonialist of the British government to stop them. This proposition does leave one wondering why almost all of the overseas territories have offshore financial services as their primary economic activity. By comparison, France's overseas territories are part of the metropolitan state. Islands in the Eastern Caribbean such as Martinique and Guadeloupe are as much part of France as Burgundy and Provence. Save for minor regional variations, these territories all have the same administrative structures, the same educational system, the same laws, taxes and standards as France. Crucially, they also have the same political structures, sending representatives to the French national assembly and having a full Cabinet minister to represent their interests. No French overseas territory is a centre for offshore finance and they are mostly net recipients of central government money, as you would expect for a less-developed region of a powerful and wealthy country.

By contrast, the British Overseas Territories are expected to be self-financing and self-regulating. A child born in the Turks and Caicos Islands will not enjoy the same educational standards as one born in Buckinghamshire. Policing, healthcare and wider public services all have lower standards than in Britain. Citizens of these islands have no representation in Britain's Parliament or Cabinet and their administration is the purview of one of the least-influential departments of Britain's Foreign Office. The administrative centre of Britain's overseas empire is a dingy corridor in the attics of King Charles Street, the Foreign Office headquarters. Faced with minimal support or interest from the colonial overlord, these isolated colonial territories, too small to have viable real economies, avail themselves of the two major advantages afforded them by Britain: control over their own tax rates, and our world-renowned legal system. The reason that a major global corporation might take the seeming risk of putting its headquarters in a tiny island controlled by a small political class, is that these islands all have Britain's Supreme Court as their final court of appeal. The oligarch or major global corporation knows that its legal and property rights are enshrined in the court sitting in Parliament Square, Westminster, not Tortola in the British Virgin Islands.

The status of Britain's Overseas Territories, and their continued involvement in offshore finance, are choices made by successive British governments. It would be possible to build up alternative industries in these territories. It would also be possible to recognise that certain geographically isolated regions of a country require extra resources and certain privileges to be able to function (something we accept, for example, for the remote Scottish islands). Finally, Britain can exert its overarching power as a colonial overlord. This is not just a theoretical power.

In 2022 the government recommended the imposition of direct rule over the British Virgin Islands in response to the corruption and mismanagement there, just as the island's premier Andrew Fahie was arrested in Miami on drugs smuggling charges. Britain could impose on the overseas territories a range of incentives and penalties to change their approach to financial services, or even simply impose the legislation outright. But it chooses not to.

Russians have a particular enthusiasm for Britain's offshore territories. Indeed, the British Overseas Territories are among the preferred destinations for money leaving Russia and in the period 2008–2018, a staggering £68 billion from Russia was lodged in these varied jurisdictions, according to the anti-corruption organisation Global Witness. Of course, this does not imply that these territories now benefit from upgraded infrastructure or widespread construction. These are paper assets, domiciled offshore to avoid tax and transparency. Offshore finance is something that Britain chooses to support because it fits neatly with the City of London's vast onshore financial services sector and with Britain's continued profile as a hub for professional services and the government's vision of Global Britain centred on the City of London.

The City of London is far more than just a wealth management centre for a global elite. It is also one of the world's primary corporate finance centres, where companies can be floated on stock exchanges, where mergers and acquisitions are financed and executed, where bond issues raise funding for businesses and governments. The sums involved in these transactions run into the billions, dwarfing the prices paid for even the grandest oligarch mansions in London. Whilst oligarchs might tire of their Londongrad property portfolios, it is here that a real strategic difference has been made to Russia and its economy, as a matter of choice, by Britain.

In 2006, the Russian partially state-owned oil company Rosneft listed a chunk of its shares on the London and Moscow stock exchanges, raising £8.5 billion in the process and earning hundreds of millions for Western bankers and advisers. As an entity, Rosneft was little more than a holding vehicle for the private wealth of Putin and his closest KGB associates. It had benefited from the seizure of the assets of Yukos, once Russia's largest independent company, whose owner Mikhail Khordorkovsky had fallen foul of the Kremlin and spent years in jail. While the Yukos acquisition was of questionable legality, the Stock Exchange appeared untroubled by the prospect of raising money for Rosneft. This was despite noisy objections from respected financiers such as George Soros, and the fact that the New York stock exchange had refused to handle the sale on compliance grounds. As Catherine Belton recorded in her book *Putin's People*, the Rosneft sale was viewed as a disgrace by Russian liberals:

> For Andrei Illarionov, the Kremlin economic adviser who by then had stepped down in disgust at the changes that were going on, the Rosneft sale was 'a crime against the Russian state and the Russian people... Western companies are actually building long-term relations with those forces in Russia that are destroying the very pillars of modern society: a market economy, respect

for private property, democracy.' But for the KGB men behind Rosneft's transformation, it was the stamp of approval they'd been working for, and allowed them to deepen their infiltration of international markets.

In this early period of Russia gaining 'the stamp of approval' through access to international markets, London's stock market was completely dominant in raising finance for Russian firms, most of them state-owned and thereby directly financing the interests of President Putin and his closest cronies. From 2002 to 2011, $39 billion was raised by Russian companies via listings on the London exchange. The next closest competitor was the Hong Kong stock exchange which raised just $2.5 billion in the same period. As David Cameron proudly noted in a speech delivered in Moscow in 2011: 'Russian companies already account for around a quarter of all foreign initial public offerings on the London Stock Exchange.'

RUSSIA AND NATO

Britain's determined enrichment of Russia's ruling classes was not happening in isolation. It was taking place against a backdrop of worsening relations between the western alliance and Russia under President Putin. Since the days of the Cold War, Britain, as a hawkish member of the Western alliance, supported military and diplomatic policies apparently designed to contain and limit Russia's power and influence. We have already seen how Britain's advocacy of military action in Kosovo unsettled Russia back in 1999. Nonetheless, this immediate post-Cold War period also saw efforts to find ways to co-ordinate Russia productively with the activities of NATO. This tendency took a renewed priority after the 9/11 terrorist attacks on New York and Washington DC.

Russia's President Putin made common cause with US President George W Bush on the issue of tackling Islamist terrorism. In Russia's case, an ongoing separatist rebellion in Muslim-majority Chechnya was treated as another front in the Global War on Terror, and the US soft-pedalled its earlier concerns about human rights there.

In 1999 and 2002, NATO welcomed new members in Eastern Europe, former allies of Russia such as the Czech Republic and also the Baltic states that had been constituent parts of the USSR. Some of America's allies, such as France and Germany, counselled caution. And George Kennan, architect of America's Cold War policy of hawkish containment of Russia, described the policy as a 'tragic mistake.' But Tony Blair, in his speech at the 1999 NATO summit, called for further enlargement of the alliance.

Immediately after the Baltic states' accession to NATO, the alliance began F-16 air patrols over Baltic territory, to Putin's intense frustration. The establishment of a NATO-Russia Council (NRC) in 2002, at which Russia would sit as an equal with NATO's existing members, was an attempt to alleviate some of these tensions.

Then, in November 2003, a revolution in the former Soviet Republic of Georgia swept a pro-Western government into power. While there is little or no evidence that America promoted the so-called Rose Revolution, as Russia claimed, there were close diplomatic links between some of the new regime and the

US Embassy in Tbilisi, Georgia's capital. For Vladimir Putin, a paranoid and resentful former officer of the KGB, this was a clear example of Western powers extending their sphere of influence to an important former Soviet republic.

For Russia, worse was to come: the following year, Ukraine, the most important and powerful post-Soviet republic, had its own 'Colour Revolution.' The Orange Revolution was a popular uprising against a corrupt government's flagrant attempt to rig an election it was set to lose. This corrupt government, with the extensive support of the Russian authorities, even went to the trouble of poisoning the main opposition candidate Viktor Yuschenko, albeit failing to kill him. After widespread mass protests Ukraine's supreme court insisted on a re-run of the election, which the reformists won, to Russian outrage. Both Georgia and Ukraine, two of the most important and dynamic post-Soviet republics, had new governments keen to develop closer relations with the West. In both cases, the role of the US and Western powers, as well as prominent NGOs such as those supported by the financier George Soros, has been hugely overstated and misrepresented by the Russian state. The risk of a 'Colour Revolution' breaking out in Russia appeared to be one of Putin's main concerns. Under this paranoid world-view, the Colour Revolutions were Western-inspired conspiracies to encircle Russia and undermine its legitimate interests in the former Soviet republics.

It was not the West's fault, and certainly not Britain's, that Putin and his Russian nationalist supporters baselessly chose to interpret the Colour Revolutions – positive national affirmations of democratic development – as hostile acts. However, these events played straight into Russia's paranoid fears of encirclement, coupled with more recent wounded pride in the aftermath of the collapse of the Soviet Union. One event in particular had chilled Putin. As the Iron Curtain was being torn down across Europe in 1989, a crowd had surrounded the headquarters of the Stasi (East Germany's secret police) in Dresden and then turned towards a nearby KGB installation. A KGB officer on duty called a Red Army tank division to ask for protection. As the BBC's Dresden correspondent explained: 'The answer he received was a devastating, life-changing shock. "We cannot do anything without orders from Moscow," the voice at the other end replied. "And Moscow is silent".' That KGB officer was Vladimir Putin and this visceral illustration of the frailty of power has had a life-long effect. By 2005, he was describing the end of the Soviet Union as the 'greatest political catastrophe of the [20th] century.' Russia's fear of encirclement and its lack of a natural western frontier has spooked its leaders for most of the modern era. A hugely influential book in Russia is the 1997 work by the Russian neo-fascist Aleksandr Dugin, *The Foundations of Geopolitics: the Geopolitical Future of Russia*, which proposes carving up Europe into spheres of influence in order to counteract the perceived Atlantic threat.

In this context, it is no surprise that the decision to invite Georgia and Ukraine to join NATO was seen as a threat by Russia. In 2007, Putin delivered a blistering speech at the Munich Security Conference, observing:

I think it is obvious that NATO expansion does not have any relation with the modernisation of the Alliance itself or with ensuring security in Europe. On the contrary, it represents a serious provocation that reduces the level of mutual trust. And we have the right to ask: against whom is this expansion intended? And what happened to the assurances our Western partners made after the dissolution of the Warsaw Pact? Where are those declarations today? No one even remembers them. But I will allow myself to remind this audience what was said. I would like to quote the speech of NATO General Secretary Mr Woerner in Brussels on 17 May 1990. He said at the time that: 'The fact that we are ready not to place a NATO army outside of German territory gives the Soviet Union a firm security guarantee.' Where are these guarantees?

There was enough uncertainty around promises not to expand NATO for Russians to claim that they had been misled. But this was not heard in London which continued to support the plan for Georgia and Ukraine to join NATO. What was the strategy underpinning Georgia and Ukraine's membership? And if either country were attacked by Russia, would NATO be prepared to operate its Article V commitment to treat an attack on one as an attack on all? Would NATO be willing to enter into World War III for Georgia?

At the NATO summit in Bucharest in April 2008, the contradictions in the case for Georgia and Ukraine joining the alliance were laid bare: while both countries had pro-Western governments, they had militaries with no interoperability with NATO member-states, they had extensive integration with

Russian structures, weapons systems and military culture and, in the case of Georgia, they had ongoing territorial disputes with Russia.

It is important not to mistake the Ukrainian army of 2022, having enjoyed extensive training from NATO forces, with that of 2008. In 2008, neither Georgia nor Ukraine was ready to join NATO. In 2022, Ukraine certainly is. Many experts in 2008 were uncomfortable with the prospect. For example, John Lough, who represented NATO in its office in Moscow, described the 2008 invitation to Georgia and Ukraine as 'very rash' and Fiona Hill, a US-based Russia expert working at the time at the National Intelligence Council, advised against. Nevertheless, President George W Bush invested significant personal energy and political capital in lobbying for the new would-be members. France, Germany and the Netherlands made very clear their opposition. According to a former official who attended the summit, Britain sat on its hands, not wanting to disagree publicly with the Americans.

In April 2008, NATO did not agree to allow Georgia and Ukraine to join the pathway to full membership. But at the same time it stated that the two countries would join NATO at some point in the future, without any specific timeframe. This was arguably the worst possible outcome. It allowed Russia to fear Georgia and Ukraine's future membership while not offering those countries the protection implied by it. At the same time as the NATO summit, President Putin had written to the leaders of two breakaway regions of Georgia, South Ossetia and Abkhazia, referring to both as 'president' and talking of Russia's 'practical' support to the statelets. In doing so, Putin was being deliberately provocative, undermining Georgia's territorial integrity. In South Ossetia, by August 2008, separatists had begun artillery attacks on Georgian installations. The Georgians responded with the seizure of a town in South Ossetia. With remarkable speed and direction, which pointed to a carefully prepared plan, the Russian military surged into Georgia, under the pretext of protecting their allies. Russian warplanes bombarded Georgian cities well past the frontiers of South Ossetia. At one point, it looked as though Russia would march on the capital, Tbilisi. With no international military support, Georgia desperately sued for peace, welcoming a ceasefire stitched together by France's President Sarkozy. The five-day war left Georgia fatally weakened and its NATO ambitions in tatters.

Had Georgia been a NATO member, would Russia have dared send troops into South Ossetia or into Georgia proper? Russia might have judged that NATO would not be prepared to go to war for Georgia. NATO's Article 5 on collective defence is a key factor here. It is important to understand what it actually says rather than what it is believed to say. Article 5 does not commit NATO members to automatically declare war on any country that attacks another member. In fact, its wording is more circumspect:

> The Parties agree that an armed attack against one or more of them in Europe or North America shall be considered an attack against them all and consequently they agree that, if such an armed attack occurs, each of them, in exercise of the right of individual or collective self-defence recognized by Article 51 of the Charter of the United Nations, will assist the Party or Parties so attacked by taking

forthwith, individually and in concert with the other Parties, such action as it deems necessary, including the use of armed force, to restore and maintain the security of the North Atlantic area.

Any such armed attack and all measures taken as a result thereof shall immediately be reported to the [United Nations] Security Council. Such measures shall be terminated when the Security Council has taken the measures necessary to restore and maintain international peace and security.

This text, and therefore NATO membership, is not a guarantee of military action in defence of alliance members. Had Georgia joined NATO in 2008, there is no guarantee that NATO members would have leaped to a full military defence of Georgia. At the time of publication, Georgia's NATO ambitions remain in suspended animation. Russian forces are stationed both in Abkhazia and South Ossetia, and Russia has recognised the independence of these two areas, creating two improbable would-be independent countries. By the same token, Ukraine's President Zelensky, previously committed to NATO membership, now states publicly that this is no longer an option.

Britain has kept reliably to its line that Georgia and Ukraine 'will be' members of NATO, without apparent consideration of how and when or why their membership would improve transatlantic security. The admirable policy objective of holding to a firm line on Russian expansionism does not necessarily require the admission of Russia's neighbours to NATO, a policy which may have reduced, rather than improved, Europe's security. But Russia's extreme aggression towards Georgia and Ukraine makes this a debate that it is impossible to have with any sense of balance or insight.

POISONINGS IN BRITAIN

Russia's growing aggression has not been limited to the post-Soviet countries. On 4th March 2018, Sergei Skripal and his daughter Yulia were found unconscious on a park bench in the historic cathedral city of Salisbury in Wiltshire and rushed into hospital. Skripal had been a double agent inside Russia's GRU military intelligence agency, secretly passing information to MI6 for nearly ten years. He was transferred to Britain in 2010 as part of a complex spy swap involving Russia and the USA. Inexplicably, he lived under his own name in a quiet cul-de-sac in Salisbury and, according to a wide range of reporting, continued to work with the intelligence services of Britain as well as its allies in NATO. Between 2012 and 2018, Skripal's wife, son and older brother had all died in questionable circumstances. Nevertheless, Skripal unfathomably had no security or special protection. Skripal had been targeted by a deadly nerve agent known as Novichok, unique to Russia. It had been placed by a pair of GRU operatives who were recorded on a variety of CCTV cameras as they progressed through southern England. The Skripals spent nearly a month fighting for their lives in hospital and were lucky to survive. Another Salisbury resident, Dawn Sturgess, died after spraying the chemical, which was in a fake perfume bottle, onto her arm.

The Novichok deployment was the first use of a nerve agent in Europe since World War II and an extraordinarily pro- vocative act by the Russians. It was a classic case of Putin testing the West for a reaction, probing to see how far he could push. He was sending a deadly message. Traitors to Russia were never safe.

However, Skripal's targeting was not unprecedented. Alexander Litvinenko was a former KGB officer who had settled in England after publicly criticising Putin's regime. In 2006, Litvinenko met two Russians in a London hotel, believing he was going to be discussing business opportunities. The meeting was in fact a murder by appointment: Andrey Lugovoi and Dmitry Kovtun had slipped polonium-210, an extremely dangerous radioactive isotope supplied by Russia's security services, into Litvinenko's tea. Because Litvinenko was a fitness enthusiast it took him three weeks to die, giving him enough time to work out what had happened. As Litvinenko helpfully explained from his deathbed to the detectives from Scotland Yard sent to investigate: 'I have been poisoned by the Russian Special Services on Putin's order.' Litvinenko died in agony on 23rd November 2006. Two days earlier, a haunting photo had been taken of him lying in a hospital bed, staring at the camera, his head devoid of hair and a bloodstain on the pillow, surrounded by complex medical machinery, tubes and wires. Litvinenko made a deathbed statement to the world.

You may succeed in silencing one man but the howl of protest from around the world will reverberate, Mr Putin, in your ears for the rest of your life. May God forgive you for what you have done, not only to me but to beloved Russia and its people.

There were howls of protest, but the British government's response was initially cautious. As a former senior official involved with Russia policy at that time observed, there was considerable debate within Whitehall whether or not to hold Putin and the Russian government directly responsible. Litvinenko had made a name for himself investigating Russian gangsters and there was speculation that he had been targeted by organised crime figures, rather than by the Russian state itself, although only state operatives would have been able to get access to polonium-210. But in the earliest stages, some British officials argued that Litvinenko was a maverick who had possibly brought the problem upon himself. Britain made limited diplomatic expulsions and resisted attempts to delve too deeply into the matter. Litvinenko's widow Marina fought a lonely battle for a public inquiry to be held. In 2013 Theresa May, at that time Home Secretary, confirmed that she had blocked a public inquiry in order not to offend the Russians. The Foreign Office ensured that material relating to the Russian government's role was not released to the coroner.

With the embarrassing experience of appearing to have been soft on Russia over Litvinenko, it was not surprising that Theresa May, as Prime Minister, was determined to appear forceful in her response to the Skripal attack. In March 2018, the UK expelled 23 Russian diplomats assessed to be intelligence officers working under diplomatic cover and in co-ordination with the USA, Germany, France, Poland and a score of smaller countries, over 100 were expelled across the world. A Russia specialist from a Western intelligence agency told me that this global reaction was probably more impactful than Putin had anticipated.

INVASION OF UKRAINE

Writing this in 2022, the assassinations in Britain feel like quaint spy capers in comparison to Russia's full invasion of Ukraine. But Russia's invasion of Ukraine began in 2014, not 2022. The events of 2014 in Ukraine were a partial rerun of the Orange Revolution. Pro-European Ukrainians removed a corrupt, decadent pro-Russian president from power and embraced a far-reaching association agreement with the European Union. Except that this time Putin responded by annexing Crimea and surging irregular forces into the Donbas region. A war rumbled on in eastern Ukraine between Russian proxy forces (often with Russian special forces on the ground alongside them) and the Ukrainian army. Crimea was swiftly absorbed into the Russian Federation, with a new bridge across the Black Sea ensuring its physical connection to its new overlord.

Britain was completely blindsided by these events. The UK embassy in Kyiv had very limited resources as a result of years of cuts. The defence intelligence staff had to resort to rehiring retirees, so thin was its Russia team. As with Georgia there appeared to be little ability for British analysts to understand the complex cultural and historic baggage that the region of Crimea held for ordinary Russians, among whom the annexation was wildly popular. The inability of the UK to have a sophisticated understanding of Russia's strategic intentions becomes easier to understand when we learn that much of the core analytical capability inside the British government has been reduced or simply discarded. In 2015, the former soldier, diplomat and MP Rory Stewart observed:

We got rid of the Advanced Research and Assessment Group, which did the basic Russian analysis, we sacked our Ukraine desk officer and the defence intelligence service reduced its Russian analysis.

In the years following 2014, Putin appeared to have become obsessed with the idea that Ukraine must not be allowed to choose a pro-Western, democratic path. In 2021, in a 5,000 word article allegedly written by the President himself, Putin outlined the *Historical Unity of Russians and Ukrainians.* Putin's contention was that Ukrainians and Russians are one people.

However this was no brotherly comity, but a clearly hierarchical relationship in which Ukraine was subsumed into Russia, having no independent right of existence. The article describes Ukraine as dominated by 'neo-Nazis' and under 'direct external control' with 'NATO infrastructure.' Putin signposts his hostile intentions, writing: 'I am becoming more and more convinced of this: Kyiv simply does not need Donbas.' Almost exactly seven months later, Putin would recognise the two Russian-held regions of Donetsk and Luhansk as independent countries.

At that moment, in early 2022, more than 150,000 Russian troops massed on the Ukrainian border, insisting, in addition to the independence of the two occupied regions in the Donbas, that Ukraine demilitarise and 'denazify' and that it accept Russian sovereignty over Crimea. These were demands that Ukraine could not – and did not – agree to. For Ukraine's President Volodymyr Zelenksy, a native Russian speaking Jew who had lost close relatives in the Holocaust, they were also chillingly offensive. But

Zelensky, who had publicly and repeatedly lobbied for Ukraine's membership of NATO, appeared unmoved by widespread Western intelligence of a full-scale Russian invasion of his country. On this occasion, the spooks were correct, and Russia invaded on 24th February 2022. Putin appeared increasingly unhinged in his obsessions with NATO membership, and Ukraine's 'drug-addicted, neo-Nazi leaders.' His decision seemed entirely irrational and self-defeating, and the poor initial performance of his military in the face of stiff Ukrainian resistance further underlined the stupidity of his decision.

2022 proved to be a historical turning point – a *zeitenwende* in the words of German Chancellor Olaf Scholz. European countries such as Germany, which had relied heavily on trade with Russia, including its energy supplies, committed to break their dependence and rebuild their underfunded militaries. Sweden and Finland, after centuries of neutrality, decided to join NATO. And Britain's Prime Minister Boris Johnson celebrated the UK's prompt action in supplying weapons to the Ukrainian military. But the turning point had in fact been almost exactly eight years earlier, in March 2014. Putin's first invasion of Crimea and the Donbas was the first time since World War II that one European country had invaded another. This was a moment for the rules-based international order, if it had any meaning at all, to take effect, for countries to put maximum pressure on Russia. Instead, Britain determinedly tried to keep to business as usual, raking in Russian money and helping Russian businesses raise more of it on our stock markets. And even after March 2014 a secret briefing document for Britain's National Security Council recommended that responses to Putin's flagrant breach of international law should not 'close London's financial centre to Russians.' Britain saw its national security priority as continuing to make it easy for the Kremlin and its allies to wash their money through London.

THE CONSERVATIVES AND RUSSIA

The Tories' enthusiasm for Russian money is perplexing when you consider the party's heritage. Margaret Thatcher, whom British Conservatives almost universally revere, was the firmest, most hawkish Western leader during the Cold War. And, importantly when it comes to foreign policy towards Russia, Boris Johnson appears to be operating firmly in Thatcher's tradition. As Prime Minister he has never been known to take a publicly pro-Russia stance on an important matter of international policy. (As a newspaper columnist he wrote articles praising Putin, but his record as a columnist is so varied that it is difficult to ascribe any firm opinion to him.) Notoriously, as Foreign Secretary in October 2016, Johnson called for protests outside the Russian Embassy in London, the sort of the thing you never do as a foreign minister unless you want your own embassy in the target country's capital city to be surrounded by a baying mob. In 2017, Johnson found himself internationally isolated at a G7 summit as he attempted to push for additional sanctions against Russia to punish its support of the Assad regime in Syria. Even traditional supporters of Johnson and the Conservatives, such as the former British Ambassador to Washington, Chistopher Meyer, wondered: 'How on earth did Boris get himself out on this limb?'

Shortly after this summit, Britain's relations with Russia were about to get much worse as a result of the Skripal poisoning. But Britain carried on letting the Russians use London as their primary financial hub.

In late 2017, En+ Group, a multi-billion dollar Russian energy and metals company floated on the London Stock Exchange raising around £1 billion from the sale of shares. At the time, En+ Group was controlled by Oleg Deripaska, an oligarch reportedly close to Putin. The headquarters of the business was technically in the British offshore finance territory of Jersey (corporation tax: 0%). In spite of being under sanctions, state-owned Russian banks VTB and Gazprombank were involved in the share listing. VTB both had a significant stake in En+ and had loaned the business almost $1 billion. En+ also was the controlling shareholder of Rusal, an aluminium company founded by Deripaska. As Parliament's Foreign Affairs Committee reported, quoting Harvard scholar Emile Simpson:

Rusal's own website says that it supplied military material to the Russian military that was potentially used in Syria. That arguably should have attracted the attention of the regulators, given that the EU has sectoral sanctions on the Russian defence sector.

While the regulators appear not to have worried, other institutions were raising concerns. According to the *Daily Telegraph*, MI6 regarded it as a 'scandal' that Deripaska had been allowed to raise significant sums using British institutions. Causing particular outrage was the role Rusal played supplying materials used in the production of Russian weapons including Buk missiles. Russian forces used a Buk missile to shoot down a civilian Malaysian airliner over Ukraine in 2014, killing all 298 on board. While En+ was causing ructions at MI6 headquarters, in another of Britain's most august institutions, the House of Lords, it was viewed rather differently by Lord Barker of Battle, a former energy minister and Conservative politician. Lord Barker, En+'s executive chairman, was paid a $4 million bonus by Deripaska for his work in securing the lifting of US sanctions on En+. He resigned from En+ in March 2022 after Russia's invasion of Ukraine. Barker was not the only member of the House of Lords to rake it in from Russia's riches: many other lords and ladies worked for Russian state-owned oil refiners and energy firms, shipping lines and banks.

In March 2018, in the immediate aftermath of the Salisbury poisonings, Theresa May told the House of Commons: 'There can be no question of business as usual with Russia.' But business continued exactly as usual, making a mockery of this statement and the wider diplomatic response to the attacks. Within days of May's tough statement, Russia used the British markets to issue bonds raising nearly $5bn for Russia's energy giant Gazprom, effectively the Kremlin's piggy bank, and sovereign bonds issued by the Russian state. Russian state-owned bank VTB exploited a loophole in the sanctions regime to take part in the issue of the sovereign bonds, further enriching Russia. In 2021, major Russian companies were still raising billions on the London stock exchange, as if nothing in Putin's behaviour gave cause for concern.

In 2022, with Russian forces pounding the streets of Kyiv and Kharkiv, killing civilians and committing war crimes, the UK appeared to be the weakest link in putting sanctions on Russian military aggression. Lists of sanctioned entities issued by the EU were not followed up by Britain, or done so sluggishly. Sanctions on VTB, Russia's second largest bank, were issued with a 30-day grace period, effectively allowing the targets to move their assets to safety in another jurisdiction. France announced plans to seize 'yachts, houses and bank accounts' of Russian oligarchs believed to be supporting the Kremlin. Britain lagged behind, citing the complexities of having left the EU – itself ironic since proponents of that move had argued it would give the UK more freedom of manoeuvre.

As the Foreign Affairs Committee concluded, these were not a set of unconnected coincidences. Russia uses London as a base for its financial transactions, whether transactions of the state or of its wealthiest individuals. This activity is a deliberate and calculated strategy to undermine international norms, and to embed British institutions and individuals within that process. Britain's response has been partial, piecemeal, and ineffective. Faced with the need to match its supposedly hawkish international policies with similarly firm domestic financial regulations, Britain has repeatedly failed to take the necessary action.

As if to prove the government's resistance to change in this area, an official report by the Intelligence and Security Committee of Parliament on Russian influence was blocked from publication by the government, which insisted there were 'no successful examples' of Kremlin interference in British politics. This claim was dropped when the government asserted that there had in fact been Russian interference in the 2019 general election, while also confusingly insisting that it was not necessary to investigate the possibility of interference in the 2016 referendum on Brexit.

SENDING ARMS TO UKRAINE

During the period of Russia's first invasion of Ukraine, the British were begged to supply weapons by the Ukrainians. Prime Ministers David Cameron and Theresa May always refused, as did Boris Johnson while he was Foreign Secretary. In 2016, Johnson sought a 'normalisation' of relations with Russia and was a vocal advocate of the policy of sending only non-lethal equipment to Ukraine. Once Russia had invaded Ukraine for the second time, the British government, and particularly Boris Johnson, did their best to rewrite this recent history. It is undoubtedly true that the British were among the first to supply weapons to the Ukrainians early in 2022. But the Americans had in fact led the way four years earlier, and other countries such as the Baltic states began to support Ukraine militarily at the same time as Britain. Johnson's claims to be 'leading' in its support to Ukraine are debatable. In absolute terms, several European countries have supplied more weapons and aid, and most European countries have supplied more than Britain, relative to the size of their economies. Every large country in Europe has taken many more Ukrainian refugees. So Britain has a policy of talking loudly about its support for Ukraine but not necessarily putting its money where its mouth is.

In particular, as the UK rushes to change laws in response to the invasion, imposing new sanctions and tightening anti-money laundering controls, it needs to invest in the prevention of financial crime. As witnesses to an inquiry into Russian corruption by Parliament's Foreign Affairs Committee observed, the relevant bodies in Britain for tackling high-level financial crime lack resources, staff, expertise and the high-level political backing needed to carry out their work. The issue of political backing is of particular importance. As Foreign Secretary, Boris Johnson made it clear to the inquiry that he did not see it as a priority for the government to be involved in the fight against corruption and financial crime. As the report records:

We repeatedly asked the Foreign Secretary what the FCO and the Government more broadly could do to help stop the flow of corrupt money into the UK. He appeared to suggest, however, that there was no real role for Government in this process.

This hands-off approach has real-world impacts. Britain relies upon suspicious activity reports (SARs), filed by businesses, to track financial crime, whereas other countries, such as Australia, automatically track all transactions over a certain threshold. SARs rely on institutions (companies, banks, law firms etc) to reach a conclusion on whether activity has been suspicious and then report it via a cumbersome and outdated IT system, with a clear risk of perverse incentives. According to the National Crime Agency, a specialist force which has tackling serious and financial crime as part of its remit, SARs succeed in stopping less than one per cent of the estimated £100 billion in illicit funds that passes through the UK each year. So for every £1 billion that is detected, £99 billion of dodgy money washes through the UK annually. Even at these rather meaningless levels of interception, the government refuses to invest the resources necessary to analyse the SARs that are filed. Around 80 staff are expected to analyse and investigate nearly half a million reports annually. The Financial Action Task Force, a global organisation dedicated to helping countries tackle financial crime, has concluded that Britain's SARs system is not working. Businesses such a lawyers, accountants and trust companies, all of which have significant intelligence on financial crime, are under-reporting suspicious transactions. This is not surprising as filing a report brings unwelcome scrutiny and administrative burdens. And Britain's Financial Intelligence Unit is a 'serious concern,' under-resourced, providing questionable intelligence and unable to interact meaningfully with similar units in other countries, thereby undermining the international fight against money-laundering. In 2022, Transparency International, the global anti-corruption campaign group, described Britain as a 'safe haven for corrupt individuals, their allies and assets.'

Even after the 2022 invasion, Britain finally sanctioned prominent Russian oligarchs such as Roman Abramovich, the owner of Chelsea football club. But there was no evidence that Britain was giving its specialist law enforcement agencies the additional resources necessary to rigorously police financial crime.

Although one cannot rule out the possibility that the outlook of the odd individual may have been altered by Russian money, I do not believe that a pro-Russian conspiracy sits at the heart of the British state. What is almost certainly at play is the peculiarly British aversion to long-term planning over short-term gain, particularly where that gain stuffs the bank accounts of upper middle class professionals. Faced with the choice between making it easy for money launderers and criminals to spend their money in London and the longer-term global benefits of propriety, Britain has always kept the dirty money flowing. £99 billion annually buys a nation of blind eyes. Where this represents an especially serious failure is that, as a financial hub for the Russian elite, Britain could have probably influenced Russia – and the growth of a kleptocratic Kremlin – more profoundly than almost any other Western state. Not through hawkish national security policies, or by championing new members of NATO, but by closing down Russia's access to Britain's skilled professionals and our treasure islands.

8. CHINA: THE GOLDEN ERROR OF KOWTOW

'If you folks go forward with the decision to include Huawei, it will have a direct and dramatic impact on our ability to share information with you. Period, end of story.'
Mick Mulvaney, White House Chief of Staff, February 2020

CHINA, THE COMING POWER

Russia was by no means the only intrusive authoritarian state that succeeded in capturing Britain's establishment. Another far more powerful country was slowly increasing its power and influence, engaging in a process of 'elite capture' that brought Britain to the brink of destroying the Five Eyes alliance, the world's most successful intelligence network, as well as seriously undermining Britain's reputation for shrewd national security policies.

Russia is a declining economy over-reliant on fossil fuels with a rapidly shrinking population. Its ability to cause chaos does not reflect its fundamental strength, rather it reflects its ability to probe the weaknesses of its adversaries. On the other hand, China is already a global superpower and may well be the next hyperpower. While there are similarities between China's goals and the objectives of Russia, these are mostly superficial. Russia's corrupt ruling elite, and particularly President Putin, has a narrow belief that whatever is bad for the West must be good for Russia. China, or more properly the Chinese Communist Party which controls all aspects of life and institutions in China, has a far-sighted, long-term strategy guiding its relations with other countries, including Britain. The Chinese Communist Party is not trying to get countries to adopt its version of communism, or 'socialism with Chinese characteristics,' as the China scholar Charles Parton has identified, rather, it seeks to ensure that the world holds no barriers to its continued success. In practical terms, this means three things:

1. A complete acceptance by outsiders of its methods of governance, including its disdain for human rights and its approach to ethnic and religious minorities
2. A global economy that is entirely favourable to China's interests, ideally on terms that are disadvantageous to economic rivals, and
3. Widespread acceptance of China's widest territorial claims, including Tibet, Xinjiang, Hong Kong, Macao, Taiwan and even the heavily-disputed South China Sea.

While the ultimate aim is preserving the Chinese Communist Party's continued domestic power-base, this objective necessitates aggressive intervention in foreign countries to achieve those outcomes. It needs there to be politicians, civil servants, think tanks and advisers around the world ready to defend and adopt policies that are in line with its aims, and a steadily increasing level of enthusiasm for its model of governance. It wishes to present its core interests as inviolable and its continued rise as inevitable. The US-led global alliance needs to be dismantled to allow China to be a superpower after its own fashion, not according to a standard forced on it by outsiders.

China's foreign policy has essentially become the application of its economic muscle to effect a carrot and stick approach to dealing with foreign countries: the obedient are rewarded and the non-compliant threatened. Countries are defined by the Chinese Communist Party into three broad categories: adversaries, neutral and friends. On a global scale, it wants to build the broadest possible coalition of friendly countries in order to isolate and neutralise the principal enemy, the United States. For Britain, seen by the party as one of America's firmest allies, the objective has been to ensure that the UK's interests are sufficiently bound up with China that it stays out of any future conflict between the US and China. As a primary objective this means moving the UK out of the enemy category into the neutral category, with a long-term goal of making the UK an obedient ally of China. This strategy is known as the 'United Front,' developed from Mao Zedong's original idea to bring on side, or to isolate and destroy, those who are neutral or opposed to the party. The United Front is an especially important aspect of China's projection of power internationally, reflected in the fact that all Chinese officials involved in foreign affairs work, no matter which department they belong to, have United Front objectives on which they are assessed for their annual appraisal.

Britain's relations with the Chinese Communist Party have gone through several transformations in recent years. In 2012, the Prime Minister, David Cameron, and his deputy, Nick Clegg, met the exiled Tibetan spiritual leader, the Dalai Lama, in London. The brief and largely formulaic encounter caused howls of outrage from China's leadership. Although it had taken place away from government premises, and although the Dalai Lama has no political or military power, it was seen as a public, official meeting. The Chinese responded with customary hyperbole, claiming that the meeting had 'seriously interfered with China's internal affairs' (it is unclear how: the Dalai Lama has not entered China in decades). It came on top of a rocky two years in which Cameron had been accused of having lectured the Chinese on human rights. The subsequent impact on Britain's standing with Asia's emerging hyperpower was real, and painful. Ministerial meetings were cancelled and British diplomats in Beijing were frozen out of key briefings. Cameron had come to power in 2010 with little experience or understanding of world affairs. He thought he could take a different approach on China, advocating human rights where his predecessors had been mercantilist pragmatists. In fact, he had badly misjudged his China policy. His decision in 2012 to allow Scotland a referendum on independence was seen as a further irritant. While China is quick to accuse other countries of meddling in its internal affairs, it took a publicly hostile stance on the referendum. For China, the idea that an integral part of a country might secede as a result of a lawful democratic process is anathema and offers particular risks to China's claims over Taiwan.

In an embarrassing sidebar to the overall relationship, there was an improbable role for pig semen. As part of a desperate attempt to rebuild relations, Cameron had promised that Britain would supply pig semen to China, a country with an insatiable appetite for pork. But Britain's hogs failed to deliver the goods and the shipment never came. All this had a real-world impact. At a time of considerable economic pressure for the UK, China's investment was going elsewhere. In 2013, according to OECD figures, China invested more in France, Germany, the Netherlands and even Sweden than it did in the UK. A major rethink was needed and George Osborne, Cameron's Chancellor of the Exchequer (finance minister), spearheaded the new approach. Where Cameron talked of human rights and democracy, Osborne's focus was firmly on trade, investment and economic opportunity. No Chinese investment in the UK was to be questioned, no Chinese policy was to be criticised, no Chinese initiative was to pass by without UK support. Osborne tacitly supported China's most controversial actions, such as its territorial claim in the South China Sea, even when it took the highly provocative step of building artificial islands there for military aircraft.

On a carefully choreographed visit to Beijing in September 2015, George Osborne hailed a 'golden era' of relations between Britain and China. Osborne travelled in high style as part of a huge delegation of politicians, business leaders and cultural figures, with the National Theatre performing Chinese renditions of successful productions. The complexity and pomp associated with the visit was reminiscent of President Richard Nixon's ground-breaking visit to China in 1972. Osborne telegraphed to the world that Britain was revolutionising its relationship with China, making Britain an uncritical outlier among countries in the Western alliance. In Osborne's own words, Britain was 'taking a risk' in its relationship with China. The 'risk' – seen in other Western capitals as 'an unprecedented act of kowtow' – became even more inexplicable when Britain doubled down by inviting China's leader Xi Jinping to Britain for a lavish state visit. Diplomats and intelligence officers, both from Britain and its close allies, were in despair at this craven stance. As one observed:

The most charitable spin we can put on the current China policy of the British government is to say it is a pure mercantilist, unprincipled, self-serving decision aimed at attracting short-term investment.

The decision to open Britain's doors to China was borne out of desperation. Its proponents argued that the best way to deal with communist China was to embrace its participation in the international trading system. The difficulty with this open-door approach was that almost all China experts, even those who advocate pleasing Beijing, agree that if you succumb to Chinese pressure, it only leads to more Chinese pressure. This soon became clear when China got involved in sensitive aspects of Britain's national security, on terms that would never be reciprocated in the other direction. In October 2015, a month after Osborne's trip to Beijing, China General Nuclear Power Group, owned by the Chinese state and sanctioned in America for attempting to steal sensitive nuclear technology, announced it was investing £6 billion in a controversial nuclear power plant in the west of England at Hinkley Point. This was followed by a further investment by the group at a nuclear power plant in Sizewell in Suffolk on the east coast. Aside from the Hinkley Point project being questionable under the EU's state aid rules, many commentators drew attention to the fact that no British firm would be allowed to invest in something as sensitive as nuclear technology in China. Similar Chinese investments were made in North Sea oil, in transport and in the financial sector, where Osborne adjusted regulations to develop London as the leading offshore hub for trading the Chinese renminbi.

For China, Britain was a useful target. It was not just an ally to be prised free of American influence, it was, for all the post-war decline, still a country that mattered. A major economy, a nuclear power, a permanent member of the UN Security Council and a finance powerhouse. But China also targeted Britain's world-leading research universities and its role as an exemplar of security and intelligence good practice within Europe. So China began a series of actions to buy up universities, institutions and individuals. It was a process of elite capture of decision-makers in Britain. And it was a practical manifestation of the United Front policy – the collection of friendly decision-makers, institutions and political groupings all over the world. In 2016, the International Liaison Department of the Communist Party of China claimed that the party had the support of more than

240 political movements and 280 think-tanks and NGOs from 120 countries. In Britain, mainstream political parties have little in common with the Marxist authoritarianism of the Communist Party of China, but it has not prevented major Chinese businesses scooping up a huge range of key influencers and decision-makers onto their boards and advisory teams. One was Labour's Peter Mandelson, a force behind the premiership of both Tony Blair and Gordon Brown and the former chief trade negotiator of the European Union (and arguably, therefore, the most powerful trade official in the world). Lord Mandelson's advisory company, Global Counsel, worked for a major Chinese-owned private equity fund that acquired Western tech firms, hoovering up potentially sensitive intellectual property in the process.

In the House of Lords, contacts between Chinese people and British parliamentarians flourished. Lord Chadlington, a friend of the Conservative leader David Cameron and George Osborne, built a successful business empire with extensive links to China. A senior member of the Chinese Communist Party, Li Xuelin, who became Lady Bates when she married a former Tory minister, donated almost £200,000 to the Conservatives, giving her an entrée to the 'Leaders Group' of party donors with direct access to Cabinet ministers.

In the House of Commons, Barry Gardiner, a member of Labour's Shadow Cabinet with responsibility for trade issues under Jeremy Corbyn, received more than £200,000 in donations from a law firm run by Christine Lee, a senior figure in the Chinese Communist Party and an adviser to the Chinese Embassy in London.

British members of the European parliament also received funding from China. One, Nirj Deva, then MEP for the Southeast of England, failed to declare a Chinese state-funded trip to China, including business class flights and a stay at a luxury hotel. He later lobbied for the telecoms company Huawei. Deva said he had 'no relationship' with Huawei, adding that his only concern had been to give the company a 'level playing field.'

Perhaps more than any other company, Huawei exposed the flawed thinking at the heart of Britain's China policy. As a company, it was highly successful at scooping up the upper echelons of the British establishment as employees and consultants. A former head of Britain's diplomatic service was a paid adviser to Huawei, while the company employed the British government's former chief information officer, John Suffolk, to head its cyber security assurance.

Of course, there is no suggestion that any individual mentioned here has done anything illegal or improper. They were simply taking advantage of legitimate business opportunities, career advancement, or personal interests, as is perfectly normal in a free society that trades with countries around the world. But in most cases it is hard to imagine Beijing tolerating the reverse situation in authoritarian China. For instance, it is impossible to imagine the Chinese Communist Party allowing a major British telecoms company, such as Vodafone, to employ the former most senior technology specialist in the Chinese government.

For China, Huawei is a key strategic asset as the world's largest seller of telecommunications equipment and the leader in 5G technologies. The vision for 5G is the 'internet of things' – where most everyday objects have online connections through 5G technology. In such a world, a breach of internet security offers a hostile entity information on literally every aspect of someone's life, from their private communications, to their domestic living arrangements. China is one such hostile entity, offering, as a recent US Department of Justice statement explained, 'a safe haven for cyber criminals in exchange for those criminals being "on call" to work for the benefit of the state.' While there has been endless speculation that Huawei equipment offers a 'back door' to China's hackers and intelligence collection efforts, no firm evidence has ever been produced to prove this. It is almost certain, however, that, if a Western intelligence agency had found such a capability, it would not reveal its discovery, preferring to monitor China's activities. Huawei clearly has very strong links to the Chinese state. A major online leak of the resumes of Huawei employees revealed startling connections to China's military and intelligence agencies. In one case, an R&D engineer simultaneously served as a Ministry of State Security representative. This individual 'engaged in behaviour that describes planting information capture technology or software on Huawei products.' He also worked on 'building lawful interception capability into Huawei equipment' on projects both domestic and international. So, if Huawei's equipment was not formally compromised, it was far from risk free. Under China's 2017 National Intelligence Law, any Chinese 'organisation or citizen' is obliged to assist or cooperate with China's intelligence agencies. This would therefore extend an obligation to Huawei to offer such support or information as required by the Chinese government.

Indeed, it was just this risk that led the British government to institute the Huawei Cyber Security Evaluation Centre in response to concerns that increasing quantities of Huawei equipment were present in Britain's telecommunications networks. At this centre, Huawei employees supervised by Britain's signals intelligence agency GCHQ undertook the task of evaluating each piece of Huawei equipment before it was allowed into Britain's networks, an activity that reveals the extraordinary national security concerns generated by over-reliance on this company's products. While this work was sensitive, it was not secret, and the Huawei Cyber Security Evaluation Centre produced annual reports. Its 2019 edition came to a stark set of conclusions:

> [Our] work has continued to identify concerning issues in Huawei's approach to software development bringing significantly increased risk to UK operators, which requires ongoing management and mitigation; ... No material progress has been made on the issues raised in the previous 2018 report; ... The Oversight Board continues to be able to provide only limited assurance that the long-term security risks can be managed in the Huawei equipment currently deployed in the UK; ... The Oversight Board advises that it will be difficult to appropriately risk-manage future products in the context of UK deployments, until the underlying defects in Huawei software engineering and cyber security processes are remediated.

While this cautious advice might appear to point in a single direction, the British government chose to ignore it. Britain had adopted a 'see no evil' approach and, in January 2020, the government announced that Huawei would be allowed in Britain's 5G networks. This was a coup for the company on its own terms – it was the first major G7 economy to allow Huawei such a key role. But it was also a strategic victory. Whether or not Huawei, founded by a former senior officer of the Chinese army Ren Zhengfei, represented a specific risk to communications security, it certainly represented a major increase in China's power and influence. For China, it was not just about getting Britain to accept Huawei in the 5G networks, but also about Britain as a model to other countries. As a member of the Five Eyes intelligence alliance and, with France, the greatest military power in Europe, Britain was seen as a national security exemplar. If Britain, with all its experience in intelligence and cyber security could 'manage' the risks of Huawei equipment in its 5G networks, this would send the clear message that other countries in Europe, the world's richest and largest economy, could safely follow suit. Britain was China's bridgehead into Europe.

Among our closest allies, the news was greeted with dismay. The Five Eyes intelligence grouping comprises Australia, Canada, New Zealand, the United States and Britain. Australia had banned Huawei equipment from its 5G networks in 2018. New Zealand indicated that it would take a similar line. Canada still appeared to be making up its mind, but had acted on an extradition request by the United States for a senior Huawei employee, enraging China in the process who responded by taking two Canadians hostage. The United States was implacably opposed to Huawei's involvement in national communications networks. In 2014, it had banned the Chinese firm from government contracts. Four years later, it issued a further warning to American companies against doing business with Huawei. FBI Director Christopher Wray said in testimony to the Senate Intelligence Committee in February 2018:

> We're deeply concerned about the risks of allowing any company or entity that is beholden to foreign governments that don't share our values to gain positions of power inside our telecommunications networks that provides the capacity to exert pressure or control over our telecommunications infrastructure. It provides the capacity to maliciously modify or steal information, and it provides the capacity to conduct undetected espionage.

If a close ally chose to incorporate Huawei equipment in its 5G networks, the United States would review its intelligence sharing. As Robert Strayer, US deputy assistant Secretary of State for cyber, international communications and information policy, made very clear:

> If other countries insert and allow untrusted vendors to build out and become the vendors for their 5G networks we will have to reassess the ability for us to share information and be connected with them in the ways that we are today.

As we saw at the opening of the chapter, in early 2020 Donald Trump's chief of staff Mick Mulvaney spelled it out in the starkest terms, just in case the message had not landed:

We are very much concerned that integrity of that information is hardwired into your computer systems, and if you folks go forward with the decision to include Huawei, it will have a direct and dramatic impact on our ability to share information with you. Period, end of story.

Britain's embrace of Huawei was destroying the world's most durable and effective intelligence-sharing alliance.

AN ULTRA-NATIONALIST STATE

Britain's uncritical embrace of China did not come at a neutral time, or even at a time when the argument could be made that 'working with' China led to Beijing improving its human rights and adherence to the rule of law. On the contrary, the so-called 'golden era' of UK-China relations coincided with China's evolution into an ultra-nationalist authoritarian state, owing much to the continued rise of its President Xi Jinping. Communist China has always had a strong sense of national pride, perhaps unsurprisingly for one of the world's oldest and most influential civilisations. Under communist rule, China has been an authoritarian state from the start. Prior to Xi, China's authoritarianism was less aggressive externally. Deng Xiaoping, China's leader from 1978 to 1989 and instigator of the market-economy reforms that have transformed the country's fortunes, emphasised the fusion of communist ideology with capitalist modernisation. Under Deng, the Chinese Communist Party constitution clarified its priority as economic growth under socialist rules: 'The endeavour to build China into a prosperous, strong, democratic and highly civilized modern socialist state [...] taking economic development as the central task.' The same document commits China to 'a foreign policy of independence and peace,' reflecting Deng's advice to, 'hide your strength, bide your time, never take the lead.' Under Deng, China was a one-party state, but not one that sought to dominate other countries far beyond China's borders. Under Xi Jinping it has been transformed into a one-man dictatorship, with Xi leading a multi-year purge of his opponents. This purge has encompassed thousands of officials including former Politburo members and associates of his presidential predecessors Hu Jintao and Jiang Zemin.

This process crossed an important boundary in March 2018 with the adoption of the new Chinese constitution that made it possible for Xi to be president for life. It added 'Xi Jinping Thought on Socialism with Chinese Characteristics for a New Era' to the official ideology of the state. The centrality of a single person, in this case Xi, to all aspects of China's rule, both in terms of repression and development, is typical of authoritarian populism, as is the gradual rewriting of history to minimise the contributions of earlier leaders such as Deng and Mao.

Xi Jinping's personal brand of populist nationalism is new to China. To paraphrase Donald Trump, Xi is going to 'make China great again.' Xi has promised a 'great rejuvenation' – which he calls the 'Chinese dream' and which he means restoring China to its historic power and glory. Xi's book of essays on this subject, *Xi Jinping Thought*, was published in English in 2014, reflecting another of his priorities – projecting China's power

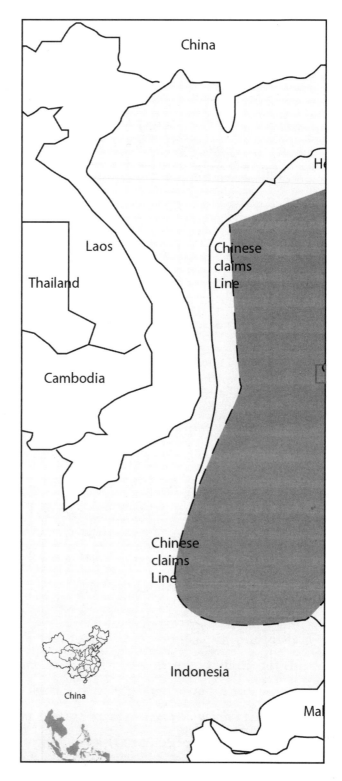

4. China's 'nine dash line' extends its territorial claim deep into the South China Sea

© Canbury Press

China

H[e]

Laos

Thailand

Chinese claims Line

Cambodia

Chinese claims Line

China

Indonesia

Mal

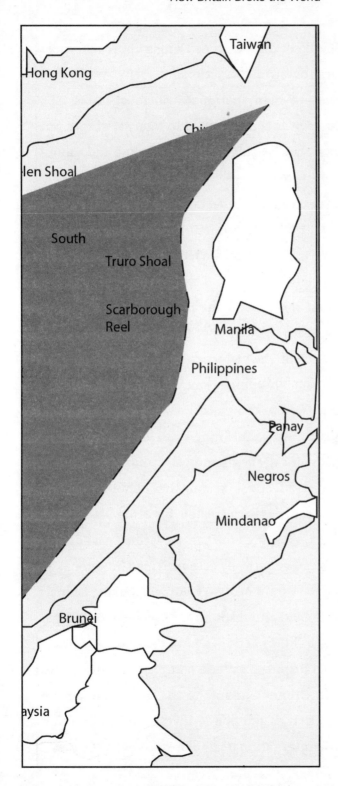

internationally. The book differs from Deng's approach, most notably in its desire for 'stronger national security.' While this sounds like a feature of many national leaders' agendas, Xi's consolidation of his power is not limited to internal purges but extends to significantly increasing military spending and a more aggressive foreign posture.

This has its most extreme manifestation in the South China Sea, a complex maritime environment where Brunei, China, Malaysia, Philippines, Taiwan and Vietnam have conflicting claims on various islets and reefs. The significance of these territories is not their miniscule land area but the rich energy resources that lie beneath the waters of the South China Sea, as well as the importance of the waters to global maritime trade routes. Brunei, Malaysia, Philippines and Vietnam have all made claims that relate closely to the coastlines of their countries. China's claim, often known as the 'nine-dash line' (because it is marked on maps with nine dashes looping deep into the disputed territory) is maximalist, effectively seizing the offshore economic interests of all other countries in the region. In 2016, a UN tribunal rejected China's claim, pointing out that the various islands and reefs were not capable of generating extended maritime zones as they were too small to sustain ordinary human activity. China's response was at once bold and disdainful of international legal norms. Threatening military action, China continued to create new islands in these disputed waters, complete with runways for military aircraft. Other claimants to the same waters have engaged in similar activities, but none with the level of ambition or the indifference to international law displayed by the Chinese.

While China has received far less opprobrium, its behaviour in the South China Sea is in some ways similar to Russia's seizure of Crimea in 2014. It is hard to see how the South China Sea dispute can be resolved in the long-term without some kind of military clash with the United States, which could easily escalate into a major war.

The rise of Chinese authoritarianism has also been seen internally and most tragically in the establishment of a network of prison camps in Xinjiang, north-western China. They are packed with large numbers of Uyghurs, a non-Chinese ethnic group that follows Islam and which enjoyed independence from China at certain points in the early 20th Century. According to official Chinese leaked documents, the camps were built across Xinjiang between 2017 and 2020. Ostensibly for 'voluntary re-education,' they are in reality vast compounds for indoctrinating Uyghurs into Chinese communist thinking and destroying their culture. One million Uyghurs are estimated to have been imprisoned, including children. There are credible reports that both Uyghur prisoners and other marginalised groups have been murdered in detention and their organs harvested for transplants. The United States has classified China's treatment of the Uyghurs as a genocide.

In addition, Xi's China has harnessed the resources of modern communications technology to create a historically unprecedented surveillance state. Facial recognition technology, linked to surveillance cameras and tracking of individual smartphones means that most Chinese citizens' communications, movements and even moods are constantly monitored. The

Chinese government has introduced a 'social credit' system in which people's credit rating, interactions with the state and reports of their behaviour affect their eligibility for jobs and other opportunities.

In areas regarded as at risk from instability, such as Xinjiang, the Chinese authorities have created immense databases of individuals' fingerprints, DNA and even facial expressions. With China seeking to control its Uyghur minority, as the *Financial Times* reported, 'mandatory surveillance software is installed on residents' mobile phones to scan for Islamic keywords and pictures.' These vast datasets are then linked to cameras that scan crowded areas and have frequently been used to alert police to be able to apprehend undesirables or wanted criminals. Unencumbered by human rights and privacy questions, China leads the world in these technologies and is busily exporting them to other countries. Huawei's involvement in surveillance in Xinjiang is a confirmed fact.

As the coronavirus pandemic swept around the world after an outbreak in Wuhan, China's lack of transparency over the initial outbreak and even attempts to blame America for the virus led to a collapse in its international reputation. As the virus developed, China restricted access to the area despite repeated pleas from the international community to allow their experts to work alongside the Chinese. Even Donald Trump was reduced to begging Xi Jinping to let his pandemic intelligence specialists into the country, to no avail. Aside from a distasteful lack of candour on the part of the Chinese, this refusal to co-operate with the international community has cost lives. The degree to which public health doctors were left battling a virus they did not fully understand was hugely exacerbated by the failure of the Chinese Communist Party to co-operate with the international community in an attempt to cover up its own failings. In the early days of the virus, asymptomatic transmission – the way that those who don't appear to be ill can spread Covid-19 in the air – was little understood. China would have known that this was taking place in January 2020: had this knowledge been clearly and honestly shared, the entire global trajectory of the pandemic could have been markedly different. Hundreds of thousands of lives may have been saved in the first months of the outbreak.

This disquiet at China's conduct in relation to the vaccine was exacerbated by its aggressive and provocative behaviour in Hong Kong, where a 36 year old treaty governing the territory's status after its handover from British colonial control to Chinese administration was torn up by the Chinese Communist Party in June 2020, as most of the world was grappling with the pandemic. At a stroke, the special status of 'one country, two systems' was jettisoned in favour of full Chinese government control of Hong Kong. Britain responded by offering a route to full British citizenship for Hong Kong holders of BNO passports (a sort of hybrid-British status). Meanwhile, escapees from the concentration camps in Xinjiang began to give first-hand testimony of their terrible experiences and videos emerged of mass prisoner transfers on railways, redolent of the darkest moments of the 20th Century. The possibility of 'normal' relations with China, let alone a 'golden era' appeared both remote and unwise.

Against this backdrop, Britain's approach to Huawei became unsustainable. It was naïve at best and cynical at worst. A major rebellion of Conservative MPs against the government was seen off by a change of policy, which was justified by the excuse that US sanctions had made Huawei no longer a workable partner. In truth, with or without those sanctions the government was about to lose a vote on the subject and had to back down. But Britain's exposure to Chinese power was not limited to one telecoms company. As we have seen, China had entered Britain's nuclear power sector and most leading British universities. In addition, China's sovereign wealth fund owned a strategic share in Thames Water, Heathrow Airport and the National Grid's gas distribution network. The China National Overseas Oil Company owned a major proportion of Britain's North Sea oil. For years, Britain's politicians lazily argued that China's money did not come with strings attached, only to profess outrage when China threatened to retaliate to the Huawei decision by taking business away from other British firms.

Even after the Huawei decision, the depth of China's penetration of Britain's national strategic assets remained a live issue. In September 2021, Boris Johnson was accused of operating a deliberate 'strategic void' on China to avoid taking necessarily difficult decisions.

Ultimately, those that understood the Chinese Communist Party best, such as the Mandarin-speaking former Australian Prime Minister Kevin Rudd, knew that (in Rudd's words) 'China respects strength, not weakness.' Britain's failure to show strength under Cameron and Osborne reflected the fact that it lacked the institutions and expertise to manage China's behaviour. While those that supported close ties with China spoke darkly of siding with the United States in a future superpower conflict, the immediate strategic question was about protecting Britain's interests, something successive governments have failed to do. Indeed, the evidence suggested that countries that had fallen foul of the Chinese Communist Party (such as Australia after 2018) had still seen their overall trade with China grow year on year. The 'golden era' had been a costly error.

9. SAUDI ARABIA, OIL AND INFLUENCE

'I was tricked. I am also a victim of terror.'
Saudi bomber Ahmed Abdullah Al-Shayea

'I am on the side of the truth, and I am on the right path. My only guilt is defending my country.'
Saud Al-Qahtani, ringleader of the Jamal Khashoggi assassination

The convoy of vehicles sped through the desert. An anonymous compound loomed out of the barren landscape. After rigorous security checks by heavily armed soldiers we were allowed inside. A collection of low, nondescript but comfortable buildings were spaciously laid out inside the high walls, with a modern mosque in the centre, its dome shining in the harsh sunlight. It looked like a strange hybrid of convention centre and military base. Dr

Al-Hadlaq, a jovial Saudi in flowing, brilliant white robes, greeted us. We were at the Prince Mohammed Bin Nayef Center for Advice and Care, Saudi Arabia's terrorist rehabilitation centre. It was 2009 and as the head of the Foreign Office's countering violent extremism team, I was visiting as a bag-carrier to then-Foreign Secretary David Miliband. We had heard that Saudi Arabia, known for its savage punishments and routine use of torture, had started to deal with terrorism not by coercion but by rehabilitation, recognising that extremism is often as much about mental health as it is about moral turpitude.

The centre was undoubtedly impressive: we were shown art therapy studios, where former extremists were encouraged to make sense of their trauma through Islamically-orthodox abstract paintings. Serious, extravagantly-bearded clerics devoted hours to re-indoctrinating their charges. At the heart of the centre's rationale was the very Saudi belief that more (not less) religion was the way to reform extremists. Their terrorist violence had been a function of misunderstanding Islam. With correct teaching, a monthly stipend and lavish personal attention, they could return to the correct path. As fascinating as those ideas were, the tour had felt largely theoretical. The compound exuded the quiet of an alternative therapy centre, a world away from bombings, gunfire and terrorist violence. But our Saudi hosts had saved the best until last. We were shown into a room where a young man in a loose-fitting white shirt stood bashfully flanked by his minder and translator. The young man had delicate, strangely handsome features. Strange because he was also heavily disfigured, with extensive burns on his face and missing most of the fingers on one hand. He was Ahmed Abdullah Al-Shayea and he had survived his own suicide bombing.

Speaking in a quiet, diffident voice through an interpreter, Al-Shayea told his story to a rapt audience of David Miliband, his bag carriers, and the accompanying media. Al-Shayea had grown up in a normal Saudi family environment. Like millions of other young Muslims, particularly those in the Arab world, he had been outraged at the invasion and occupation of Iraq by non-Muslims and believed Muslims had a duty to resist. He had travelled to Iraq in 2005, at the height of the insurgency, after a friend had shown him a fatwa saying that he didn't need either his parents' permission or that of the king of Saudi Arabia (both unorthodox interpretations of traditional Saudi teachings). Al-Shayea claimed that he had not gone to Iraq to be a 'martyr' but to be a fighter. However, lacking any military experience or training, he was like many of the other young recruits to the Iraqi insurgency. He had enthusiasm, belief and commitment, but few useful skills and was quickly frustrated by the lack of training. In Al-Shayea's account, one day a leader of the jihadists asked for volunteers for suicide bombings. Nobody raised their hand, but a few weeks later Al-Shayea found himself driving a truck loaded with 26 tonnes of explosives. He claimed to have been told that he was merely a driver, delivering the truck from one location to another. If this was true, he was a remarkably credulous one, for his fellow fighters had initially ridden with him before jumping out of the truck and speeding away in a pre-arranged getaway car. Al-Shayea's truck detonated in an explosion that killed 12 civilians and injured many more. In a bizarre twist of ballistic science, Al-Shayea himself was blown clear of the explosion and survived. He was mistaken for another victim of the attack and taken to hospital. Only later did the authorities realise that he was the bomber.

Al-Shayea maintained that he was a victim of terrorism. He had never planned to set off a suicide bomb, and he was therefore 'only' responsible for the lesser crimes of unauthorised participation in the jihad. Like everyone else, he had been tricked by the extremists. As I listened to his tale, two thoughts sprang to my mind. The first was that this programme for deradicalisation appeared not to involve remorse. Al-Shayea didn't take responsibility for the deaths of 12 people. This was something that had been done to him. His victimhood was apparently no different to those he had killed. It was also notable that he repeatedly emphasised that it was 'the Iraqis' that had done these things to the largely Saudi volunteer fighters.) The second thought was that I knew I had heard this story somewhere before. If only I could remember where....

Then it came back to me. The suicide bomber who survived. I had heard this story from one of the many international consultants and experts who'd worked in Iraq over the years. At a meeting with the Ministry of the Interior in Baghdad, the Iraqis had expressed their view that the flood of Saudi jihadists that had come to fight in the Iraqi insurgency was propelled by the hardline, anti-Shi'a Islam prevalent across Saudi Arabia. They described an extraordinary story of a suicide bomber who had survived his own bombing and had been mistaken for another victim of the attack. He was a Saudi whose identity had become clear when other mysterious Saudis had come to the hospital and offered doctors vast sums of money to discharge him with no questions asked. This had the opposite effect: the doctors realised something was up and alerted the security services. According to the Iraqis, who were in no doubt that Al-Shayea had intended to carry out a suicide operation, the subsequent investigation demonstrated that almost every person involved in the plot was a Saudi, not an Iraqi.

As we stood listening to Al-Shayea's apologia, it was clear that we were not supposed to know the Iraqi side of the story. Whether Al-Shayea was a terrorist from a Saudi-led bombing cell or a confused young man tricked by Iraqis into mass murder remained unclear to me. But his story was an illustration of the queasy discomfort at the heart of Saudi Arabia's record of Islamic extremism. On the one hand, the Saudis sought to defeat terror with more, stricter, orthodox Islam whose distinguishing feature was an unquestioning obedience to the House of Saud. On the other hand, the star turn of their deradicalisation campaign was apparently unwilling to take responsibility for his actions, and may have been deliberately misleading his audience about his deeds.

A KINGDOM FOR A STAGE

Saudi Arabia is not like other countries. Starting with its name, it is the portion of Arabia ruled by the Al-Saud family. The entire country exists as the fiefdom of a single dynasty. The Al-Saud were one of a series of warring tribes that had struggled for control of central Arabia, one of the remotest and poorest places on earth, over the 18th and 19th Centuries. In the first three decades of the 20th Century, the Al-Saud family waged successful military campaigns on the peninsula, led by 'Abd Al-'Aziz, known as Ibn Saud. He commanded a brotherhood of radical Sunni Islamists who would not be out of place in a modern jihadist group. In 1925, Ibn Saud seized Mecca from the Hashemite family that had ruled the holy city for the preceding 900 years. In 1932, the Al-Saud's established rule of the current kingdom began.

From the very start, Saudi Arabia was tied into a hardline version of Islam. The Al-Sauds owed part of their strength to their longstanding partnership with the followers of Muhammad Ibn 'Abd Al-Wahhab. This fundamentalist Sunni movement, known as Wahhabism, emphasised close adherence to the original practices of the prophet Muhammad and the removal of any 'innovation' in religion. This forbade much traditional religious practice. As a consequence, Wahhabism regards other sects and traditions as idolatrous and worthy of persecution. In essence, the Saudi-Wahhabist state was based on violent repression of its opponents and firm religious support for the Al-Saud rulers.

Had its barren plateau yielded nothing more than sand, Saudi Arabia might have remained a geopolitical desert. But, in 1938, just a few years after the fundamentalist Al-Sauds had taken charge, came the discovery of oil, which transformed the fortunes of the region and the dynasty. The existence of the world's most important oil reserves elevated this coalition of religious hardliners and feudal rulers from obscure regional alliance to a major global force. Armed with petrodollars, the Saudis set out to reshape global Islam. In the post-World War II years the Arab world was dominated by Arab nationalism and to some extent secularism, with rulers such as Egypt's Nasser and Syria's Hafez Al-Assad at the helm of their countries and dominating regional affairs. But in 1973, in response to Israel's successful counter-attack in the Yom Kippur War, the oil-exporting countries of the Gulf, led by Saudi Arabia, demonstrated their global power by instituting an oil embargo on Israel's Western allies. The price of oil surged from $3 per barrel to nearly $12, and Western economies found themselves in desperate straits. Saudi Arabia was able to use its new-found power and economic strength to export its interpretation of Islam across the world. As the French scholar Gilles Kepel identified, Saudi Arabia's da'wa (Islamic outreach) fell on fertile ground. Arab nationalism had resulted in repression, humiliation and failure at the hands of Israel's military. In particular, the new class of educated urban poor and lower middle classes were shut out from the power structures of the Arab nationalists, where party membership and military rank dominated political influence. Saudi Arabia's ultraconservative, sectarian Islam provided a perfect counterpoint to these populations looking for meaning in a world that had proved profoundly disappointing. It was also, in the view of many, divinely-ordained. God had given power and wealth to Saudi Arabia, the guardians of the two holy cities of Mecca and Medina.

The Islamic outreach had a second purpose: to distract attention from the profoundly un-Islamic antics of the Saudi ruling family. From austere desert warriors in the early years of the 20th Century, the black gold rush of oil revolutionised the lives of the Al-Saud, just as it changed the trajectory of their country. While some Saudi royals remained hardworking, religiously observant public servants, others became debauched playboys. Outside the kingdom, in exclusive villas and casinos in the fleshpots of Mediterranean Europe and in private palaces in the mountains of Morocco, the Saudis developed a reputation for all the things their religion appeared to forbid: drinking, drug-taking and prostitution. Due to the huge numbers of children that many princes had, the royal family grew rapidly and, in 2020, there were around 15,000 persons of royal status. Even lesser princes enjoy a royal stipend and various security privileges. As royal family members, they are also very unlikely to be targeted by the kingdom's feared religious police. A leaked US diplomatic cable from 2010 gave a vivid description of a party attended by a member of the American consulate staff in Jeddah, complete with dancefloor, DJs, well-stocked bar and 'working girls.'

EXPORTING OIL AND RADICALISM

As the princes partied, Saudi Arabia exported Wahhabism, funding the construction of new mosques worldwide, ideologically-quiescent Imams and charitable activities. But it also imported people in their millions to service the rapidly growing Saudi economy – workers from all over the Islamic world who adopted the religious practices of their new home and eventually took them back to their country of origin. The Saudi religious model remained officially quietist, emphasising the importance of obeisance to the established ruler (whether that ruler was the king of Saudi Arabia or the Queen of England). But an inevitable result of the export of Wahhabist theology around the world has been to teach millions of Muslims to disdain the traditional practice of religion in their own society and to be more sympathetic to the arguments of Islamist militants. The Saudis acknowledge that they have fostered conservative sectarian Islam, but have persistently denied a role in the creation of radical militant Islam, pointing out that Islamist militants from Al-Qaeda to the Islamic State regard the Saudi kingdom as their enemy. However, in real life, there is often much overlap. A country that stops followers of other faiths from practising their religion, that carries out brutal punishments based on shari'a (Islamic law) and whose clerics deliver fiery sermons on the perfidy of Jews and Shi'ites, can easily see its version of Islam act as a pathway to more extreme and militant practices. And in certain key cases Saudi officials have facilitated terrorism, particularly where that terrorism has taken place outside the borders of the kingdom of Saudi Arabia. Perhaps the most striking example of this comes from what remains the largest terrorist attack in history: that on the United States on 11th September 2001.

Fifteen of the 19 terrorists who hijacked planes and flew them into targets in New York and Washington on 9/11 were Saudi citizens (showing the degree to which Wahhabism can lead to a violent extremist interpretation of Islam). But there was also official Saudi involvement in the preparatory stage of the attacks.

In January 2000, two of the ringleaders of 9/11, Nawaf Al-Hazmi and Khalid Al-Mihdhar, travelled to California to begin pilot training. They had never before spent time in a Western country and, as the 9/11 Commission Report noted, it was unlikely that they would have travelled to the United States without arranging to receive assistance from one or more individuals beforehand. While getting established in California, the two relied heavily on the community at the King Fahd mosque in Culver City, which was funded by the Saudi state and had an Imam, Fahad Al-Thumairy, who was also a Saudi diplomat. According to the 9/11 Commission, Al-Thumairy was 'an Islamic fundamentalist... associated with a particularly radical faction within the community of local worshippers.' In later court filings it emerged that another Saudi diplomat, Mussaed Ahmed Al-Jarrah, 'tasked al-Thumairy and al-Bayoumi [another Saudi at the King Fahd mosque] with assisting the hijackers.' Al-Jarrah's role was a closely guarded secret until May 2020 when the FBI accidentally revealed his name in a sloppily-redacted document. While the debate continues to rage, this disclosure proves beyond doubt a connection between Saudi Arabia's embassy in Washington DC and the 9/11 attackers.

Some will see this as proof of a conspiracy by the Saudi state to conduct the 9/11 attacks. The reality is more complex. While huge sums have flowed from Saudi citizens and charitable entities to Islamist militants, very little of that can be attributed to official Saudi state policies or instructions. And the Saudi state is very good at working with Western governments against terrorism. Nonetheless, the tens of billions of petrodollars estimated to have flowed from Saudi sources into Wahhabist proselytism have had an impact. As William McCants, an expert on terrorism has observed, the Saudis are 'both the arsonists and the firefighters.' While a combination of factors are usually at play in terrorism and radicalisation, it seems reasonable to conclude that a world without Saudi-financed, ultraconservative, intolerant interpretations of Islam would be a world with fewer Islamist terrorists and it might have been a world without Al-Qaeda and the Islamic State.

In addition to the Saudi-led onslaught on traditional religion and diversity, within the kingdom of Saudi Arabia, the worst human rights abuses are normalised as part of the established legal order. Notoriously, Saudi Arabia still carries out public beheadings, stonings to death and amputations. Such sentences follow trials where evidence is extracted through torture and access to justice is minimal. These traditional forms of Islamic justice are decried by the British government when practised in other contexts. The Foreign Office website has a section on its work in Afghanistan which talks of 'barbaric punishments such as amputation' carried out by the Taliban. By contrast, in a statement to Parliament, Foreign Office minister Tobias Ellwood said: 'The human rights situation in Saudi Arabia reflects widely held conservative social values and, as such, needs to move at a pace that is acceptable to its society.' The minister was speaking three days after the Saudis had publicly executed 47 people, mostly by beheading.

MORE FUEL TO YOUR FIRE

There is no doubt that Saudi Arabia represents a fundamental challenge to the core values of individual freedom, respect for the rule of law, and responsible international citizenship that characterise the democratic world. If it sat only on sand, Saudi Arabia would be a pariah state, subjected to the harshest sanctions and threatened with humanitarian intervention. But it is, of course, the world's key supplier of oil to international markets. Of particular importance, Saudi Arabia has historically been the 'swing producer' of oil. This means that Saudi Arabia can, on its own, shape the world price. This is a function both of Saudi Arabia's oil production volumes (it vies with Russia and the United States for title of world's greatest producer – the lead alternating between the three in the years between 2015 and 2020) and its ability to flex those volumes. This latter point is more important. Unlike the US and Russia, Saudi Arabia's oil production is under the control of a single state-owned entity, Saudi Aramco, the world's largest oil company. If Saudi Arabia wants to change the global price of oil, it can do so by raising or lowering production. This should not be mistaken for a simplistic power: if the oil price rises above certain levels, global demand will fall, meaning that the overall revenues for Saudi Arabia may also fall. Nevertheless, Saudi Arabia has the greatest power over global energy prices.

In addition to the ability to shape global energy prices, Saudi Arabia has persistently spent the largest proportion of GDP of any country on its military. Put simply, Saudi Arabia buys vast quantities of weapons from Western countries, notably from the United States and Britain (and to a lesser extent, France). This profligacy does little for Saudi Arabia's security. Most notably, in 1990, Saudi Arabia felt sufficiently threatened by Iraq that it summoned a global coalition to defend its northern border, even though Iraq is poorer and has a smaller population. Although Saudi Arabia has one of the world's best-equipped airforces, its pilots are notoriously incompetent and often crash in undemanding situations. Saudi Arabia sees its primary threat as emanating from Iran and its allies in the Middle East, notably pro-Iranian militias in regional countries such as Iraq, Syria and Lebanon. However, there is no realistic evidence that Saudi Arabia could effectively contain Iran, either in a conventional conflict or in proxy wars. As the noted expert on Gulf military affairs expert Michael Knights observed in 2017, 'there's nobody in the Iranian General Staff that's afraid of Saudi Arabia on the ground.... The fact is, Iran is better at doing this stuff.'

However, Saudi Arabia's arms sales buy not only weapons, but global influence. Indeed, Saudi Arabia's influence in Britain may be less due to its oil wealth than its purchases of British-made fighter jets. In 1986, against fierce French competition and after considerable lobbying by the British government in which Margaret Thatcher had played a prominent role, Saudi Arabia agreed to buy over a hundred British-made fighter jets and a wide range of support and training packages in the 'Al-Yamamah' deal (the name translates to 'dove'). The transaction was so important to the newly-privatised British Aerospace (BAE) that the Saudis received the first Tornado jets to emerge from the production line, ahead of the RAF for whom it had been developed. The deal was highly controversial from the start. It had only become possible due to a setback in Saudi-American relations, meaning that America would not sell F-15s to the Saudis, and it led Israel to express its dismay to the British government. Ahead of the deal's conclusion, Thatcher was petitioned by US congressmen urging her not to go ahead.

Al-Yamamah was the first of many linked arms deals that were, in the view of BAE chairman Mike Turner, worth up to £80 billion over a forty-year timespan. In the words of the *Financial Times*, it was, for Britain, the 'biggest sale ever of anything to anyone.' It also proved to be highly controversial. The contract, undertaken between the two governments, was highly secretive. Paid for in crude oil, it meant that the exact sums garnered may never be known, but it also had knock-on effects for other industries (for example, it undermined the UK's North Sea oil sector). The secrecy also masked a range of business practices that would normally be unethical and possibly illegal. Reporting at the time of the original agreement suggested that bribes of £600 million had been paid in 1985 (equivalent to £2 billion in 2020 terms) to secure the deal. Repeated and detailed allegations of bribes and commission payments emerged over the years. In 1989, the National Audit Office began an inquiry. Three years later, this report was suppressed. A later criminal inquiry by the Serious Fraud Office was dropped in 2006 when the Saudi government threatened to suspend intelligence co-operation – a devastating ultimatum when an active Islamist terrorism campaign was unfolding on British soil. Britain's reputation for transparency and anti-corruption fell sharply and the decision to halt the inquiry was subsequently found to have been illegal. So egregious was it that the world's leading anti-corruption watchdog, the Organisation for Economic Cooperation and Development, voiced its 'serious concerns' and sent inspectors to London to ascertain the reasons for it. This was by no means the end of the matter. In 2010, BAE pleaded guilty to criminal charges and paid a fine of almost $450 million for allegations of corporate bribery in an unusual joint Transatlantic corruption investigation.

It is easy to come across as unworldly when discussing Saudi Arabia. For all the distaste that we might feel for the lack of freedoms for Saudi women (until 2018, banned from driving) or the cruelties of its criminal justice system, or its corruption, there is an element of realpolitik in dealing with this country. If Britain refused to supply Saudi Arabia with fighter jets, they would almost certainly fly in from another country. The Tornado (and later Typhoon) jets were assembled mostly in the post-industrial north-west of England, generating significant employment and economic benefits.

The problem with this argument is the warping effect of Saudi's money on Britain. The Al-Yamamah deal has bent the institutions of the UK out of shape and weakened the country's international reputation. Britain has become beholden to Saudi Arabia. London is desperate to placate the notoriously touchy rulers in Riyadh, even at the expense of its own armed forces. On numerous occasions, Britain's Royal Air Force has missed out on upgrades to its equipment, because the Royal Saudi Air Force has taken priority. Both with the launch of the Tornado and its successor, the Typhoon, the RAF found its own essential aeroplanes were delayed in order to service the valuable Saudi customer, even as Britain's planes were required in active military campaigns in places such as Afghanistan and Libya. And the existence of the Saudi contract has meant that BAE has become 'too big to fail.' Increasingly, it is the entire British defence industry. This means that the British government usually has little choice in its own procurement decisions. BAE effectively controls the market, whether for planes, ships or munitions.

The influence that BAE has in Britain means that BAE operates as if it were a state-owned company. As Robin Cook, former Foreign Secretary, ruefully noted, 'the chairman of BAE appeared to have the key to the garden door to No 10. Certainly I never knew No 10 to come up with any decision that would be incommoding to BAE.' This influence would be crucial when Saudi Arabia changed its behaviour and actually started to use its planes, in an ill-judged war in Yemen.

BOMBING YEMEN

The legendary home of the biblical Queen of Sheba, Yemen lies at the southern end of the Arabian peninsula. It is a distinct and unique part of Arabia: more fertile, geographically varied and historically more able to support settled populations than the arid deserts of Saudi Arabia. Yemen's rugged mountains have allowed religiously diverse populations to maintain their autonomy and their distinctive practices over centuries. It is no surprise that one of the last Jewish communities of the Middle East has existed in Yemen until the present day, surviving as a reflection of the weakness of the modern Yemeni state and the inhospitable terrain that militates against centralised control.

The current conflict there has its roots in the year 897, when an Islamic scholar called al-Hadi was invited to Yemen to rule over tribes living in the mountains of southern Arabia. The 9th Century tribes that welcomed al-Hadi became adherents of Zaydi Islam, which remains the faith of a significant proportion of the population of Yemen, particularly those living in the north of the country. Technically speaking, it is a branch of Shi'a Islam, but it is historically distinct from the 'twelver' Shi'a Islam practised in Iran, Iraq and Lebanon.

Ordinarily, Zaydis and Sunnis found it easy to live alongside one another, but such harmony did not survive the pernicious influence of Saudi Wahhabism. Yemen's Zaydis live in the mountains bordering Saudi Arabia and as such were particularly susceptible to the influence of their powerful neighbour. For years, tribal leaders in this region were happy to take Saudi money in return for an alignment with the kingdom's interests, but they did not welcome Saudi interference in their religious life. However, Saudi Arabia's relentless promotion of Wahhabist teachings and denigration of Shi'a (including Zaydis) was a source of resentment in the Zaydi community. Of particular concern were the antics of Moqbel Al-Wadei, a Saudi-funded hardline Sunni shaykh who had set up a network of schools in Dammaj, in the heart of Zaydi country. While Al-Wadei was not an active supporter of terrorism, his institutions had been a finishing school for generations of jihadists, including the notorious 'American Taliban,' John Walker Lindh.

Zaydis were not passive in response to this provocation: they began their own programme to revive their faith, particularly among the younger generation. This movement developed a more radical militant side led by the prominent Zaydi Al-Huthi family, whose battle cries were 'Death to America! Death to Israel! Curse the Jews!' This development of the 'Huthis' came at a sensitive time: Yemen's longtime President 'Ali Abdallah

Salih, a master of balancing the complex coalitions that make up the fragile Yemeni state, found himself co-operating with Western countries on counter-terrorism while at the same time continuing his long-term policy of having discreet relations with Sunni Islamists. Salih, who knew how to pique the interest of his Western interlocutors, tried to claim that the Huthis were receiving material support from Iran, on the basis that their Zaydi Shi'ism made them attractive to the Iranians. This was, at best, simplistic. While the Huthis' slogans were based on Iran's, their movement in its early days was wholly rooted in the local politics and history of Yemen's northwest highlands.

At meeting with President Salih during the first Huthi uprising in 2004, the President, a wily, energetic personality (and himself a Zaydi), declared that Iran was behind the Huthis and asked for Western assistance to counter this threat. Salih could provide no evidence whatsoever for these allegations, beyond the fact that some of the Huthi leadership had spent time in Iran. During the same period Salih claimed that a southern separatist movement had Iranian support (again, without evidence).

The rise of the Huthis coincided with the slow-motion collapse of the Yemeni state. A separatist movement in the south of the country began to gain ground at the same time as Al-Qaeda gained in power and capability in the south and east of the country, partly as a result of being displaced from Saudi Arabia. This was happening as the Yemeni state was facing increasing social pressure after years of corruption from Salih's regime and growing regional inequality. For Zaydis this was a particularly potent message during the Arab Spring in 2011, which stretched the country to breaking point. President Salih agreed to stand down as part of a complex power-sharing deal, but he declined to leave the battlefield, taking a large part of the country's armed forces with him. The country was engulfed in a multi-factional civil war. The various sides were Yemen's official government, the Huthis, loyalists to Salih, a southern separatist movement, Al-Qaeda, the Islamic State and a range of tribal militias who frequently changed sides.

While there was no evidence of Iranian support to the Huthis in 2004, this became a self-fulfilling prophecy. Sunni countries in the Gulf, especially Saudi Arabia and the UAE, mounted an effective campaign to portray the Huthis as part of an Iranian plan to encircle the oilfields of the Gulf, an argument which found a ready audience in Washington and London. As fighting escalated, the Huthis did start to receive limited support from Iran. In 2013 an Iranian ship loaded with weapons destined for the Huthis, including sophisticated anti-aircraft missiles, was seized off Yemen's coast. These weapons had been loaded onboard in an Iranian military dock. The Islamic Republic's protestations of innocence were unconvincing.

Salih, now out of power but leading a rebel movement, demonstrated his endless capacity for reinvention by allying himself with the Huthis in 2014, against whom he had previously fought six wars. The Huthi-Salih alliance was able to seize control of Yemen's capital Sana'a in 2014, directly against Iran's orders (there is evidence that Iran was entirely opposed to the Huthi-Salih alliance). Yemen's new President, Mansour Hadi, abandoned his capital and retreated to Aden, pursued by a Huthi army. With

Aden also close to falling into Huthi hands in March 2015, Hadi was evacuated to Saudi Arabia. From there, more prisoner than guest, he called for international intervention.

The Huthis' seizure of Sana'a and the escape of President Hadi changed the dynamics. What had been a civil war became a regional conflict. But something else also changed these dynamics: a new king in Saudi Arabia, and the rise of an unknown youngster to a position of extraordinary power.

A PRINCE FROM A NIGHTMARE

In January 2015, King Abdullah of Saudi Arabia died at the age of 90 after a period of ill-health. At that time, the Saudi norm was for the succession to the throne to pass through brothers. As expected, Abdullah was succeeded by Salman, the sixth brother to ascend to the throne. What was unexpected was the appointment of one of Salman's youngest children to the powerful role of Minister of Defence. Muhammad bin Salman, known everywhere as MbS, was little-known outside Saudi Arabia at the time of his appointment. Unlike other Saudi princes, he had not been educated abroad, had not been trained at a Western military academy such as West Point or Sandhurst, and was not a feature on the diplomatic circuit. MbS was initially dismissed by many ill-informed observers as a frontman, a prince of limited accomplishments, known to be close to his elderly father, who would act as a cipher for the king. They could not have been more wrong. Yemen was the proving-ground of the man who would transform Saudi Arabia.

Almost the first decision that MbS took as Defence Minister was to launch a campaign of airstrikes against Huthi targets in Yemen. After years of buying cutting edge fighter jets and not using them, the Saudis were finally putting their formidable air force to use. Supported by smaller airforces from across the Arab world, the bombardment began immediately. The only problem was that the Saudis either didn't know how to minimise civilian casualties or they didn't care. Their very first airstrike killed up to 23 civilians in Sana'a, including women and children, according to Human Rights Watch. In the following years, repeated violations of the laws of war appeared to have been committed by the Saudis, mostly caused by indiscriminate, or at least poorly-targeted air-raids. By late 2020, the Saudi-led coalition had carried out more than 20,000 airstrikes, killing nearly 9,000 civilians and injuring many more. Airstrikes frequently hit civilian targets including hospitals, schools, refugee camps and densely-populated residential neighbourhoods. In May 2015, the Saudis declared the entire northern Yemeni province of Sa'ada a military target. At the time its population was around 50,000, almost of all of whom were civilians. This was clearly a violation of the laws of war. At the same time, the Saudis established a blockade of Hudaydah, the main port serving northern Yemen. Unsurprisingly, this resulted in a famine.

By 2019, the death toll from Yemen's civil war passed 100,000 civilians. It would be incorrect and misleading to suggest that the Huthis were the wronged party in this conflict. They bear much of the responsibility for the outbreak of the war, even if their underlying grievances had some legitimacy. Huthi rebels have killed plenty of civilians and they have a track record of human rights violations, imprisoning perceived opponents and use of torture. Huthis also repeatedly seized food from humanitarian agencies, diverting it from needy civilians to their own commanders. However, the majority of direct civilian casualties of the war were caused by airstrikes carried out by the Saudi-led coalition. Undoubtedly, the Huthis were cynical opponents who would mix fighters in with civilian populations. This required intelligent and humane targeting on the part of the Saudis, which did not occur. Repeated studies by independent groups have judged that Saudi air attacks have amounted to war crimes. And they continue: investigations in September 2020 point to recent airstrikes that appear to have targeted civilians – another war crime. Furthermore, the blockade of Yemen's ports is largely responsible for the famine and disease that have ravaged the country.

For a country that grants its own citizens minimal rights, the Saudis' indifference to the plight of Yemeni civilians is perhaps unsurprising. The surprise is the willingness of Britain and America to support the Saudi war effort. In spite of having one of the world's best equipped air forces, the Saudis are not capable of carrying out a campaign of airstrikes without complete reliance on Britain's engineers, technicians and weapons. As a leading British expert on Saudi Arabia's military, General John Deverell, remarked: 'The Saudi bosses absolutely depend on BAE.' Another BAE employee spelled it out very clearly to a Channel 4 documentary: 'They couldn't do it without us. If we weren't there, in seven to 14 days there wouldn't be a jet in the sky.'

British engineers, targeters, analysts and 'liaison officers,' some from the RAF, have worked hand in glove with the Saudis to enable their inexperienced and ineffective military to carry out its campaign. This is in addition to the British bombs that Saudi planes drop onto Yemeni civilians and, occasionally, military targets. In the years since the start of the Saudi air campaign, BAE sold £15 billion worth of arms and services to Saudi Arabia. British-made bombs, such as the Raytheon Paveway, MBDA's Brimstone and Storm Shadow, as well as cluster munitions, have all been dropped over Yemen. In the case of cluster munitions, which leave unexploded 'bomblets' that linger for years, killing children and vulnerable civilians long after the conclusion of a conflict, both the Saudis and British government misled the public about the malevolent application of these weapons in the conflict. In May 2016, the British defence minister Philip Dunne told Parliament:

We assess that no UK-supplied cluster weapons have been used, and that no UK-supplied aircraft have been involved in the use of UK cluster weapons, in the current conflict in Yemen.

Later in the same year, a Saudi military spokesman responded to photographs of UK-made cluster bombs found in Yemen by claiming these images had been manipulated, and repeated Dunne's denial. In December 2016, the British government eventually conceded that UK-made cluster munitions had been dropped on Yemen. These munitions are loaded onto planes by technicians supervised by British contractors. Under Britain's adoption into law of the international Convention on Cluster Munitions, since 2010 this would constitute illegal activity for any British person. Almost every country in the world has banned cluster munitions. The British government has taken no action in this case. Saudi Arabia is one of the few countries that is not a signatory to the convention.

INTERNATIONAL ISOLATION

Britain has become increasingly isolated in its support for the Saudi campaign. Germany suspended its arms sales in 2018 after the Saudis tricked Jamal Khashoggi, a dissident Saudi journalist, into coming to their consulate in Istanbul, where he was killed, dismembered and his body fed into an incinerator. A series of European countries followed suit, as did Canada. France continued to sell weapons to the Saudis, in far smaller quantities than the British supplies, and maintained that these were not being used in the Yemen conflict. In Europe, only Britain remained a forceful proponent of Saudi Arabia's strategy in Yemen. In essence, this strategy has been to bomb the Huthis into submission. History contains no examples of a guerilla movement being defeated solely by airstrikes. Perhaps in recognition of that, the Saudis, with allies such as the United Arab Emirates, deployed ground forces in Yemen in 2018. Britain continued its enthusiastic involvement, deploying special forces on the ground in Yemen, confirmed by credible reporting in 2019. That year the cross-party House of Lords International Relations Committee concluded that arms sales to Saudi Arabia for use in the war on Yemen were 'unlawful.' The same committee observed that Britain relied on inadequate, self-serving investigations carried out by the Saudis to confirm the legality of the military actions, rather than carrying out independent investigations. Under successive Conservative prime ministers, the government ploughed on, only briefly suspending arms sales after a court judgement in 2019, before resuming them a year later.

Throughout this period Britain appeared to have no clear strategy for the Yemen conflict. It professed a desire to see the conflict resolved and offered its support to the UN envoy. In speeches, parliamentary debates and broadcast interviews, British ministers would repeat the well-worn line that there was 'no military solution' to the conflict. This was a disingenuous line to take from a country that had allowed itself to become a party to one side of the military conflict, even to the extent of deploying troops on the ground.

The war in Yemen has been disastrous for Saudi Arabia, too. It has reduced Saudi Arabia's security while leading to humanitarian catastrophe in Yemen. Just as the US invasion of Iraq led to the considerable strengthening of Iran's presence, the Saudi intervention in Yemen has bolstered Iran too, around Saudi Arabia's southern border.

Plucked from obscurity and with no experience, surrounded by terrified yes-men, MbS may not know his true reputation. But many others do know: 'Everything he touches turns to shit,' observed a senior American diplomat and veteran of the US Embassy in Riyadh, in a private conversation. The Yemen war may have been MbS's most egregious failure, both in terms of civilian lives lost in Yemen and in the cost to Saudi Arabia's own security, but there are a wide range of other examples of his inadequacy as a national leader. In June 2017, Saudi Arabia, with the UAE, announced it was suspending its diplomatic relations with its immediate neighbour Qatar and instituted an air and sea blockade. This was a highly provocative act towards a wholly import-dependent country. Saudi Arabia had accused Qatar of financing terrorism and in particular of having sent hundreds of millions of dollars to the Islamic State, as well as being too close to Iran with whom it shares a major gas field. While Qatar and Saudi Arabia had a different perspective on relations with Turkey, Iran and the Muslim Brotherhood, they had worked closely together in Yemen and Syria right up to the moment of the blockade. Amid a welter of claims and counter-claims, Saudi Arabia has largely failed to persuade the world that Qatar is a sponsor of terrorism. It is not that the charge is entirely baseless, but that it was a little rich, coming from Saudi Arabia. Both sides have invested significant sums trying to discredit each other in paid-for posts in the international and social media. The situation was not helped by President Trump apparently being unaware that his country's biggest Middle East base was in Qatar, meaning that he appeared to briefly take Saudi Arabia's side in the dispute.

MbS clearly thought that his swift action would lead to a swift Qatari capitulation. In fact, the opposite occurred. Faced with an interruption to their normal supply chains, Qatar turned to Turkey and Iran, the very countries that MbS had demanded they distance themselves from. Qatar's young emir, Tamim bin Thani, became a national hero because he was seen to have stood up to bullying from an over-mighty neighbour. After an initial period of nervousness in the international business community with companies unsure whether they should pull out of Qatar, things have largely settled down. Qatar continues to be close to its Western allies and remains the world's largest exporter of liquefied natural gas. The embargo has strengthened its relations with Turkey and Iran. Meanwhile, the Saudis have literally been digging in. They are considering spending billions of dollars on a canal to separate the Qatari peninsula from the Saudi mainland, turning it into an island. Much of the dispute was de-escalated in a public ceremony between Saudi Arabia and Qatar at the start of 2021, but the Qataris will not quickly let go of their new-found autonomy after years of living in the Saudis' shadow.

This is not the place to list all of MbS's failures. At one point he kidnapped the Lebanese Prime Minister. In another moment he sent assassins to Canada to murder an exiled former security chief. He has imprisoned various members of his immediate family whose achievements and experience contrast favourably with his own.

Nevertheless, Boris Johnson has hailed the Crown Prince as a 'reformer' who 'deserves our support.' One element of Britain's support was a desperation to list the shares of the Saudi national oil company, Saudi Aramco, on the London stock exchange. By some measures the world's largest company, Aramco's stock listing, another of MbS's personal initiatives, was viewed as a 'prize' by a range of major stock exchanges around the world. The problem was that the Saudis did not welcome the ordinary standards of compliance and transparency that apply to a publicly listed company in an advanced economy. In its enthusiasm to secure the Aramco listing for London, Britain went the extra mile to satisfy the Saudis. Legislation that had been introduced specifically in response to a series of failures of foreign owned companies listed on the London stock exchange was exempted by the Financial Conduct Authority (FCA) under a special new 'premium' category created to help Aramco. As a senior corporate governance manager in the City observed in an interview to the *Financial Times*: 'It looks like the FCA is consulting on amending the existing listing rules to accommodate the peculiarities of one company, which is not a very effective strategy for regulating the market as a whole.' In off-record conversations that I had at the time with Foreign Office staff, it was clear that the FCA had adopted these new regulations for the specific purpose of securing the Aramco listing, however much this was denied by the FCA.

The question of relations with Saudi Arabia is difficult for every Western democracy. Whatever we might think of its strict policies, it is naïve to assume that we can ignore the country. But it is equally naïve to believe that a megalomaniac and aggressive prince will respond positively to critical engagement from the outside, even if he has undertaken superficial social reforms. This is all the more the case if our engagement is weak, as both Yemen and Aramco demonstrate. The uncritical approach to Saudi Arabia is also to ignore the obvious, undeniable trajectory of global economics. The end of the fossil fuel era looms. Saudi Arabia's influence is expected to wane correspondingly, whatever MbS does. For years, Saudi Arabia has had a set of reform plans for a post-oil economy, varying in their ambition and plausibility. MbS's version of these, known as Vision 2030, has slightly more urgency. But there no credible reason to believe that Saudi Arabia will be able to create a dynamic or successful post-oil economy. In fact, the future for Saudi Arabia looks bleak. As global demand for Saudi hydrocarbons collapses and the world moves to net-zero carbon emissions, Saudi Arabia has a large and young population, accustomed to extensive social welfare and subsidies, unaccustomed to operating in a competitive global marketplace.

THE SAUDIS AND THE AMERICANS

No discussion of Saudi Arabia's recent history is complete without mentioning the United States. Historically, America's Presidents have been close to Saudi Arabia, reflecting both its central economic role in hydrocarbons and a belief, possibly misplaced, that Saudi Arabia is central to stability in the Middle East. During the years of the War on Terror, Saudi Arabia successfully retained its proximity to America as a strategic partner and co-operated closely on counter-terrorism. However, in the same period, America's domestic production of hydrocarbons was rapidly increasing. Counting both oil and gas, America has for some time been a larger producer than the Saudis. Saudi Arabia has a much more predictable, stable production from a single mega-company, Aramco. But the underlying point remains: Saudi Arabia's command of world oil markets is not what it was at the beginning of the millennium.

A second factor comes into play here: the long-term demand crisis for hydrocarbons. The world has, in fact, already reached peak oil demand, according to the respected BP Energy Outlook, which has been tracking energy usage since 1951. The 2020 edition foresees declining oil demand in all scenarios. Should commitments to a net-zero global economy gain traction, oil demand is predicted to plummet in the next 20 years, to levels not seen since the 1970s. In this case, Saudi Arabia's strategic importance to the United States and the wider world becomes limited. In geopolitical terms, Saudi Arabia is eventually likely to command similar attention to a country such as Sudan: poor, populous, regionally important but largely ignored.

Under Barack Obama, America had already begun a cautious distancing, as part of his 'pivot to Asia.' However, this pragmatic policy was to reckon without the power of personalities. In particular, President Trump and his 'bromance' with Muhammad bin Salman. There may of course be a simpler explanation. Trump made an intriguing choice for his first foreign visit as the leader of the 'free world': Saudi Arabia. On his return, the self-proclaimed 'Master of the Deal' started to make increasingly bold claims for the scale of Saudi investments that he had negotiated. By 2018, Trump claimed to have ensured $450 billion of Saudi investment into the United States, of which $110 billion was an arms deal, creating 500,000 to 600,000 new American jobs. This was not true. In the year prior to these outlandish claims, the United States exported $16 billion of goods to Saudi Arabia. Possibly as many as 500 new jobs could be attributed to a growth in trade with the Kingdom. But what really mattered to Trump was his own personal wealth and that of his immediate family. Here, the results were more impressive. Since the 1990s Trump had received tens of millions of dollars in payments from a range of Saudi royal and governmental sources for various real estate transactions. Even as President, Trump came to benefit personally from Saudi officials making extensive use of his hotels in New York and Washington DC. In 2019, according to reports, 'a senior executive from the Trump Organization visited Riyadh... "trying to get a deal" for a Trump hotel in Riyadh.'

Trump's point-man for Middle East affairs was his son-in-law, Jared Kushner. This was welcomed by Gulf Countries that are ruled by close-knit family networks that view business, politics and dynastic affairs as inseparable. It is far easier for a Saudi prince to deal with an American prince than with a professional bureaucracy such as the State Department. The Saudis knew they were onto a good thing with Kushner, who had no background knowledge of the Middle East (this was noted in an internal Saudi assessment, leaked to a Lebanese newspaper). Kushner's engagement with the region involved active work with MbS on a range of policy issues. In 2017, Kushner had given MbS a green light for his disastrous Qatar escapade and they also found common cause over mutual hostility towards Turkey and Iran. At the same time, Kushner's private business interests benefited from undisclosed Saudi funding and since leaving office he has launched a group to promote business interests between Gulf countries and Israel. In this light it is hardly surprising that the Americans, led on Middle East policy by Kushner, supported the Saudi war on Yemen. This changed significantly in 2021 when the new Biden administration ended sales of offensive weapons to the kingdom. In his first foreign policy speech as President, Joe Biden announced the appointment of a special envoy to lead peace efforts in Yemen.

In spite of the US lead, and a direct appeal from one of the most influential American Senators to Britain to follow suit, the UK continued to plough an increasingly lonely furrow, supplying weapons and supporting the Saudi war. As late as June 2021, in an official visit to Riyadh, Foreign Secretary Dominic Raab praised the Kingdom's 'pivotal role in regional stability' and described the Yemen war as a 'shared security challenge.'

Britain's active complicity in Saudi Arabia's war on Yemen reflects a deeper problem: the narrowness of the British manufacturing sector and an over-reliance on defence exports. The risk for Germany to stop selling arms to Saudi Arabia, and for France to refuse to sell arms that could be used in the war on Yemen is far lower. According to the British government's own figures, in the years from 2008 to 2017, Britain's arms sales have far exceeded those of Germany in every one of those years and exceeded France in every year except 2015 and 2016. Germany's manufacturing sector dwarfs Britain's; France's is consistently larger. For either of those countries to decide to reduce or stop its arms exports to Saudi Arabia has less impact on the overall economy. For Britain, the impact is far greater and it is concentrated on a single dominant defence company (BAE) whose political connections are unparalleled. Brexit makes this situation all the more difficult: our access to export markets in our nearest, democratic neighbours in Europe, has reduced. Therefore we need to increase, not reduce, our dependence on emerging economies, many of which have questionable human rights records.

As we have seen, the long-term economic prospects for Saudi Arabia are bleak. And the Kingdom is increasingly turning away from Western arms suppliers that tend to come with annoying human rights considerations and an inquisitive media. In August 2021, the Saudis signed a military cooperation agreement with Russia, a country unlikely to complain about violations of international law. And in December 2021 US intelligence satellites demonstrated that the Saudis were building ballistic missiles with support from China. Ultimately, the British economy could easily survive the loss of the Saudi defence business. But the greatest impact would be felt by the legions of retired generals, ambassadors and politicians who make a living from the Saudi arms sales ecosystem. As an example of state capture, the Saudis have done an impressive job with the UK.

The basic justification for Britain's enabling of Saudi Arabia's destructive behaviours over the decades has been the idea that we can rely on the Saudis to provide the world with oil in a consistent and price-stabilising way. But when Russia's invasion of Ukraine caused oil prices to shoot to historic highs, the Saudis proved that this reliability was a myth. In March 2022, the *Wall Street Journal* reported that the White House 'unsuccessfully tried to arrange calls between President Biden and the de facto leaders of Saudi Arabia and the United Arab Emirates.' Faced with the biggest energy and security crisis in post-World War II history, it turned out that neither the Saudis nor the Emiratis were willing to turn on the taps to help the Americans, their long-term protectors. MbS felt personally slighted by President Biden's decision to release an official intelligence report on the Khashoggi murder, which stated: 'We assess that Saudi Arabia's Crown Prince Muhammad bin Salman approved operation in Istanbul, Turkey to capture or kill Saudi journalist Jamal Khashoggi.' MbS apparently complained to a visiting journalist that 'human rights law wasn't applied to me' and complained that his feelings had been hurt by the accusations.

Britain's Prime Minister Boris Johnson had been careful not to be seen as critical of MbS. Indeed, he had accepted Saudi hospitality in the form of a lavish, £14,000 trip to the Kingdom just days before the Khashoggi murder. The *Spectator*, a right-wing British magazine normally supportive of the British Prime Minister, speculated that his reticence on MbS might be because the Saudis had 'kompromat' on Johnson. Whether or not this was a factor in his decision-making, he avoided making direct criticism of MbS. After the brush-off received by President Biden, Johnson announced that he would be travelling to the Kingdom to plead directly with MbS. He, too, returned empty-handed: the Saudis refused to increase oil production. Oil and gas prices remained sky-high. Europe continued to be held to ransom by its reliance on Russia's energy exports. While Britain has benefited financially from the Saudi's billions, it found out that the friendship did not extend to Riyadh helping out with its key commodity. In this sense, Britain's decades-long policy to let Saudi Arabia poison global Islam with sectarian bigotry, export terror, prosecute a merciless war in Yemen, while supplying it with the weapons and expertise to do so, has failed.

Britain deludes itself that the Saudis' conduct in the Yemen war has improved as a result of its engagement, even as millions face starvation and children lie dead from British bombs. The UK wants to believe that the Saudis can be a positive force because it needs their money and their oil, not because their actions give London any reason to believe so. This delusion takes us back to the Saudi deradicalisation centre. As a metaphor for the Saudis' relationship with the UK, it is apposite: we want things from Saudi Arabia so we try to persuade ourselves that what they are doing is beneficial to our wider interests, in spite of glaring evidence to the contrary. Graduates of the Saudi deradicalisation programme have returned to terrorism, including Said Ali Al-Shihri and Muhammad Al-Harbi who, after being released for their 'successful' completion of the programme, became leadership figures in Yemen's branch of Al-Qaeda. And no delusion is more powerful than the story of Ahmad Al-Shayea, the man who survived his own suicide bombing and who, we are supposed to believe, was himself a victim of terrorism, not responsible for his own actions. In November 2013, this star pupil of Saudi deradicalisation left Saudi Arabia to join the Islamic State in Syria.

10. INDIA AND THE POLITICS OF EMPIRE

*'They were dragged out of their houses. Someone cut them down…
another set them ablaze.'*
Mangilal Jain, describing the 2002 riots in Gujarat

*'Even then if a puppy comes under the wheel, will it be painful or not?
Of course it is.'*
Indian Prime Minister Narendra Modi commenting on 2002
anti-Muslim pogroms

It was February 2002 and Ehsan Jafri was running out of options.
A violent Hindu mob had surrounded the largely Muslim housing
compound where he lived in Gujarat state in western India. As a
former MP, he was seen as a leader in his community. Neighbours
and associates had congregated at Jafri's house, believing that a
distinguished retired politician would be protected. In the past,

during riots, Jafri had been able to call up police protection. Later, a member of the mob confirmed that the police had let them continue unmolested. '[The police] kept away from Hindus.... They told us that everything should be finished within two-three hours.'

BANNED FROM THE US

As chief minister of Gujarat before becoming India's Prime Minister, Narendra Modi failed to prevent communal violence in 2002 which led to the deaths of at least 1,000, mostly Muslim citizens. Many respected scholars have concluded that these killings were a deliberate pogrom against Muslims and accuse Modi of significant involvement. As a result, Modi was banned from entering the United States and Britain for several years. An Indian Special Investigative Team found in 2013 that Modi had not intentionally caused these deaths, although several of his senior officials have been found guilty. Modi's leadership appears to have set a pattern of normalisation of communal violence. Lynch mobs, often targeting Muslims, have become so commonplace that in 2018 the Supreme Court of India recommended that parliament enact specific legislation to outlaw the problem. These mobs appear to be increasing and are often defended by Modi's senior ministers.

Modi was re-elected in a landslide victory in 2019, and oversaw an expansion in anti-Muslim policies. In late 2019, for instance, Modi's government enacted a new citizenship law. This ostensibly held that only non-Muslim immigrants from neighbouring countries could become Indian citizens. It's the case that most of India's neighbours discriminate against non-

Muslims. But India's proposed law, combined with a planned new citizenship register, would leave many Indian Muslims without access to official documentation and therefore unable to prove their right to nationality, making them a lower class of citizen. A national uproar of opposition to the measures appears to have taken the government by surprise. In a brutal response, police and vigilante groups targeted Muslim protestors. One of the key elements of authoritarian nationalism is the delegitimisation of minority and opposition groups. In the Indian context this has been done by creating a dichotomy between legitimate refugees and illegitimate 'infiltrators.' This language has repeatedly been used by Modi's right-hand man Amit Shah, widely considered a future Prime Minister of India.

A national register of citizens rolled out in the eastern state of Assam led to two million people, almost all of them Muslims, finding themselves stateless and required to prove to Foreigners Tribunals that they were in fact Indian citizens, a near-impossible task for most people in a country where access to official documentation is challenging. Human Rights Watch found these tribunals to be arbitrary and inconsistent. This discriminatory citizenship register is to be implemented nationwide and appears to contradict various international legal commitments India has made, notably the International Covenant on Civil and Political Rights.

WIPED OUT IN THE NEXT PARLIAMENT

There were plenty of reasons to believe that India's Prime Minister Narendra Modi might do badly in the 2019 general election. India's economy had not boomed in his first term. The GDP growth rate fell, as Modi's major economic campaign, 'Make in India,' fell a long way short of its targets. A quixotic decision to invalidate most of the country's paper currency in 2016 had proved chaotic and costly to many Indians. Pollsters found that Modi's party, the Hindu-nationalist BJP, was no longer seen as the solution to India's major problems. In regional elections held in late 2018, the BJP lost control of three important state legislatures. In February 2019, an Indian fighter jet was shot down over Pakistan during an escalation of the decades-old conflict between the two countries. After inflicting this humiliating blow, the Pakistanis treated the ejected Indian pilot well and returned him safely to India.

However, predictions of Modi's electoral downfall were misplaced. Modi won a landslide, embedding him as India's pre-eminent politician and leaving the primary opposition party, the Indian National Congress, on its knees. Rahul Gandhi, the Congress leader and scion of the Nehru-Gandhi dynasty that dominated India's politics since independence, even lost his parliamentary seat, which had been held by his family for nearly 40 years. After a presidential-style campaign, there was no doubt that Modi had been given a personal mandate. But his party had many practical benefits. It is significantly better-financed and organised than any other political force in India. As the political wing of a much larger Hindu cultural movement, the BJP has literally hundreds of millions of volunteers on the ground who can mobilise voters.

The BJP also had another proven advantage – the politics of national populism, in this case, Hindu-nationalist populism. Hinduism is undeniably one of the cultural foundations of the Indian sub-continent. But since independence in 1947 the Republic of India has been a multi-cultural, multi-faith mosaic of languages, traditions and histories. Its constitution, in part thanks to the ideals of independence leader Jawaharlal Nehru, proclaims its secular nature in its opening lines. Hindus make up almost four-fifths of India's population, the largest population of Hindus anywhere in the world. But India's second-largest faith community, Islam, is also one of the world's largest Muslim populations. There are also vast numbers of other faiths, notably Sikhs, Buddhists and Christians. The BJP's Hindu nationalism, known as Hindutva, makes a downtrodden non-Hindu minority inevitable.

Hindutva is a highly contested concept, and a detailed study is beyond the scope of this book. However, there is plenty of evidence that the focus on ethno-religious, cultural hegemony of Hindus shares much with European fascism. Within the Hindutva movement, particular organisations, notably the Rashtriya Swayamsevak Sangh (literally, 'National Volunteer Society') and the Vishva Hindu Parishad (literally, 'Universal Hindu Council') became powerful organisations. Both have been at the heart of Hindu nationalism throughout the 20th and 21st Centuries in India, all the while operating in lockstep with the BJP political party. It was an activist with Rashtriya Swayamsevak Sangh who assassinated Mahatma Gandhi in 1948. Another of the group's activists, whose life has been faithfully devoted to Hindutva, was Narendra Modi, a member from the age of eight. BJP figures frequently deliver speeches that target Muslims and lead to communal violence against Muslim populations.

In these violent outbreaks, a pattern emerges. There is violence on both sides, but the casualties are overwhelmingly Muslims. India's police appear to turn a blind eye to Hindu mobs. In January 2020, when a government supporter shot at Muslim student protesters in Delhi, the police took no action. A few weeks earlier, at the same location, when students protested, police had stormed the mainly-Muslim university, teargassing and beating students. Modi's new citizenship laws are likely to render tens of millions of Muslims stateless. The resulting disenfranchisement of India's Muslims would further embed the BJP's electoral advantage.

None of this is likely to trouble Modi very much. His victory was enthusiastically celebrated by like-minded politicians. Donald Trump tweeted: 'Great things are in store for the US-India partnership with the return of PM Modi.' Trump had started up a 'bromance' with Modi, with the two of them jointly hosting a huge rally of Indian-Americans in September 2019. Their relationship reached a climax in February 2020 with Trump addressing 100,000 people at a stadium in Gujarat on subjects relatively new to him such as cricket and Bollywood. Like all beautiful relationships, there was something in it for both sides: Trump was able to appear the acclaimed international statesman in a US election year, courting the important Indian-American vote; Modi could demonstrate that the US endorsed his controversial policies and favoured India over its long-time rival Pakistan.

Another populist nationalist politician who found it useful to have a strong relationship with Modi was Britain's Boris

Johnson. While Britons of Indian heritage have tended to support the Labour party, a concerted effort was made by Johnson's Conservatives to gain their support. As a largely economically-successful, upwardly mobile group, British Indians are prime targets for the Conservatives. As Labour leader between 2015 and 2020, Jeremy Corbyn had not helped himself by taking a seemingly pro-Pakistan position on the vexed issue of Kashmir, a disputed territory with India. Amid fury from British-Indian groups the party's chairman Ian Lavery had to backtrack, promising that 'the Labour party will not take a pro-Indian or pro-Pakistan stance on Kashmir.' The Conservatives were able to make hay. Johnson gave an interview to an Indian media outlet talking darkly of 'anti-India forces' at work in Britain (meaning the Labour party). On an earlier visit to India before he became Prime Minister, Johnson had given a rambling speech in favour of Modi for which he was paid more than £100,000. 'Modi is a firecracker,' he said. 'I have formed a very positive impression of him. He came to meet me when I was London's mayor. He then went and held a rally at Wembley. And I knew we were dealing with an absolute political phenomenon because he got a huge number of people to support him.'

Modi repaid the favour. The UK branch of the Overseas Friends of the BJP campaigned for the Conservatives in 48 marginal seats in the 2019 British general election. The President of the Overseas Friends of BJP UK, Kuldeep Singh Shekhawat, spelled out the strategy in clear terms: 'If the entire Indian community in the UK votes Tory, we will see a swing of around 40 seats to the Tories. This will swing the actual election result.'

Johnson's 2019 election victory was warmly welcomed by Modi, amidst talk of an incipient 'special relationship' between the two countries. It was a stunning turnaround for Modi who, seven years earlier, had been living under a boycott by the UK, effectively banning him from entering the country.

COMMUNAL VIOLENCE

In February 2002, a train passing through the Gujarati city of Godhra caught fire, killing 58 people, including many women and children. Most of the victims were members of the Vishva Hindu Parishad, returning from celebrating the demolition of an historic mosque, part of a campaign to erase India's Muslim heritage. Initial rumours suggested – wrongly – that a Muslim mob had set fire to the train. The ruling BJP, and its Chief Minister Modi, endorsed a day of protest to take place the following day. A housing compound favoured by Muslims, known as the Gulberg Society, became a target of Hindu extremists. Its high walls were blown up with gas bottles and houses were set on fire. Women were raped and burned alive. Children were not spared. Muslim men were forced to call out Hindu slogans before being chopped up by the mob. According to Sanjiv Bhatt, who was at that time Gujarat State deputy commissioner for intelligence, Modi was kept appraised of these events throughout the day.

The former MP Ehsan Jafri's house had become a last refuge, crowded with about 100 desperate, terrified people. As Jafri's son Tanveer explained to me when we spoke in late 2020, it was inconceivable that the police were unable to help: the office of the police commissioner in Ahmedabad was just three to four kilometres from Jafri's house. The husband of one of the women sheltering in Jafri's house happened to be in the police commissioner's office when Jafri called. There was no doubt that the call took place, but the police did nothing. After fruitless calls to the police, Jafri tried calling politicians and other contacts he had built up over the years. But nobody could (or would) do anything. In desperation, Jafri played his last card. He called Modi directly, pleading for help. As Tanveer Jafri recounted, those in the room with Jafri could tell things were going wrong. The call did not last long and Jafri was furious by the end. 'Modi was abusing me,' he explained to the bystanders. A desperate man, his house surrounded by a bloodthirsty crowd, begged the chief minister of his state for assistance, Modi, and in return received invective. One witness to these events reported that Modi had taunted Jafri, expressing astonishment that he was still alive.

The mob was now closing in. Parts of Jafri's house were on fire and the refugees huddled into an inner room, urgently trying to douse the flames with water from the kitchen. Outside, the attackers formed a human chain to pass cans of kerosene to feed the flames. Jafri called out to the mob: 'Spare these people, I'm coming out, do what you want with me.' A group of men dragged him away, and chopped him into pieces before burning his body parts. Jafri's sacrifice did not save the others. The house was overrun and people dragged outside where they were piled on top of one another, before being set alight. Only 31 of the 69 dead could be identified. The others were disfigured and burned beyond recognition.

Modi has maintained his innocence and ignorance, claiming to have had no knowledge of what was happening until later in the evening, after the key events had taken place. Unfortunately for his credibility, there are numerous witnesses to the phone calls, briefings and meetings that occurred throughout the day as events unfolded. The Gujarat riots in 2002 had left between 1,000 to 2,000 dead and more than 150,000 displaced. According to the independent Concerned Citizens Tribunal, this was 'an organised crime perpetrated by the state's chief minister and his government.' It was noted that Modi had incited reaction by driving the charred bodies burned in the Godhra train across the state in a motorcade. Modi's involvement went beyond incitement, however. According to a set of 'sting' interviews recorded by the investigative magazine *Tehelka*, perpetrators described Modi's role in clearing the decks to allow the violence to take place. One member of a Hindu militant youth movement said:

He had given us three days... to do whatever we could. He said he would not give us time after that.... He said this openly.... After three days, he asked us to stop and everything came to a halt....

A senior police commissioner recalled that Modi had said that Hindus ought to be allowed to 'vent their anger' at the Muslims – a clear instruction to police to stand aside as the mobs rampaged.

Later in 2002, Modi embarked on a *'gaurav yatra,'* a term for a 'journey of pride.' Modi toured Gujarat delivering speeches to huge crowds. The speeches varied from place to place, but the core message was the same untruth: Hindus had been victimised in the Godhra train fire but nobody had retaliated. The existence of violence against Muslims was simply erased from history.

Many of these speeches can still be viewed on YouTube. In one, Modi succinctly delivers his key message: 'They've defamed Gujarat so much... in response, I had to embark on this Yatra!' 'Who will save Gujarat from the Merchants of Death?' asked a campaign song. Some of the speeches were specifically delivered on the site of killings earlier in the year, and jaunty slogans rang out about Modi as the person to 'give terrorism a jolt' ('terrorism' in this context being a dog-whistle term for Muslims).

FROM INTERNATIONAL PARIAH TO GLOBAL DARLING

Modi's role in the events of 2002 may have been debated in India, but much of the international community took a clear position. Britain boycotted Modi, having no contact with him and ensuring that he was unable to visit the UK. Similarly, the US State Department denied Modi a diplomatic visa and withdrew his existing tourist visa as he was deemed 'responsible for or directly carried out, at any time, particularly severe violations of religious freedom' rendering him 'ineligible for a visa to the United States.' An official statement from the US Embassy in New Delhi made the reasons abundantly clear:

> As head of the State government in Gujarat between February 2002 and May 2002, [Modi] was responsible for the performance of state institutions at that time... reports document the violence in Gujarat from February 2002 to May 2002 and cite the Indian National Human Rights Commission report, which states there was 'a comprehensive failure on the part of the state government to control the persistent violation of rights of life, liberty, equality, and dignity of the people of the state.'

Modi was prepared to be almost as ruthless with his own side as he was with India's Muslims, ensuring that anyone who stood in his way was removed. Haren Pandya, a ministerial colleague of Modi in Gujarat state government who was known to have given evidence of Modi's actions at the time of the riots was forced to resign for his 'indiscipline.' Within a year, Pandya had been murdered in Ahmedabad. Conveniently, the murder was blamed on militant Muslims working with Pakistani intelligence. In September 2011, this allegation was dismissed. In a scathing judgement, a Gujarat court found:

The investigation has all throughout been botched up and blinkered.... The investigating officers concerned ought to be held accountable for their ineptitude resulting into injustice, huge harassment of many persons concerned and enormous waste of public resources and public time of the courts.

In an article in the Indian magazine *Seminar*, the political psychologist Professor Ashis Nandy reflected on interviewing Narendra Modi at some point before 1992, long before Modi had reached any position of power or influence. It is worth quoting this at some length:

Modi... met virtually all the criteria that psychiatrists, psycho-analysts and psychologists had set up after years of empirical work on the authoritarian personality. He had the same mix of puritanical rigidity, narrowing of emotional life, massive use of the ego defence of projection, denial and fear of his own passions

combined with fantasies of violence – all set within the matrix of clear paranoid and obsessive personality traits. I still remember the cool, measured tone in which he elaborated a theory of cosmic conspiracy against India that painted every Muslim as a suspected traitor and a potential terrorist. I came out of the interview shaken....

The opinions of psychology professors, or the international boycott did little to undermine Modi's domestic standing. His relentless promotion of Gujarat as an investment destination served to raise his profile and popularity across India and internationally. Viewed as a capable administrator, he was, unusually for a man of his seniority, not personally corrupt (although he has been happy to see his associates and allies get rich). He appears to live an ascetic life, focused solely on his work and his faith. By 2012, under Prime Minister David Cameron, Britain decided its boycott was no longer sustainable. Gujarat was a major hub for foreign investment and Britain wanted a slice of the action. And Modi was continuing to rise: looking inevitable as a candidate for Prime Minister by the BJP, it was no longer possible to hope that he would remain a merely provincial figure. In October 2012, the British High Commissioner Sir James Bevan, held an official meeting with Modi. In the bland language of a Foreign Office press release, it was said that they had discussed ways to 'develop co-operation between the UK and Gujarat across a very broad range of fields, including education, science and innovation, energy and climate change, and trade and investment.' A 'Core Script' produced for internal use by the Foreign Office around the same time spoke of the shared 'core values of democracy, pluralism and tolerance.'

At this point, Britain's relations with India were, at best, confused. The same 'Core Script,' spoke of Britain and India's 'long history of collaboration on development,' somehow managing not to mention colonialism. Post-colonial guilt was a thing of the past for Cameron's 'liberal' Conservative government. As William Hague, Cameron's Foreign Secretary, explained, Britain was in a 'new and equal partnership' with former colonies. 'We have to get out of this post-colonial guilt,' Hague had continued. 'Be confident in ourselves.... It's a different generation. Britain is seen in a different light.' In James Bevan, Britain had a perfect exponent of this new approach. According to a 'User's Guide' about himself, which Bevan would distribute to his junior colleagues, he was not a traditional British diplomat. Unlike those that had joined the Foreign Office from ancient private schools and elite universities, Bevan had attended an ancient grammar school in Buckinghamshire, followed by a leading university. With this profoundly different perspective, Bevan had been appointed 'Director-General, Change and Delivery' of the Foreign Office, which gave him a mandate to modernise the hidebound institution.

Bevan took this reforming zeal with him when he became Britain's High Commissioner to New Delhi. His message was clear: we have shared history with India and our shared values of democracy, an independent judiciary and cricket are all things that we hold dear and in common. Of course, for many Indians this 'shared history' involved colonial subjugation, humiliation and massacres. Very few Britons appear prepared to engage with the fact that the partition of India and Pakistan, the final act of Britain's imperial rule, led to hundreds of thousands, and possibly millions of deaths. During an excruciating moment in a speech in December 2012, Bevan was cut off in his stride as he extolled the common virtues of free market democracies. As Dean Nelson of the *Daily Telegraph* reported: 'An elderly Sikh gentleman stood and said he'd been jailed for campaigning for democracy and independence. Why hasn't Britain apologised for that?' The High Commissioner reportedly 'squirmed,' arguing, rather like Hague, that he hadn't been born at the time and that in any case he wanted to focus on the future. As Nelson pointed out, at that time there were more than eight million Indians alive who were at least 15 at the time of independence (August 1947), many of whom had faced arrest, violence and summary justice under an authoritarian colonial regime.

Bevan's meeting with Modi was followed by another awkward decision for Britain on how to deal with its imperial past. In 2013, David Cameron visited India and journeyed to Amritsar, where British troops had massacred hundreds of peaceful protesters in 1919. At the time, the commander responsible, General Reginald Dyer, was relieved of his command but feted as a national hero on his return to Britain and given a huge sum by a grateful public, enabling him to live out his days as a country gentleman in Wiltshire. In 2013, after a heated internal debate in Whitehall, it was decided that Cameron would 'mark' the 'deeply shameful' event on his visit, but would not go as far as apologising, for fear of creating an expectation of apologies for other imperial outrages. At the time, Britain was making more consequential decisions for its relationship with India.

For all the talk of cricket and shared values, the rationale behind the push to engage with Modi and increase ties with India was commercial. The first section of the Core Script given to British civil servants explained: 'the UK aims to double its bilateral trade with India by 2015. India seeks to increase its bilateral trade with the UK to £24 billion by 2015.' A crucial element of this ambition was the prospect of a trade deal between the EU (including, in 2013, the UK) and India. For Europeans, the opportunity to sell sophisticated manufactured goods to India was a priority. A particular issue for the UK was the reduction of the high tariffs imposed by India on Scotch whisky. India wanted its citizens to get visas to come to Europe, especially the UK. The shared imperial history did have meaning in some practical aspects: Indians were more likely to want to visit the UK, either for work or pleasure, than any other European country. Immigration was an increasingly sensitive subject for a British Conservative government that had promised immigration of less than 100,000 people per year, against a reality of double that number in 2013 and more than 300,000 in 2014 and 2015. Leading this anti-immigration policy was Cameron's Home Secretary, Theresa May, who sought to portray herself as a hardliner on the subject, insisting on preventing foreign students from remaining in the UK after completing their studies.

The EU–India trade negotiations foundered on the UK's unwillingness to make the trade-off between conflicting political priorities. Britain had the ambition to double its exports to India, but it was unwilling to entertain India's desire to ease its citizens' ability to visit Britain. Things took a particularly difficult turn when Theresa May announced a plan for visitors from 'high-risk' countries in Africa and Asia (including India) to pay a £3,000 security fee in order to be able to get a visa to visit Britain. The plan caused dismay in India and other affected countries, where lawyers announced their intention to challenge the 'discriminatory' measures. While the bond scheme was eventually dropped, the EU–India trade talks did not survive Britain's hostility to migration liberalisation. In 2017, a document from the EU parliament's influential trade committee concluded that, with the UK out of the EU and no longer able to object on the grounds of immigration and whisky tariffs, progress towards an EU–India deal was much more likely.

In 2014, when Narendra Modi became Prime Minister of India, Britain's decision to end its boycott of him had proved prudent, if craven. Although his father had been murdered in 2002 by Gujarati mobs apparently allowed the space to rampage by Modi, Tanveer Jafri remained committed to India's democratic ideals: 'People voted him to power,' he told me. 'You can't help it, except by democratic means.' A similar transition occurred in Britain in 2016, with Theresa May taking over from David Cameron as Prime Minister following a vote of members of the Conservative Party. May was trying to lead Britain into its future after its exit from the European Union. Improving economic relations with the wider world beyond Britain had become one of the key justifications for the vote to leave the EU, and India, a key emerging economy, was a top priority. Britain would show the world the opportunities now available to it having decided to leave the EU by forging a trade deal with India. However, Britain still wanted to avoid difficult choices. This was borne out in a disastrous visit to India by Prime Minister Theresa May in November 2016. India's priorities had not changed: it hoped that a trade deal would form part of a wider agreement that would make it easier for its nationals, especially its service professionals, to make short work visits to Britain. There was also a hope that students would once again be allowed to work in the UK after completing their studies, if only for a brief period. May appeared unable to understand the linkage between this and India granting Britain's exporters better access to India's markets. At a fraught meeting with Modi she doubled down, saying that India had to 'take back' its existing nationals that had overstayed their visas, before any question of liberalising the migration regime. May's officials, according to private conversations I had at the time, were dismayed. Needless to say, UK access to India's markets was not improved.

The unthinking approach in our relations with India even played into the Covid-19 crisis. In early 2021, Britain was again trying to seal a trade deal with Modi's India. The main change in the interim had been that Britain had actually left the European Union, arguably on terms that made such a deal all the more urgent. The other major development was Covid. India had seen surging cases which threatened to overwhelm the country's medical system. Social distancing is not feasible in the crowded conditions in which many Indians live. However, these environmental difficulties were made much worse by Modi's political activities. He was fighting a regional election in West Bengal and convened huge rallies attended by thousands. In addition, in March 2021, the Kumbh Mela festival was allowed to proceed involving millions of pilgrims travelling to the River Ganges to take a ritual swim. It is perhaps unsurprising that a devout Hindu such as Modi was keen for this festival to go ahead, but it may still be surprising that he encouraged attendees in advertisements claiming the festival was 'clean' and 'safe.' Modi eventually backtracked, in the middle of the festival once millions of pilgrims had already travelled, saying the Kumbh Mela 'should now only be symbolic.' The exasperated vice president of the Indian Medical Association described Modi as a 'super spreader' of coronavirus. Subsequent studies have confirmed that pilgrims from all over India spread and caught the virus, before returning home with the infection ensuring it reached all corners of the country.

In common with Boris Johnson, Modi had a reputation for bumptious rhetoric which often bore little relation to the truth. In January 2021, Modi briefed the World Economic Forum that India had defeated Covid. This was repeated in a BJP resolution in late February proclaiming:

It can be said with pride that India not only defeated Covid under the able, sensitive, committed and visionary leadership of Prime Minister Shri Narendra Modi, but also infused in all its citizens the confidence to build an 'Atmanirbhar Bharat' [self-reliant India].

Modi's government remained extremely sensitive to criticism. In late April it took legal action against Twitter to remove content critical of its pandemic response. One of the most worrying aspects about India's Covid crisis was the emergence of a new variant that was significantly more transmissible. The British government was aware that this variant had reached Britain by 1st April 2021, but chose not to restrict travellers from India to the UK. At exactly the same time, realising the Covid threat in South Asia, visitors to the UK from Pakistan and Bangladesh were mandated to quarantine in hotels ('red-listed') on arrival. But India was exempted from these measures for a further 17 days. As the consistently well-connected Westminster journalist Alex Wickham wrote the following month:

Despite Downing Street's strenuous denials, there is barely anyone in Westminster who doesn't think the government held off putting India on the red list because Johnson had a trade trip to the country planned.

In the end, the visit could not go ahead as India's Covid outbreak spiralled out of control, with images of mass cremations of the victims. But the decision came too late. Britain had imported India's highly-transmissible Delta Variant and Covid cases surged. Between May and June, Britain moved from having one of the lowest caseloads of Covid in Europe to the highest. Europe's leaders became reluctant to allow British travellers back onto the continent. Britain had made an ethically questionable but seemingly pragmatic choice to recognise Modi – once his political ascent was inevitable. But faced with the need to recognise the realities of making a trade arrangement with India, the question of allowing Indians to visit Britain more easily has proved an impossible barrier. Our relations with India illustrate a dysfunctional foreign policy: capable of endorsing an arguably fascist leader but incapable of making the trade-offs necessary, such as allowing talented Indian students to study in greater numbers at British universities, to achieve a trade deal that is viewed as an essential element of its economic future.

As we have noted, Britain's actions will have had very little impact on Modi's rise, which is rooted in the realities of India's domestic politics. But at a time when another authoritarian strongman, Vladimir Putin, has been able to upend Europe's security, the risks of India under Modi should not be underplayed. The world's largest, increasingly oppressed Muslim minority, in a country that is becoming steadily less democratic, represents both a human rights and a security challenge for the future. Given that India's population in 2022 was 1.4 billion, we should not underestimate the seriousness of the issue. Giving Modi an easy ride for the sake of a trade deal will not serve Britain's, or the world's interests. What might we do differently? The first thing would be to recognise that a future trade deal with India will not be transformational for the UK in any case, so it is not something worth compromising our values for. Britain is not a significant trade partner for India and it is unlikely to become so in the future. In recent years, Britain's trade with India has equalled its trade with medium sized European countries such as Belgium and Sweden. The second thing might be to observe Modi's India from a safe distance. Far from giving him validation and encouragement, facilitating the further slide into authoritarianism, Britain should observe strict neutrality while maintaining our support for India's constitutional values of secularism and democracy.

11. THE US AND THE UK 'SPECIAL' RELATIONSHIP

'They are arrogant, fundamentally hostile to us, and they wish to dominate world politics.'

Winston Churchill, speaking about American naval expansion in 1927

SPECIAL OR SPECIOUS?

Various experts and practitioners (in some rare cases, expert practitioners) have described Britain's foreign policy as having two 'pillars': the transatlantic relationship with the United States and our engagement with Europe. These pillars are relationships: the so-called 'special relationship' with the United States and the rather less special relationship with Europe. Let's deal with the 'special relationship' first, in this chapter.

Britain has claimed for itself a unique ability to work with America, forged in the fires of World War II and the natural affinity that Winston Churchill had for his American mother's country. This special understanding of America enabled Britain to assume it was the bridge between the US and Europe.

A third pillar is sometimes added to the Atlantic-Europe structure: Britain's privileged role in international relations, most notably our permanent membership of the UN Security Council, which gives the UK a veto on resolutions (although we have not used this on our own since 1972). Whatever the number of pillars, the structure they support is the same: the liberal international order, in which a transatlantic alliance boosts Britain's engagement with Europe and its international connections.

Some countries have questioned the simplicity of this world order. Notably, France, in its own way both Atlanticist and strongly European, did not choose to support American foreign policy at every turn. When France's President Jacques Chirac questioned the United States' conception of a unipolar world and suggested a multipolar alternative as early as 1999, he was greeted with hostility both in America and in Britain. After the bitterness of the 2003 Iraq war which Chirac strongly opposed, Blair dismissed the French President's views as 'dangerous' and 'pathetic.' For Britain's Prime Minister, the policy of supporting America's every move was not open for debate.

As we have seen, the rules-based international order started to fall apart in the 1990s. In a speech in 2019, Britain's then-Foreign Secretary Jeremy Hunt was obliged to acknowledge:

All is not well... the rules-based international system is under greater strain than for many decades – and the evidence is all around us.

This order would eventually collapse with Russia's invasion of Ukraine in February 2022. As the indispensable, exceptional nation, the US may be the keeper of the global rules, but it also considers itself above those rules. When the US decided to invade Iraq after 9/11 it did not see itself as needing any particular authorisation. It was Britain that needed a UN resolution to justify the conflict, as President Bush accepted through 'gritted teeth' as early as August 2002. And America continues to play by its own rules, whether in its decision to use torture on detainees during the 'War on Terror,' its hostility to the International Criminal Court, or its decision to walk away from an international treaty with Iran on nuclear issues, even though Iran was complying with that treaty. Therefore, being an uncritical supporter of America sometimes clashes with supporting a rules-based international order. It could be said that uncritical support for America undermines the liberal international order. As the Iraq Inquiry concluded of this contradiction:

The circumstances in which it was decided that there was a legal basis for UK military action were far from satisfactory.

To understand Britain's relationship with Europe, we have to understand Britain's relationship with America. Our belief that we have a uniquely special relationship with the United States was one of the core justifications for leaving the European Union. 'Global Britain', in this argument, was not just another member of the European political club to be treated equally with Belgium and Bulgaria, but a bigger player, if not quite America's equal, certainly its peer. We did not need the buttress of European Union membership to be able to pursue our relations with America.

A SECURITY RELATIONSHIP

There is no doubt that a strong relationship with the world's greatest power is important. America is the UK's largest bilateral trading partner and the greatest source of foreign direct investment. But it is above all a security relationship. At the secret heart of this mutually beneficial connection is the anglophone 'Five Eyes' intelligence network (mentioned in Chapter 8 in the context of Huawei and China). Particularly in the field of signals intelligence, the geographical spread of the partners and their technical capabilities makes this an unmatched global capability. The revelations from Edward Snowden, a rogue former contractor at the US signals service, the National Security Agency, give a sense of the extraordinary capacity of the Five Eyes signals network. Snowden, although not a staff member of the National Security Agency, had access to sensitive documents both from the agency and its partners. Over several months in 2012 and 2013 he made copies of nearly two million sensitive intelligence reports, revealing mass surveillance programmes. One of the most striking revelations was the fact that the National Security Agency intercepted the calls of 35 world leaders, including Germany's Angela Merkel.

From an intelligence perspective, the value of the Five Eyes network is unquestioned. The question is whether it implies a wider political network. Does it place a requirement on Britain to ape America's foreign policy? The evidence from other members of the Five Eyes is that it does not. For example, in 2003 Canada did not participate in the US-led invasion of Iraq, specifically because the operation did not have a UN authorisation. This did not appear to have led to any substantive, long-term change to the Five Eyes arrangements, because they are fundamentally operational, not political. In a similar vein, in 2021, New Zealand has taken a softer stance towards China than other Five Eyes partners, but this has not affected that country's participation in the Five Eyes. And while the Five Eyes is significant, it is not a unique intelligence relationship. As Snowden revealed, in addition to the Five Eyes, the signals agencies of Denmark, France, Germany, Italy, the Netherlands, Norway, Spain, Sweden, Switzerland, Singapore as well as Israel all have deep co-operative relationships with the National Security Agency. While all of these countries might be loosely described as members of the Western alliance, they represent a very broad range of foreign policy traditions and approaches. It is almost the point of an intelligence relationship, carried out in the shadows and with little or no public scrutiny, that it doesn't require overt political alignment between the countries involved. In fact, the United States has been able to take this to extremes, carrying out deep co-operation on intelligence matters with countries that it has very little in common with, such as Pakistan or Algeria. So, membership of the Five Eyes is not in itself a reason for Britain's 'special' relationship with America.

Britain deludes itself about the 'Special Relationship.' In a world where the US is a single military superpower, it is not surprising that for all countries, their relationship with that single superpower is a relationship of special importance. This is particularly the case for any country that shares a tradition of democracy and particularly those dependent on the Atlantic security alliance. As President Obama said:

> **For more than two centuries we have stood together in friendship, and because of our unwavering commitment to the cause of liberty, I'm confident that we'll continue to stand together, strong and free, for all the centuries to come… long live the alliance between our two great nations.**

He was talking, of course, about the United States's relationship with France. Similar speeches will have been given by American presidents with reference to (among others) Canada, Australia, the Netherlands, and of course Britain. It is only Britain that believes that this relationship is supremely special to America. For decades it has been abundantly clear that our relationship with America is similar to that of other major European countries. Helmut Schmidt, Germany's Chancellor in the late 1970s and an energetic promoter of transatlantic relations, observed that Britain's 'Special Relationship' was so special that only one side knew that it existed. In 1962, a former US Secretary of State, Dean Acheson, had clarified America's views on Britain, noting:

> **Great Britain has lost an empire and not yet found a role. The attempt to play a separate power role – that is, a role apart from Europe, a role based on the 'special relationship' with the US, this role is about played out.**

Acheson's curt dismissal is all the more wounding because it is undeniably true.

Undeniably, some British Prime Ministers have forged particularly strong connections with their American counterparts. In an era when American politics was dominated by north-eastern elites of Anglo-Saxon heritage, an obvious cultural affinity existed between the British and American ruling classes. John F Kennedy may have had Irish heritage, but his father had been America's ambassador to the United Kingdom and he developed deep links to Britain's ruling classes. JFK's sister Kathleen had been married to two British aristocrats in succession and the young John Kennedy spent some of his formative years in Britain. At the time of his presidency, his relationship with British Prime Minister Harold Macmillan was particularly close. Throughout the Cuban Missile Crisis Kennedy and Macmillan spoke to discuss the details of strategy. In the 1980s, Margaret Thatcher and Ronald Reagan were similarly intimate, united in their determination to defeat the Soviet Union and bring neo-liberal economics to their respective countries.

Even when British and American leaders started off on a difficult footing, they have often ended up being firm allies. George W Bush, elected in controversial circumstances in 2000, was not an obvious partner for Tony Blair, who had been politically and personally aligned with his predecessor Bill Clinton. Blair's wife Cherie, on the flight with her husband for their first meeting with Bush, remarked: 'I don't expect that they are looking forward to this any more than we are.' After this inauspicious start, the only positive thing that the new President could find to say about his connection with Tony Blair was that they used the same brand of toothpaste. However, in the light of the 9/11 attacks the two formed an intense bond driven by a shared moral purpose, as they saw it, to tackle Islamist extremism.

When America elects a new president, a peculiarly British tradition takes place. In its own way this tradition is as quintessentially British as the Royal Family, the Changing of the Guard at Buckingham Palace and tea taken at four o'clock. The tradition is the febrile, toxic obsession of the British political and media class in trying to get the new American President to say that he regards his relationship with Britain as the most special of his international connections. This statement has to be topped off with an unseemly transatlantic dash by the British Prime Minister to be the first international leader to be photographed with the new President or at least to be the first to take a transatlantic phone call. For British politicians, a particular priority is to get photographed ahead of the French or Germans. By 2009, Barack Obama did not appear very interested in performing his part of this strangely pointless ritual. In the immediate days following Obama's inauguration, British Prime Minister Gordon Brown's staffers frantically tried to schedule a meeting with Obama. Eventually the new President agreed that his first meeting with a foreign leader would be with a British Prime Minister. The only problem was, he met the wrong one. To Brown's chagrin, ex-Prime Minister Tony Blair was the first world leader to shake hands with Obama. With deadening predictability, this was reported as a humiliation by the British media. Articles that attempted to analyse the actual agenda of transatlantic relations took up fewer column inches than harrumphing over Obama's decision to move a bust of Churchill from one part of the White House to another.

This frivolity hit a nadir over the question of gifts ritually exchanged between Brown and Obama. The practice of giving gifts between world leaders is a strange hangover from a pre-modern era where items of real personal value were exchanged between monarchs and princes. In almost all modern democracies, a gift given officially from one country's leader to another is never for the personal use of the recipient. These gifts are normally valued, logged and stored in government warehouses, rendering them useless. And yet the apparent mismatch of gifts between Brown, who gave Obama a hand-made pen holder crafted from the same timbers as those used to make the President's Oval Office desk, and Obama, who appeared to have picked up a stack of DVDs at the airport duty free, was further cast as evidence of the threats to the 'special relationship.'

Obama saw less value in his relations with Britain than some of his predecessors. That is self-evident. The more important question is to ask why this should be the case? Obama's own background, which he had detailed in books published before his presidency, set him apart: much has been made of his Kenyan father. Perhaps more significant was his age – the first (and still in 2022, only) US President born after 1960, as well as a childhood spent in the Pacific: in Indonesia and in Hawaii. Britain's decision to base its foreign policy so heavily on a relationship with a single country was based on the flawed assumption that the country in question did not regard its own interests and priorities as evolving. The United States of the post-World War II era, anglophone, dominated by the Eastern seaboard, intimately connected to Britain and Europe, is not the same as the US in the 21st Century: increasingly Hispanic and Asian, focused on the Pacific basin, reliant on trade with China but at the same time, viewing China as its biggest threat. A look at the evolution of America's trading partners spells this out in raw, numerical terms. In 2004, the top European exporters to the United States were Germany and the United Kingdom, in that order. By 2021, Germany remained in place as one of the top five exporters to America. But the UK had fallen significantly, behind rising Asian powers such as South Korea, Vietnam, Taiwan and India, but also behind European countries such as Italy and Switzerland. A trade deal isn't going to change the fact that we aren't very good at making things to export to the Americans.

Britain's foreign policy has required successive US Presidents to behave as if it was still the 1970s. Unsurprisingly, they are disinclined to do so. The fact the British political and media establishment cannot grasp this fairly simple concept tells us a lot about the challenges the UK faces in adjusting to a new global reality. The election of Donald Trump took this journey to a painful place. As a white nationalist, whose mother was born in Scotland, Trump himself was culturally attached to the traditions of Anglo-Saxon transatlantic relations. But his foreign policy agenda, to the extent that it was coherent, was based on the idea of America First, a slogan he repeated in his inaugural address and at numerous subsequent occasions. Nevertheless, Prime Minister Theresa May rushed to Washington DC and invited the new President for a state visit to Britain. In the arcane world of royal protocol this was a controversial decision, as state visits had not previously been offered to newly installed leaders. Theresa May, a fervent monarchist, was said to have put the Queen in a 'very difficult position,' in the words of Peter Ricketts, a former head of the diplomatic service. Things got worse when widespread protests broke out at the prospect of a visit from the new President and parliamentarians expressed their dismay at the prospect. Eventually, Trump's visit was downgraded but was still largely a disaster – Trump declared in an interview that Theresa May had 'wrecked' the Brexit negotiations because of her failure to follow his advice and pursued a personal vendetta against London's mayor Sadiq Khan. There were widespread protests and the President was viewed to have made a fool of himself during his meeting with the Queen. If the objective was to get a trade deal with America, that didn't happen either.

In practical terms, Trump believed that America did not need alliances. He tried to walk out of America's most important trading arrangement with its neighbours Canada and Mexico. He tried to end security relationships with Japan and South Korea. And he obsessively attacked NATO, believing it to be a type of joint bank account into which the other allies were not paying an agreed sum, rather than it being mutual defence alliance. While there is no doubt that many European powers spent far less on defence as a proportion of their GDP than America, in many cases this was for reasons that were in line with America's own strategic interests. Notably, Germany's military remains constitutionally confined to defensive operations as a result of Germany's troubled history of military aggression in the

20th Century (although these constitutional limits have been increasingly loosely interpreted). By a similar token, America's vast defence budget exists largely because America chooses to maintain its unquestioned global hegemon status, not because of an arbitrary target set by NATO. In fact, had European powers consistently all spent as much proportionally on defence as the United States, the US would probably have lost its sole superpower status and unquestioned leadership of NATO.

The US Defense Secretary may not have used Trumpian language, but the message was pretty clear: 'A dim if not dismal future' awaited NATO members if they failed to accept the 'blunt reality… to be serious and capable partners.' The President used the words 'free riders' to describe allies that were happy to encourage the US to initiate complex conflicts in places like Libya, but were not capable of sustaining these military engagements. However, in these examples, the Defense Secretary was Robert Gates, and the President in question was the impeccably multilateral Barack Obama. The phenomenon of America scolding its European allies was not unique to Trump, even if the ignorant, narcissistic manner of his pronouncements was. In the light of Russia's invasion of Ukraine in 2022, Germany declared its intention to spend €100 billion on defence, but European under-spending on their militaries has been a bugbear of transatlantic politics for the past two decades, before and after the Trump years.

AMERICA FIRST

The increasing dysfunction of America's politics means that its leaders of all political stripes are likely to be inwardly focused.

After the trauma of the Trump years, America remains cautious of alliances and disinclined to share its decision-making with its allies, even its self-appointed 'special' friends. In April 2021, President Biden announced the withdrawal of United States troops from Afghanistan, without consulting European countries, including Britain, that also had troops deployed there. Biden carried out this withdrawal with no regard for the views of European allies. There was bold talk in Britain of us leading a separate mission to Afghanistan, without the Americans. But the brutal truth is that no European power, including Britain, could operate such an intervention without American help. The right-wing in America is increasingly inclined to isolationism, consumed with internal culture war struggles, tinged with paranoia and racial resentment. But the liberal tendency, while more instinctively internationalist, is not instinctively Atlanticist. Obama wanted to 'pivot to Asia.' Before the invasion of Ukraine, Biden's major foreign policy initiatives were to engage global democracies to contain China and to engage China to contain climate change. With that in mind, one of Biden's priority areas of activity has been to revive the Quadrilateral Security Dialogue, known as the 'Quad', an Indo-Pacific grouping of the USA, Japan, Australia and India. This collection of countries, all seeking to counterbalance China's increasingly assertive behaviour, remains high on Biden's agenda even after the eruption of the Ukraine crisis.

Britain is not an irrelevance in this area: in September 2021, Britain, with the United States and Australia, surprised the world by announcing the 'AUKUS' security alliance, focused on sharing

UK and US nuclear submarine technology with Australia, as well as wider security and intelligence co-operation. As part of the deal, with only a few hours' notice, the Australians cancelled a pre-existing deal with France for submarines worth €35 billion. The French were furious and reacted by withdrawing their ambassadors in Canberra and Washington, a highly unusual step that almost never occurs between close allies. The French Ambassador in London remained in place, however. Not because Britain was seen as less at fault but because, in the words of Defence Minister Jean-Yves Le Drian: '[w]e have recalled our ambassadors to [Canberra and Washington] to re-evaluate the situation. With Britain, there is no need. We know their constant opportunism. So there is no need to bring our ambassador back to explain.' The situation was possibly made worse by the dismissive tone of Boris Johnson who urged President Macron to '*prenez un grip and donnez-moi un break*' – remarks that were actually targeted at his political base in the UK that would enjoy any excuse for a cross-channel spat.

In spite of the AUKUS announcement, we should not mistake this for Anglophilia on the part of President Biden who identifies strongly with his Irish heritage. During his election campaign, he declined a request for an interview with a BBC journalist with the response, 'I'm Irish.' In the following chapter, the way in which Britain's dismissive treatment of the Republic of Ireland in the context of Brexit has worsened our relations with America is explored in further detail. But it is worth noting that Biden's only visits to the UK have been to attend multilateral events, the G7 and climate change summits, suggesting that he does not prioritise bilateral engagement with the UK at present. Undoubtedly, the Ukraine invasion has dragged America's focus back to Europe. But this does not mean that America sees this through a US-UK prism. America's engagement on the issue is profoundly with continental Europe, centred on Brussels – the headquarters of NATO and the European Union – rather than with London.

The evolution of America's foreign policy demonstrates that the United States has no particular reason to privilege a relationship with a single northwestern European power, let alone Britain. And Britain, by the same token, has no particular reason to privilege its relationship with the United States. As we saw in an earlier chapter, had Tony Blair been able to distance himself from George W Bush's plan to invade Iraq, it is quite possible the invasion would never have happened. This would have had immeasurable benefits for global security which would still be felt today. Even if the US had gone ahead and invaded Iraq without Britain, our own country would almost certainly be better off as a result. Both in terms of public trust in politicians and key institutions such as intelligence and diplomatic services, and in specific terms of lives lost and changed, it is hard to imagine anything except upsides in a counterfactual world where Britain avoided the Iraq war. So we must accept that if this is a 'special' relationship, it comes with costs, as well as benefits.

This is not to suggest that Britain's relationship with the United States is insignificant or unimportant. It remains one of the more important bilateral relations that America enjoys, alongside those with other similar powers such as France and Germany. But, on the American side it is pragmatically focused, depending on what we can bring to the table. If Germany transforms its military, as it has announced that it will, at the same time as Britain's is set for a real-terms decline, it is easy to imagine Germany vying with France to become a preferred partner for the US military in Europe. What Britain must decide in the immediate future is whether it is logical for a European country in the 2020s to build its foreign policy around a relationship with the United States and the wider world, to the exclusion of its neighbours in Europe? This was the unanswered question at the heart of the debate about Britain leaving the European Union, which is the subject of the next chapter.

12. BREXIT: ISOLATION IN EUROPE

'I want my country back. I want freedom. I don't believe our country's ours anymore. I want Britain to be Britain.'
Brexit supporter explaining her reasons on BBC *Question Time*, April 2016

Scores of books have been written about the most important foreign policy decision that the UK has made in its modern history – the country's departure from the European Union, which resulted from a referendum held on 23rd June 2016. Tim Shipman wrote an excellent blow-by-blow account of the Brexit campaign itself. For penetrating analysis of the cultural baggage around British exceptionalism, consult the work of Fintan O'Toole. For a detailed exposition of the complexities of trade negotiations, there have been excellent guides from think-tanks such as the Centre for

European Reform and the Institute for Government. There are as many well-written opinions on Brexit as there are explanations for its underlying causes. Was it the product of persistently anti-EU newspapers reporting calumnies about the EU for decades – a process in which Boris Johnson played a prominent role as a Brussels correspondent of a national newspaper? Was it Britain's geography – arguably more an Atlantic island than a European nation, dividing our political and legal culture from Europe's? Was it our history – standing alone against Nazism in 1940 as Europe fell to the Blitzkrieg? Was it an internal Conservative Party struggle inflicted on the people of Britain, most of whom had never cared much about Europe prior to 2016? Or was it the combined effect of the financial crisis and a decade of austerity, taking hope from marginalised communities across Britain?

Brexit happened for all of the reasons offered above. There was also the all-important element of contingency. There was nothing inevitable about a vote that came out 51.9 per cent in favour of leaving the EU after a campaign dominated by lies, rancour and the assassination of an anti-Brexit Member of Parliament, Jo Cox, by a self-described, Brexit-supporting 'political activist.'

A BOLD AND UNPLANNED DECISION

From the outset *How Britain Broke the World* has sought to describe and explain the impact on the wider world of Britain's foreign policies. As we come to the end of this process it remains to examine the impact on Britain itself. While most of the case studies discussed in the book so far have not been focused on

Europe or the EU, they all illustrate the political and policy culture that made Brexit possible. They are not causes, but symptoms. Brexit itself is unusual in one important way. It is, in the words of its proponents, 'the will of the people.' Foreign policy choices are not normally taken by referendum. They do not ordinarily have the force of direct democracy. But the British state's approach to Brexit, before and after the referendum, shows once again a country that can take bold choices, but appears unable to consider the implications of them and plan for success. And it also points to a country with a confused understanding of its own ability to shape its future.

But this is not to argue that Britain is now irrelevant, 'a small island to which no-one pays any attention,' as a Russian spokesman claimed in 2013, disproving his own point by making the statement. (In fact, Britain is one of the largest islands in the world, and the fifth largest island state, after Australia, Indonesia, Japan and the Philippines.) Since the Blair years, as this book has demonstrated, Britain's foreign policy has marshalled its considerable international resources to achieve certain outputs – leading the charge on the international intervention in Kosovo; providing the intelligence that was used to justify the invasion of Iraq; the moral suasion, backed up with air-power, that moved the US to support an intervention in Libya; the sophistication and reliability of its financial sector that sucked in Russia's elite. These examples, and more, show the capabilities that go with being a top-10 global economy, as well as being, with France, Europe's largest military power and a nuclear-armed permanent member of the UN Security Council.

Britain's ability to take bold action is not in doubt. In every one of these cases, Britain showed itself capable of seizing opportunities to bring about change. Equally in every case, Britain was incapable of making a credible assessment of the implications of its actions. It was almost as if the bold output was the goal, not the long-term outcome. Brexit has proved a natural expression of this tendency. It is tempting to describe it as the 'end-point,' but there is no reason to believe that Britain will change its chronic short-termism. In Brexit, almost every part of Britain's administrative resources has been devoted to 'getting Brexit done,' but no thought or attention appears to have been devoted to the long-term outcome. Indeed, the government closed down the parliamentary committee charged with scrutinising the future relations between the UK and European Union in January 2021. At the time, transitional arrangements were still in place and Britain's new trading relationship with the EU, known as the Trade and Cooperation Agreement, was still going through widespread and well-reported teething troubles, such as the inability of Britain's shellfish exporters to sell to their key European markets and significant barriers in the way of British artists and performers to operating commercially across continental Europe.

A STRATEGIC SHIFT AWAY FROM EUROPE

Two of the core arguments underpinning Brexit are that Europe's economies are largely stagnant and that, consequently, Britain's strategic future lies instead with its close relationship with the United States. Reinforcing these points, the most dynamic economies are elsewhere in the world (notably Asia, but also the US). According to this argument, it makes sense for Britain to focus on its security relationship and its largest single trading partnership with the United States, at the same time as seeking to increase trade with Asia and other emerging economies. This raises further questions. First, is a deeper relationship with the United States something that is available to Britain, and does that relationship require Britain to be outside the European Union? Similarly, does enhanced trade with the wider world, particularly the emerging Asian economies, require Britain to leave the European Union?

It is no secret that the mainstream of America's foreign policy community believed it was in America's interests for Britain to remain in the European Union. President Obama memorably said that a post-Brexit UK would be 'in the back of the queue' of countries seeking a free-trade deal with the United States. This prompted furious responses from pro-Brexit campaigners, notably Boris Johnson, who controversially drew attention to the President's 'part-Kenyan' ancestry as an explanation for his stance. The reason this mattered to Brexit's advocates was twofold: at the heart of the Brexit world-view was the special relationship myth, where Britain's connection to America owed nothing to its EU membership; second was the fact that the European Union has never managed to agree a free-trade deal with the US. To be able to demonstrate that Brexit enabled something that the EU had not been able to deliver, would be a way of demonstrating a tangible benefit of Brexit.

One of more credible arguments against Obama's position in 2016 was that he was nearing the end of his second term and would therefore not be the Head of State responsible for bringing such a trade deal to fruition. Obama's successor, Donald Trump, could have been responsible. On numerous occasions he spoke publicly in favour of a trade deal which would, in Trump's typically overblown language, be 'massive' and 'phenomenal.' However, the 'America First' President was not going to risk being seen as a soft touch. The actual negotiations (which Trump left to the professionals) were tough and quickly got stuck on some fundamental challenges. In the UK media this became an obsession with 'chlorinated chicken' and 'selling off the NHS.' But both represented serious questions that would need to be resolved. Would Britain's food markets be open to America's agricultural produce, typically cheaper than that in Europe but produced at lower hygiene and environmental standards? If the precedent of Britain's 2021 trade deal with Australia was anything to go by, they would. Would Britain's public services, including its largest, the National Health Service, be open to contracting by American businesses? These possibilities were likely to be highly unpopular with voters and unlikely to command the support of many mainstream British politicians. But access to public contracting and food markets are normally seen as obvious elements of a trade deal. The fact was that Brexit-supporting politicians liked the idea of free trade with the United States but might find the reality to be rather less attractive.

Despite President Trump's grandiloquent language, no trade deal was reached during his single term as President. His successor, Joe Biden, made clear that such a deal with the UK was not a priority. Visiting London in May 2021, Biden's Secretary of State, Anthony Blinken, played down any hopes of a quick agreement. A well-connected former British Ambassador to the United States estimated that such an agreement was unlikely to be reached in President Biden's first term. This would mean that the promise of Brexit delivering free trade with the United States would, at best, have taken around ten years from the date of the referendum.

Simply put, the special relationship with America was not special enough to give us a trade deal after Brexit.

A WELL-PREPARED EUROPE

The faltering steps towards a trade deal with the United States reflected a wider challenge with Brexit. It was the most daunting bureaucratic and diplomatic task that Britain had faced since World War II, and one in which it struggled to achieve its lofty goals. The question here is not so much the 'why' of Brexit, but the 'how.' When Britain voted to leave the European Union, it was famously noted that no plans existed for the departure. The Prime Minister, David Cameron, forbade his civil servants from planning for Brexit because he didn't want any leak to the media that the possibility of losing the referendum was even entertained. At a meeting of European leaders in December 2015, Cameron's insouciance was on display as he explained, 'I'm a winner. I can with this.' When he failed to do so, the European Union, after a brief period of dismay, assembled a summit in its usual bureaucratic fashion (excluding the United Kingdom). The

EU swiftly appointed its chief negotiator, the seasoned former French foreign minister, Michel Barnier, who had served twice as a European Commissioner and in several other senior European roles. By April 2017 the EU had agreed and published its guidelines for the negotiations.

On the UK side, no such transparency existed. Things did not run so smoothly. Questions that probably should have been clarified ahead of the vote now loomed large. Should the narrow result (51.89% vs 48.11%) and the fact that 13 million had not voted at all have any impact on the government's next steps? Did it matter that two of the so-called United Kingdom's nations (Scotland and Northern Ireland) had voted to Remain in the EU? Having refused to address these questions ahead of time, Cameron similarly refused to address them as Prime Minister. Within hours of the result, he had announced his resignation.

Eventually, the UK assembled its negotiating team. David Davis, a veteran Conservative politician who had served briefly as a Europe minister 20 years earlier, was selected to face off against Barnier. Opinions of Davis varied. One Conservative described him bluntly 'as thick as mince,' others held him in higher regard. Whatever his standing, his knowledge and insight of the European Union or of trade deals did not remotely equal that of Barnier. The pattern was repeated further down. Barnier's deputy, Sabine Weyand, was a lifelong EU official, experienced trade negotiator and fluent in English, French and German. Her opposite number Olly Robbins, although widely regarded as one of the most talented civil servants of his generation, spoke halting French and had spent most of his previous career focused on security roles.

The significance of Davis and Robbins's lack of specialist EU experience is not about the absence of technical knowledge, which was present in other members of the UK civil service. More important was the absence of networks. Anyone with experience of diplomatic wrangling will know that the formal process of sitting across a shiny table from your opposite number is a small fraction of the whole. Successful negotiations usually require a wide range of background, off-line and informal discussions. For these to work, the parties need deep networks and an understanding of the culture and thinking of a wide range of key stakeholders. In the case of the Brexit negotiations, these key stakeholders were the EU institutions and the governments and leadership of major European powers (especially France and Germany). An article that David Davis wrote proclaimed confidently that:

> **Within minutes of a vote for Brexit the CEOs of Mercedes, BMW, VW and Audi will be knocking down Chancellor Merkel's door, together with the leaders of Europe's other key industries, demanding that there be no barriers to European access to the British market.**

Davis was a former businessman who had enjoyed international success, so a reader of his piece might conclude that his assertions were based on evidence. Perhaps he had spoken to German industry, for example? (There is no evidence that he had.) Davis's writings displayed an ignorance of German industry, of that country's politics, and the economics of trade deficits.

Not all of Britain's key players were as ill-informed on the workings of the European Union. Ivan Rogers, Britain's Permanent Representative to the institution, had spent almost his entire career focused on European issues, including some time as a secondee inside the European Commission. Rogers was clear-eyed with Downing Street and Davis about the challenges and trade-offs inherent with Brexit. For his candour, it was made clear to him that he did belong in the government's Brexit team. In his resignation letter, Rogers observed that: 'Serious multilateral negotiating experience is in short supply in Whitehall, and that is not the case in the Commission or in the Council.' Rogers exhorted his civil servants to 'continue to challenge ill-founded arguments and muddled thinking and... never be afraid to speak the truth to those in power.' Pro-government media were quick to dismiss Rogers. A typical example was an article in the *Daily Mail* calling him an 'arrogant merchant of doom' who 'threw tantrums.' Brexit-supporting MPs expressed similar views.

The inability within the British political system to balance difficult decisions with a range of unwelcome outcomes was demonstrated in the intervention in Libya and the uncritical approach towards intelligence over Iraq's purported weapons of mass destruction. So it is unsurprising that the government did not welcome those who were straightforward about the trade-offs that existed with Brexit. Sober analysts, even those who refused to declare their hand on whether or not they believed it was a good idea for Britain to leave the EU, were clear that there would be benefits and risks. Set against that balanced view was the Brexit objective not to pool any aspect of British sovereignty with the EU, to 'take back control,' as the slogan went. (This argument leaves aside the fact that the UK continues to pool sovereignty with other organisations, such as NATO and the Council of Europe, whose European Court of Human Rights continues to apply to the UK). Enthusiasts for the removal of any EU jurisdiction in the UK would argue that choice might be worth a measure of economic hardship generated from trade friction. To articulate that simple proposition – that there were costs as well as benefits – would require a political culture that recognises complexity and unpredictability and, crucially, communicates that to its electorate.

This culture was not present in the Brexit debate. Proponents of Brexit stated baldly that Britain would enjoy the 'exact same benefits' in trade with the EU after leaving as it had as a member. Michael Gove, with Boris Johnson perhaps the most significant supporter of Brexit inside the Conservative Party, stated clearly:

> **The day after we vote to leave we hold all the cards and we can choose the path we want. There is a free trade zone stretching from Iceland to Turkey that all European nations have access to, regardless of whether they are in or out of the euro or EU.... Agreeing to maintain this continental free trade zone is the simple course and emphatically in everyone's interests.**

Another cabinet minister and Brexit supporter, Liam Fox, told listeners to BBC Radio:

If you think about it, the free trade agreement that we will have to come to with the European Union should be one of the easiest in human history.

These forecasts were wholly wrong.

An aspect of this infantilisation of the public debate can be seen in the government repeatedly announcing things that are now possible 'thanks to Brexit' when they were equally possible prior to Brexit. The blue passports (as used by EU-member Croatia), the creation of freeports (found throughout the continent) and the emergency approval for Covid vaccines (clearly permitted under EU regulations) were all claimed as benefits of Brexit when they could easily have been done as an EU member. Some things which were supposed to be easier after Brexit proved to be the reverse. After Russia's invasion of Ukraine the EU sanctioned hundreds of senior political and business figures deemed to be close to the Kremlin. Britain seemed to be dragging its feet and the government claimed that, thanks to Brexit, it now was harder for the supposedly 'sovereign' Britain to implement sanctions than it had been when a member of the sluggishly bureaucratic EU.

A version of this zero-consequences-from-Brexit argument was that downsides existed only for the EU. 'They need us more that we need them,' was the message. This argument was supposedly strengthened by the fact that the UK had, since 1999, a persistent and growing trade deficit with the EU. In 2019 the EU exported approximately £100 billion more in value of goods to the UK than the UK exported to the EU. The argument was persistently made that the EU's trade surplus automatically implied that the UK had the upper hand as the EU would not want to lose access to this valuable export market. As Michael Gove had stated in his 2016 speech, 'they sell far more to us than we do to them,' which was, in his view, an advantage for Britain. At the same event, Gove's former adviser and head of the Vote Leave campaign, Dominic Cummings, claimed he had spoken to 'umpteen ambassadors' from EU member states that agreed with Gove's interpretation. Similarly, other prominent proponents of the Brexit cause, from Boris Johnson to Jacob Rees-Mogg and Steve Baker, advanced the same argument. As Rees-Mogg said in a radio interview in December 2018, it was in the EU's 'financial interest' to give the UK what it wanted.

From the outset of the Brexit negotiations there were certain immutable facts that were never articulated by its advocates. One of these was that, despite our large trade deficit with the EU, perhaps more important was the difference in size between the two economies. In 2019, the EU's GDP (stripping out the UK) was €14 trillion. The UK's in the same year was €2.4 trillion. In these circumstances, the smaller party claiming to 'hold all the cards' is a deliberate lie.

Another immutable fact was that the UK's land border with the EU (between the independent Republic of Ireland and Northern Ireland, part of the UK) required freedom of movement and frictionless trade between the two territories. While EU membership was seen as an important buttress of these freedoms, they were in fact the product of entirely separate treaties: notably the Good Friday Agreement of 1998 but also

The UK's trading isolation in Europe after Brexit

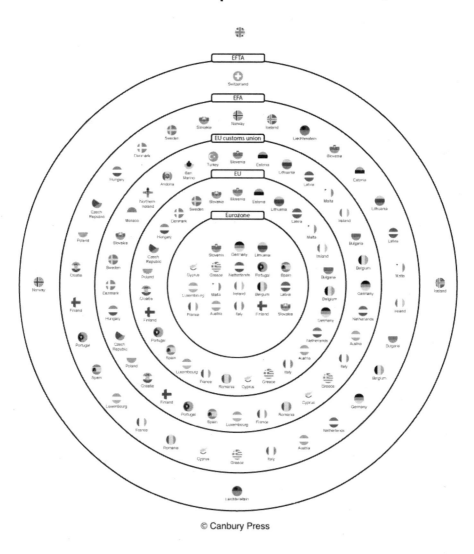

earlier agreements dating back to Irish independence in 1923. In or out of the EU, the UK had made prior commitments to avoid a border on the island of Ireland. If the UK chose to leave the freedom of movement arrangements of the Single Market and the open trade arrangements of the Customs Union, Northern Ireland would need to be exempted from whatever Brexit deal the UK struck, effectively remaining in the EU. It was not that Brexit necessitated Britain's departure from the Single Market and Customs Union, but that Britain selected that option. There is a particular irony of a 'Conservative and Unionist Party' (to use its full name) pushing for Brexit and then breaking up the UK union to pursue its particular version of 'hard' Brexit (outside the Single Market and Customs Union).

It may be ironic, but this was the choice made by Boris Johnson in October 2019. Having resigned from Theresa May's government on the supposed basis that her Brexit proposals gave the EU too much control over Britain's regulatory frameworks, Johnson's own deal allowed an EU border inside UK territory, between Great Britain and Northern Ireland (thereby avoiding the Irish border problem). This was surprising, as a year earlier Johnson himself had said that 'regulatory checks and even customs controls between GB and NI... no British Conservative government could or should sign up to any such arrangement.' However, unlike with May's deal, Johnson took the approach that an exhausted UK population would not pay any attention to the details of his arrangement. Indeed, the purpose of the deal was not to solve the Irish border conundrum, but to offer a seemingly attractive solution to a British public facing a general election. This was the deal that would, in the words of Johnson's election slogan, 'Get Brexit Done.' Its details were immaterial. When Johnson was asked whether there would be any paperwork associated with moving goods between Northern Ireland and Great Britain under his deal, he replied: 'Tell them to ring up the Prime Minister, and I will direct them to throw that form in the bin.' This was in fact a cynical and deliberate lie, since Johnson's government had already agreed to this paperwork and to the establishment of additional border posts. The UK government website makes it very clear that an 'entry summary declaration' must be completed for almost all goods transported between Great Britain and Northern Ireland, 'before the goods arrive.' But the deal served its purpose. At the December 2019 general election, large numbers of Britons, including some that were opposed to Brexit in principle, voted a hefty Conservative majority to Get Brexit Done and move on from the seemingly intractable affair.

The degree to which Northern Ireland was under the new treaty functionally part of the EU was little appreciated on the British mainland, which was probably Boris Johnson's preferred outcome. Any person born in Northern Ireland had the right to EU (Irish) citizenship, and with it, freedom of movement throughout the EU's member states and affiliates, at the same time as being eligible for UK nationality. Any business based in Northern Ireland had, in the words of the Northern Ireland Office on its official website, 'remained in the EU's single market,' which, 'allows goods to flow to and from NI to the ROI and the rest of the EU as they did while the UK was a member of the EU, without customs checks, tariffs or new paperwork' (in stark contrast to the situation with goods moving from Great Britain to the EU). This special status for Northern Ireland was trumpeted as a 'globally unique opportunity' by the Northern Ireland Secretary, Brandon Lewis. In the same statement, Lewis enthused about, 'the unique position that Northern Ireland business now have, as an integral part of UK market & able to trade with EU.' This was the same Brandon Lewis who had announced on his personal website that he was backing Brexit because 'remaining part of the Single Market and Customs Union,' which were ruled out in his particular interpretation of Brexit, were not, 'compatible with the result of the referendum.'

A LOSS OF TRUST

From the jaded vantage point of the early 2020s, the Kosovo campaign, the starting point of this book, belonged to a different era of global politics – a prelapsarian age when public trust in politicians was at its highest. As a result, it has tended to be viewed as a success, even when some of its actual impacts were very different. By contrast, the interventions in Iraq, Libya and Afghanistan are all impossible to portray as successful. Instead, they contributed to a malaise, a loss of faith and a crisis of trust in Britain's political leaders. It is hard to disentangle this malaise from wider issues, particularly the effects of the financial crisis and the stagnation of wages in Britain. However, there is plenty of evidence that mistrust in Britain's government stems in part from the idea that, on the really big issues, voters can't be sure they will be told the truth. Certainly, this lack of trust contributed to some of the conspiracy thinking seen around the Syrian issue.

In 2015, the Labour Party made it easier for registered supporters to participate in the election for party leader. Jeremy Corbyn, a far-left candidate who had opposed the Iraq war and all other foreign interventions, swept the board. Corbyn's credibility on these issues would be severely undermined by his attempt to question the role of Russia's military intelligence agency in the attempted murder of Sergei Skripal in 2018 in the face of glaring evidence. But Corbyn was able to articulate the frustrations of many with leaders who seemed to repeat the same errors without reflection or remorse. The despair with the mainstream of politics which led to Corbyn's election was seen in some of those who voted for Brexit, hoping for a radical shift in Britain's political settlement. It is important not to dismiss the views of those who supported Brexit (as distinct from its actual delivery). It is true that some communities changed rapidly as a result of EU migration. In my view this was mostly for the better, culturally and economically, but there are genuine cases where public service provision, such as primary school places, was put under strain on the basis of changes in local demography, in part fuelled by high immigration. The appropriate remedy to this issue would have been for central government to surge school places and other services in the affected areas, rather than joining the media in falsely objectifying migrants as the cause of society's ills.

However, those who voted for Brexit got something very different – not the promised £350 million extra a week for the National Health Service, but a British government treating Brexit as a mandate to double down on the politics of cynicism and dishonesty.

TENSIONS RISE TO THE SURFACE

The contradictions at the heart of the Brexit deal, and specifically the Northern Ireland Protocol, came to the surface in September 2020, less than a year after the government had negotiated the Protocol. The same government that had reached the deal announced its plans to break international law by ignoring certain elements of that agreement 'in a specific and limited way.' If the government had expected these caveats to mitigate the concern, they underestimated. Immediately, the head of the government's legal team, Sir Jonathan Jones QC, resigned in protest. Theresa May, the Prime Minister ousted by Boris Johnson, expressed her dismay, asking: 'How can the government reassure future international partners that the UK can be trusted to abide by the legal obligations of the agreements it signs?' The dismay extended to the EU, whose Commission President Ursula von der Leyen announced:

The Commission has decided to send a letter of formal notice to the UK government. This is the first step in an infringement procedure.

The British government's plans to break international law returned to the surface in a different format a few months later. Once the Northern Ireland Protocol and the wider Trade and Cooperation Agreement with the EU had been agreed and ratified, the British decided unilaterally to increase the 'grace periods' which gave time for both sides to the agreement to phase in the new border control measures; in simple terms, Britain refused to implement its undertakings. On the UK side, this was a politically sensitive issue, made worse by the fact that Boris Johnson had lied about there being any such measures. Tensions increased in Northern Ireland as it became clear how difficult it would be to trade between Britain and the province under the new system. As a territory that had experienced a prolonged violent insurgency within living memory, the potential for a return to political violence was clear. The Johnson government decided to weaponise the risk of political violence, rather than work to limit it. It set about portraying the difficulties with the Protocol as inflicted by an unreasonable EU, rather than being jointly agreed elements of a negotiated settlement ratified by two sovereign powers. Without irony, Johnson told a Northern Ireland television programme:

If we can't make enough progress and if it looks as though the EU is going to be very, very dogmatic about it and we continue to have absurd situations... then frankly I'm going to, we'll have to take further steps.

Once again, the EU launched formal enforcement procedures to insist that the UK keep to its promises.

The UK side had deliberately misled its citizens about the impact of the post-Brexit arrangements. However, even its own advocates, including the chief negotiator of this final stage of the Brexit process, Lord David Frost, admitted that the deal did not protect British businesses. He told a parliamentary committee in May 2021, 'the processes around the boundary between GB and Northern Ireland are significant. They probably have a bigger chilling effect than we thought on GB businesses wanting to move goods into Northern Ireland and that is one of the problems that's underlying some of the unrest and political developments we are seeing in Northern Ireland.' By any measure, the deal had failed.

BREAKING INTERNATIONAL LAW

There was probably never a good time for a country that sees itself as one of the world's leading democracies to break international law. But this came at a very bad time. As British ministers themselves had been saying in a series of speeches, the rules-based international system was under increasing threat. Russia was committing war crimes in Syria with impunity; China tore up its agreement with Britain over Hong Kong, as well as seizing territories in the South China Sea; Brazil ignored international climate agreements. Even the government's supporters pointed out that, as much as Britain's plans to break international law were 'specific and limited,' the government's ability to reproach egregious violations from other countries was fatally undermined. Lord Howard, a Brexit-supporting, right-wing former Conservative leader and lawyer, expressed the problem very clearly in the House of Lords:

> **How can we reproach Russia, China or Iran when their conduct falls below internationally accepted standards, when we are showing such scant regard for our treaty obligations?**

However, from a cynical perspective, the British approach could be said to have worked. Russia's Vladimir Putin represents a useful case study of the benefits available to bad faith actors. Under Putin, Russia has been able to ignore a wide array of international norms including its invasion of Ukraine and assassinations of dissidents on foreign soil. At the same time, Russia talks loudly and selectively about other countries' violations of international law. As Philip Remler, a former diplomat and scholar at the Carnegie Endowment identified: 'In speech after speech, both Putin and [Russian Foreign Minister Sergei] Lavrov have stressed the importance of upholding international law. Lavrov often contrasts this law with an alternative that he maintains the West is promoting to expand Western interests and values.'

Similarly, Britain negotiated in bad faith with the EU, later claiming that it had signed the Northern Ireland protocol 'under duress.' Of course, this gave the lie to earlier statements that 'we hold all the cards' and, instead, suggested that this 'sovereign' country had easily been cowed by the EU. When it decided to break those commitments, claiming that the EU was showing a 'lack of flexibility' and behaving in a 'legalistic' manner, it presented the international community with a difficult conundrum. If a party to an agreement has no intention of keeping to its commitments, the remedy is not necessarily to undermine other agreements, such as the Good Friday Agreement. The EU is acutely aware that a resumption of violence in Northern Ireland will be seized upon by the British government as proof of dangerous inflexibility on the part of Europe. Just as Vladimir Putin was the main beneficiary of the rise of the Islamic State in Iraq and Syria, allowing him to claim that support to Syrian rebels was creating space for international terrorism, a resumption of violence in Northern Ireland suits the

British government's interests, allowing it to blame the EU for the rise of terrorism. As a point of historic fact, it is worth noting that senior Conservative politicians, including Michael Gove, opposed the Good Friday Agreement in 1998 and may not be credible in their protestations of support for it in the Brexit era.

By embracing bad faith approaches to international agreements, Britain undermines its reputation and trustworthiness. But just as the international community tried to continue to deal with Putin's Russia on a 'normal' basis up until the point of the invasion of Ukraine, the EU has to continue to deal with the UK. The ability of the UK to sign a deal it has no intention of upholding, in order to win an election, while knowing that it will be able to reach some kind of alternative arrangement with an EU forced to choose between political violence and a recalcitrant negotiating partner, is the ultimate endorsement of the bad faith approach.

It is also the ultimate demonstration of Britain's departure from the rules-based international system it claims to have created and upheld since the end of World War II.

CONCLUSION

'*...et penitus toto divisos orbe Britannos*'
'*...and Britain isolated from the entire world*'
Virgil's *First Eclogue*, written c.42 BCE

This book has examined two of the long-term features of the British foreign policy system. The first is Britain's enormous drive to effect major international change, combined with a lack of practical capability. Britain has considerable gusto for bold initiatives, such as the interventions in Kosovo, Libya, Afghanistan and Iraq. But it does not have the enthusiasm for considering their long-term implications. The system lacks expertise and is unwilling to listen to external experts. While very different types of policy initiative, the 'Golden Era' approach to China and the provision of money-laundering services to Russia's elite exhibited a similar weakness: a desire for a major re-alignment of Britain's economic relationships without considering the strategic implications. Brexit has proved the ultimate example of such an approach. A political class obsessed with the current 'opportunity' (leaving the European Union) has taken little or no interest in the wider implications, including when those implications, such as in the case of the Northern Ireland Protocol and the real risk of terrorist violence, become evident in short order.

The second tendency is undermining international law while talking loudly about Britain's role as a pillar of the rules-based international system. In the past, this process has had an element of subtlety. Britain sought to defend its bending of international legal norms in Kosovo and Iraq with UN resolutions and retrospective self-justification. Similarly, the intervention in Libya was justified by securing a limited UN resolution and then massively expanding the activity falling under that resolution. By the time of Brexit, Britain had ceased to feel the need to cover its tracks. Britain negotiated and agreed an international treaty with the EU and within a year announced its intention to break it and international law. Britain's proposed Nationality and Borders Bill, tabled in June 2021, outlined plans for 'pushbacks' of migrant boats crossing the English Channel, forcing refugees and migrants back into French waters. Under international law, including the European Convention on Human Rights to which Britain remains a signatory, such actions are illegal. This point was made publicly by an exasperated French Interior Minister in September 2021.

There is a tendency with books such as this one to end on a note of artificial optimism. I am not going to propose a 'ground-breaking new approach' that will fix all of Britain's problems. A belief in quick fixes is partly what has got Britain into this mess. However, the purpose of this book is not merely to catalogue a series of unfortunate events. Nor is it to suggest that Britain should not pursue its national self-interest, that our foreign policy should be softly internationalist. On the contrary, the point is that our bad policies and practices have gone against our national interests. A world in which the UN Security Council was still functional, in which Iraq and the Middle East was spared the tragic error of the 2003 invasion and all that followed, in which the Syrian Civil War had taken another course and in which Libya remained a whole country, would be a better world. And a better one for Britain. If the UK had pursued more balanced policies towards China, the UK would not now be in the difficult position of trying to build up alternative suppliers of 5G hardware for telecoms networks, having over-relied on Huawei. If Britain had stopped the Russian elite from laundering their wealth in the West, would Putin have felt less convinced of the West's fundamental, decadent weakness? Might he have hesitated before launching a full invasion of Ukraine? And of course, if Britain had left the European Union with an eye to maximising future trading options with Europe, rather than limiting them, it would be easier for UK businesses to flourish and reduce the risk of conflict in Northern Ireland.

So, what should Britain do differently? There is no point in making proposals that are politically impractical. At a time when London celebrates breaking international law and proclaims an empty foreign policy as 'Global Britain,' it may not be especially receptive to advice or suggestions. There are things that aren't going to happen whoever is in government, whether or not these are desirable from my personal perspective. Britain is not going to rejoin the European Union. The political stability required in Britain for a clear mandate to pursue this aim cannot be envisaged. And it is hard to imagine Europe readily readmitting its troublesome former member, particularly if the question of Scottish independence remains unresolved. But Britain must find a sensible means of living alongside its larger neighbour and main trading partner. In the early 2020s, the UK may be in the initial, scratchy phase of post-Brexit relations with Europe. The problems over the Northern Ireland Protocol, the belief that the UK can agree better trade deals more quickly than the EU with countries beyond Europe, and the disinclination to co-ordinate with Brussels on matters of security, foreign policy or military affairs, are all features of this phase.

But the EU isn't going anywhere, and it will continue to evolve structures that head towards a federal superstate (although I expect an actual United States of Europe is still many years away). Britain's desire to increase trade with distant but faster growing economies, notably in Asia, will never be able to replace the opportunity of having the world's largest trading bloc on its doorstep. The UK has already rushed through a trade deal with Australia (estimated by the government to bring a microscopic 0.02% uplift to GDP), which appears to be terribly one-sided against British agriculture.

It's reasonable to think that this will result in an eventual political backlash against the idea that deals with distant and marginal trading partners are a substitute for frictionless trade with Europe. At some point, British political culture might be able to take on board the necessary reality that a strong relationship with Europe, including aligning some regulation, is worth the huge benefits of frictionless trade with key markets. In the immediate aftermath of Putin's invasion of Ukraine, there were signs of the beginnings of a change in approach. Foreign Secretary Liz Truss attended an EU Foreign Affairs Council meeting, something that would have been inconceivable a year earlier. However, Truss found it hard to admit this publicly. In a video about a series of engagements in Brussels, she managed not to mention the European Union.

A RECALIBRATION

The big picture is that Britain, an important but declining country, needs to find ways of making its foreign policy better, both for its own people and for the wider world. Adopting a precautionary principle with interventions should be a feature of future decision-making. The UK is proud of having an expeditionary military, but that doesn't mean that it should rush to use it without considering the likelihood of achieving objectives. Unless the UK can demonstrate with real expertise why an intervention will not be a re-run of costly past failures, it should be not made. This is not about limiting the ability of the British military to defend the country in an emergency, but about how major decisions are debated, such as the decision to take military action in Libya.

But we need to accept that Britain's military is not, on its own, strong enough to meet the challenges of the 21st Century. In the past Britain has relied on an assumption that America will play world policeman when required, with the UK and other European nations able to make a niche commitment. The America First policies of the Trump era, and Biden's single-minded withdrawal from Afghanistan has shown that this period is over. A logical response would be to increase Europe's stand-alone military capability, particularly in light of Russia's flagrant aggression towards its neighbours. But this requires Britain to be willing to have a grown-up dialogue with the EU. As with trade, that cannot be envisaged in the short term. However, the UK can start to build smaller bridges that might prepare the way for greater ambition in the future. A very small, but positive, sign was the 2020 agreement for Sweden, Italy and the UK to work together on developing Tempest, a proposed cutting-edge fighter jet. Britain needs to seek out a series of deep engagements with Europe's more capable militaries, which will make it easier for a future government to pursue a comprehensive security deal with the EU.

But these remain limited suggestions. We need ambition; post-Brexit, Britain wants to be 'Global.' How might it achieve that? One option might be to focus on international organisations other than the EU and make a concerted effort to influence these, mainly through ensuring our personnel are well-represented in senior positions. At the start of the Covid crisis, much was made of the allegation that the World Health Organization was insufficiently robust with China because of that country's excessive influence in the organisation. Much less was made of the systematic campaign over several years by China to position its nationals at the head of a wide range of UN agencies, as *Politico* reported in April 2020. In the same period, Britain has tended to be dismissive of many of these entities, which are easily caricatured as gravy-train institutions for ponderous and lavishly salaried civil servants. The British Foreign, Commonwealth and Development Office has never prioritised getting its people into these roles. But China, with its leadership role in the International Telecommunication Union, an international body that sets technical standards for communications networks, was able to advance Huawei's standing as the pre-eminent supplier of 5G telecommunications equipment worldwide. Chinese officials also head up the UN's agriculture, aviation and economic affairs agencies.

It is not just a rising superpower such as China that can make the international system work for it. Nordic countries have been particularly successful at getting their nationals into senior positions in international organisations. According to an academic study entitled, *Who runs the international system?*:

> **Finding themselves well represented in these senior positions gives the Nordic countries an opportunity to exercise power over international institutions; they may find it to their benefit to continue to cultivate a reputation for impartiality, attaining power through legitimacy.... Moreover, the ability to shape the preferences of other states is one of the faces of power; the other states may not even realize the power they have bestowed on the Nordics.**

The same study identified a steep decline in the UK's presence in the UN Secretariat, languishing between Somalia and Argentina in the rankings. One of the ways that countries all over the world increase their influence in international organisations is via funding a Junior Professional Officer programme, which provides entry-level opportunities for suitably qualified candidates from donor countries. This creates a reservoir of talent which often results in professionals rising up through the relevant organisations. While many countries see this as a useful way to increase their global reach, Britain chooses not to participate in most of these. It is understandably myopic that the UK chooses to ignore the EU at present, but it is inexplicable that it continues to ignore a wide array of other organisations that could be leveraged to increase the reach of 'Global Britain.'

Appointing and retaining specialists to advise on foreign policy would also make a difference, but it will also be necessary for politicians to listen to their advice, which may prove harder. Politicians often claim they want to recruit experts when in fact they want to recruit ideologues that support their narrow agenda. This was particularly the case during the Brexit era when genuine trade experts were ignored, but individuals who had never worked in the field were elevated to positions of high influence. To identify and recruit real expertise into the civil service requires a different approach which may need a change of government or at least a new culture around the intersection between ideology and the national interest. But we should not fall into the trap of thinking that the civil service has the right skills and expertise internally to reposition British foreign policy as required. Whichever party is in power, our institutions need to find an easy way to bring in genuine outside expertise, whether as staff members or as advisors.

Finally, there is a question of whether power and influence are desirable ends in themselves. This book has demonstrated how Britain has been able to have a global impact, but there is little strong evidence that this has improved the everyday lives of Britons. A wide range of quality-of-life indexes, such as that compiled by the *Economist* and a similar exercise by the Organisation for Economic Co-operation and Development, tends to put the UK well behind most of its northern European neighbours, as well as Canada and Australia. British diplomats, soldiers and politicians might benefit personally from the country's influence on the global stage, but it is hard to see how this helps ordinary people who want good housing, secure employment, low crime, education for their children and affordable, reliable healthcare. The evidence suggests that small countries in northern Europe, such as the Nordic nations and the Benelux countries, have managed to offer the best quality of life to the largest proportion of the population in their countries, compared with any point in human history. Given this, the break-up of the UK union state, with an independent Scotland, the reunification of Ireland, and England and Wales as the remaining entity, may not be an awful prospect. A smaller, humbler country might focus more attention on the wellbeing of its own people and less on international posturing.

For that to happen without rancour, however, would require a revolution in how we debate these issues in this country. Can the UK learn to carry out public debate based on facts rather than prejudice? Can Britain look at itself dispassionately without falling into empty statements of grandiosity? The evidence of recent years is that there is a long way to go. But if this book helps, even in a small way, it will have served its purpose.

ACKNOWLEDGEMENTS

This book is not a memoir, but it draws heavily on the wisdom of those I have worked alongside during my time in government service who have patiently listened to my rantings and then offered greater insight and intelligence in their responses. Many of the people I owe the most to cannot be named. They know who they are and I am eternally grateful. These people collectively have centuries of experience in every corner of the world and it has been my privilege to work alongside them. Four that I can name, because they are sadly no longer with us, are Matthew Middlemiss, Charles Farr, Andrew Kent and Mark Powell. All hugely impressive in their particular fields, they taught me vital lessons that I've relied on ever since.

I have the highest possible regard for those brave citizens of Yemen, Iraq and Afghanistan that I had the privilege to work with, all of whom live with constant insecurity and risk of death, but have nonetheless decided that co-operating with the international community to improve their country is a worthwhile activity. One of the few that I can name is Pamir Patang, a brave Briton, born in Afghanistan, who has given his adopted country so much.

In developing my ideas on Britain's foreign policies and its overseas entanglements, I have to thank the endless well-lubricated evenings spent debating with the Magdalen crowd (whose members are too numerous to mention) – and the many people I spend too long arguing with on Twitter. In a slightly more formal setting I'm indebted to Shane Brighton, now a Senior Lecturer at Sussex University and an inspirational tutor on a Master's degree I pursued long ago, which set me on the path which led, eventually, to the writing of this book. My fellow student Charles Brown was also the most patient sounding-board, always underestimating his own sagacity but an invaluable help to my thinking on everything from military mishaps to global money laundering. Ben Higgins has been a source of inspiring debate and ideas, particularly with reference to the Middle East. Dan Kaszeta is always willing to discuss terrifying weapons and their application. Greg Shapland's expertise and wisdom were of great help, as was the fierce intelligence of Amil Khan.

Justin Scheck and Iyad Al-Baghdadi helped me to get my head around MbS's Saudi Arabia and Jason Pack helped me to understand Libya, even if he probably won't agree with what I've written about it. Two men with particular knowledge of Afghanistan, Dr Mike Martin and Dr Frank Ledwidge, have added enormously to my limited understanding of that place. Charles Parton's China expertise was invaluable, as was Dean Nelson's on India. I am also indebted to Tanveer Jafri who spoke to me with amazing calmness about the most painful subject imaginable, the gruesome murder of his father. My knowledge of Russia has been greatly augmented by John Sweeney and Patrick Dobbs. And particularly by Christopher Steele. As colleagues, Chris Steele and Christopher Burrows were generous in letting me write this book while I worked alongside them. My ability to think and write about Brexit owes an enormous amount to my friends and collaborators at Podmasters, in particular Andrew Harrison, Ian Dunt, Dorian Lynskey, Alex Andreou, Naomi Smith, and Ros Taylor.

This book could never have happened without Martin Hickman of Canbury Press deciding to publish an unknown middling former diplomat, so I owe him huge thanks for his excellent, patient editing and support throughout the process. Guy Vassall Adams QC offered sage advice on how to avoid legal entanglements. And thanks finally but most importantly, to Charlotte for having all the best ideas, and Matilda and Edward, for being the best reviewers, thank you so very much.

REFERENCES

Introduction
not in the 'Iraqi character.'
Cordesman, A. and Chair, A. (2003). The Current Military Situation in Iraq. [online] Available at: https://csis-website-prod.s3.amazonaws.com/s3fs-public/legacy_files/files/media/csis/pubs/031114current.pdf [Accessed 4 Jun. 2022].

Mr Trump blew apart the veneer of cordiality.
Trump Refuses to Sign G-7 Statement and Calls Trudeau 'Weak' (Published 2018). (2018). [online] The New York Times 9 Jun. Available at: https://www.nytimes.com/2018/06/09/world/americas/donald-trump-g7-nafta.html [Accessed 4 Jun. 2022].

This helped to create the new global disorder
Pack, J. (2022). Libya And The Global Enduring Disorder. S.L.: Oxford Univ Press Us.

Chapter 1
a speech outlining the government's approach to foreign policy
Robin Cook's speech on the government's ethical foreign policy. (Published 2018) The Guardian. [online] 12 May. Available at: https://www.theguardian.com/world/1997/may/12/indonesia.ethicalforeignpolicy.

bad for Britain
The Spectator Archive. (n.d.). BAD FOR BRITAIN» 25 Oct 1997» The Spectator Archive. [online] Available at: http://archive.spectator.co.uk/article/25th-october-1997/22/bad-for-britain [Accessed 4 Jun. 2022].

the 'End of History' and the victory of the liberal international order across the world
Fukuyama, Francis. "The End of History?" The National Interest, no. 16, 1989, pp. 3–18

'an ambitious strategy in which a state aims to turn as many countries as possible into liberal democracies like itself.'
Mearsheimer, J.J. (2018). Great Delusion : Liberal Dreams and International Realities. New Haven, Ct Yale University Press.

'simultaneously accelerating their development of new military capabilities.'
Kilcullen, D. (2022). DRAGONS AND THE SNAKES : how the rest learned to fight the west. S.L.: C Hurst & Co Pub Ltd.

Put simply - more people are dying in more wars and conflicts.
ucdp.uu.se. (n.d.). UCDP - Uppsala Conflict Data Program. [online] Available at: http://ucdp.uu.se/#/encyclopedia [Accessed 4 Jun. 2022].

the acceleration in the rate of decline from year to year.
Economic Intelligence Service. (1933). World Economic Survey 1932 1933. [online] Internet Archive. Available at: https://archive.org/stream/in.ernet. dli.2015.206049/2015.206049.World-Economic_djvu.txt [Accessed 4 Jun. 2022].

In 2020, the number of Free countries in the world reached its lowest level since the beginning of a 15-year period of global democratic decline, while the number of Not Free countries reached its highest level.
Freedom House (2021). New Report: The global decline in democracy has accelerated. [online] Freedom House. Available at: https://freedomhouse.org/article/new-report-global-decline-democracy-has-accelerated.. And Repucci, S. and Slipowitz, A. (2021). Democracy under Siege. [online] Freedom House. Available at: https:// freedomhouse.org/report/freedom-world/2021/democracy-under-siege.

according to an indictment from Special Counsel Mueller against a group of officers of Russia's military intelligence service (the 'GRU')
The Grand Jury for the District of Columbia charges: COUNT ONE (Conspiracy to Commit an Offense Against the United States). [online] Available at: https://www. justice.gov/file/1080281/download.

There is a risk that some political parties might come to view the payment of these fines as a cost of doing business; the Commission therefore needs to be able to impose sanctions that are proportionate to the levels of spending now routinely handled by parties and campaigners
www.electoralcommission.org.uk. (n.d.). Conservative Party fined £70,000 following investigation into election campaign expenses. [online] Available at: https://www.electoralcommission.org.uk/conservative-party-fined-ps70000-following-investigation-election-campaign-expenses [Accessed 4 Jun. 2022].

to strip the Electoral Commission of the power to prosecute law- breaking
The Independent. (2021). Electoral Commission to be stripped of power to prosecute after probe into Boris Johnson's flat makeover. [online] Available at: https://www.independent.co.uk/news/uk/politics/electoral-commission-boris-johnson-flat-b1868407.html [Accessed 4 Jun. 2022].

Chapter 2

I will fight hard to convince the staff that I am getting into the shape I was in last season.
www.panorama.com.al. (n.d.). Ka humbur vendin e titullarit, mesfushori i Besës i sinqertë: Isha... mbipeshë. [online] Available at: http://www.panorama.com. al/sport/ka-humbur-vendin-e-titullarit-mesfushori-i-beses-i-sinqerte-isha-mbipeshe/ [Accessed 4 Jun. 2022].

the reverence with which the former British Prime minister is held in Kosovo
Borger, J. (2014). Meet the Kosovan Albanians who named their sons after Tony Blair. [online] the Guardian. Available at: https://www.theguardian.com/ politics/2014/jun/20/kosovan-albanians-name-children-tony-blair-tonibler.

doctrine of international community
Blair, T (1999). Chicago Speach. [online] Available at: http://www.
britishpoliticalspeech.org/speech-archive.htm?speech=279.

the very brains of Milosevic's military apparatus and leadership
news.bbc.co.uk. (April 1999). BBC News | Europe | Nato defends TV bombing.
[online] Available at: http://news.bbc.co.uk/1/hi/world/europe/326653.stm
[Accessed 4 Jun. 2022].

Kosovo, with its majority ethnic-Albanian population, had been sullenly peaceful
Glenny, M. (2001). The Balkans : nationalism, war and the great powers, 1804-
1999. Harmondsworth: Penguin Books.

45 Kosovo Albanians were killed by Serbian security forces in the village of Račak
web.archive.org. (2003). Report of the EU Forensic Team on the Racac Incident, 17
March 1999. [online] Available at: https://web.archive.org/web/20031229235818/
http:/www.ess.uwe.ac.uk/Kosovo/Kosovo-Massacres2.htm   [Accessed   4
Jun. 2022].

The first sustained use of armed force by the NATO alliance in its 50-year existence.
Wanis-St. John, A, The Rambouillet Negotiations: A Precursor for Failure?
Diplomatic Courier. 1. 37-49 (2008)

This illusion appears to have been widely held in NATO headquarters and national capitals.
Roberts, A. (1999). NATO's 'Humanitarian War' over Kosovo. Survival, 41(3),
pp.102–123. doi:10.1080/00396339912331342943.

an army that would largely comprise American troops
Naughtie, J. (2002). The rivals : the intimate story of a political marriage. London:
Fourth Estate.

*President Clinton's support for such an offensive was restricted by unfavourable congressional
and public opinion*
DADDOW, O. (2009). 'Tony's war'? Blair, Kosovo and the interventionist
impulse in British foreign policy. International Affairs, 85(3), pp.547–560.
doi:10.1111/j.1468-2346.2009.00813.x.

*Blair himself was self-aware enough in his memoirs to acknowledge that applying those tests
to the 2003 decision to invade Iraq shows that it was a 'finely- balanced' decision.*
Blair, T. (2010). Tony Blair : a journey. London: Stanley Paul.

*the Security Council can resort to imposing sanctions or even authorize the use of force to
maintain or restore international peace and security*
United Nations (2015). United Nations Security Council. [online] Un.org.
Available at: https://www.un.org/securitycouncil/.

As Ivo Daalder, who would later serve as the US Ambassador to NATO, observed
Daalder, I.H. (1999). NATO, the UN, and the Use of Force. [online] Brookings. Available at: https://www.brookings.edu/research/nato-the-un-and-the-use-of-force/.

an expansion of the UN's capabilities and activities in the field of collective security.
Hannay, D. (2013). Britain's Quest For a Role A Diplomatic Memoir from Europe to the UN. London I.B.Tauris & Co Ltd I.B. Tauris & Co Ltd.

nearly a million of whom fled or were forced out of Kosovo.
Balanzino, S. (1999) "NATO's humanitarian support to the victims of the Kosovo crisis", NATO Review, no. 2, Summer 1999, p. 10

Professor Taylor Seybolt
Seybolt, T. (2008). HUMANITARIAN MILITARY INTERVENTION THE CONDITIONS FOR SUCCESS AND FAILURE. [online] Available at: https://www.sipri.org/sites/default/files/files/books/SIPRI08Seybolt.pdf.

to believe that humanitarian military intervention helped the world
Rentoul, J. (2001). Tony Blair : prime minister. Lancaster: Little, Brown.

according to an investigation carried out by the Council of Europe, a human rights organisation
The Guardian. (2010). Kosovo PM is head of human organ and arms ring, Council of Europe reports. [online] Available at: https://www.theguardian.com/world/2010/dec/14/kosovo-prime-minister-llike-mafia-boss [Accessed 4 Jun. 2022].

inflexible and unimaginative.
Samorukov, M. (n.d.). A Spoiler in the Balkans? Russia and the Final Resolution of the Kosovo Conflict. [online] Carnegie Endowment for International Peace. Available at: https://carnegiemoscow.org/2019/11/26/spoiler-in-balkans-russia-and-final-resolution-of-kosovo-conflict-pub-80429.

Politicians formerly known as liberals praised the Russian army for its performance there; one said it was regaining its dignity.
Gessen, M. (2014). For 15 Years, Putin Has Been Planning His Revenge for the U.S Bombing of Kosovo. Crimea Is That Revenge. [online] Slate Magazine. Available at: https://slate.com/news-and-politics/2014/03/putins-crimea-revenge-ever-since-the-u-s-bombed-kosovo-in-1999-putin-has-been-planning-to-get-even.html.

my ambitions are to reach the top of football, to achieve as much as I can. Lajmet e fundit - Zëri. (2018). Toni Bler-at e Kosovës. [online] Available at: https://zeri.info/sport/187722/toni-bler-at-e-kosoves/ [Accessed 4 Jun. 2022].

Chapter 3
How come all the good reporting I get is from SIS

Woodward, B. (2004). Plan of attack : the definitive account of the decision to invade Iraq. New York, N.Y.: Simon & Schuster.

particularly outrageous activities
Department Of State. The Office of Electronic Information, B. of P.A. (2004). Zarqawi Letter. [online] 2001-2009.state.gov. Available at: https://2001-2009.state.gov/p/nea/rls/31694.htm [Accessed 4 Jun. 2022].

first advocated military intervention in Iraq as early as 1992
Cirincione, J. and Cirincione, J. (2019). Origins of Regime Change in Iraq. [online] Carnegie Endowment for International Peace. Available at: https://carnegieendowment.org/2003/03/19/origins-of-regime-change-in-iraq-pub-1214.

We do not seek to impose an American solution or a foreign opposition on the people of Iraq
"Saddam Hussein's Iraq", US Department of State, September 1999, https://nsarchive2.gwu.edu/NSAEBB/NSAEBB167/13.pdf [accessed 13 January 2020]

make the case for hitting Saddam's regime over its plan to produce weapons of mass destruction[WMD].
Vulliamy, E and Beaumont, P. (2001). Secret US plan for Iraq war. [online] Available at: https://www.theguardian.com/world/2001/dec/02/afghanistan.iraq [Accessed 4 Jun. 2022].

like fraternity brothers
White, R.D. (2008). George Tenet and the Last Great Days of the CIA. Public Administration Review, [online] 68(3), pp.420–427. doi:10.1111/j.1540-6210.2008.00879.x.

all the good reporting . Woodward, 2004

'phenomenal access' to Iraq's biological and chemical weapons programme
The three official inquiries touching on intelligence on Iraq's WMD programmes, the Hutton Inquiry, the Butler Inquiry and the Chilcot Inquiry, provide extensive and well-documented evidence of the intelligence produced by MI6 to make the case for war with Iraq.
Iraq (Chilcot) Inquiry. (2017). [online] Available at: https://webarchive.nationalarchives.gov.uk/ukgwa/20171123122743/http:/www.iraqinquiry.org.uk/the-report/.
"Review of Intelligence on Weapons of Mass Destruction", known as The Butler Inquiry. (2004) [online] Available at: http://news.bbc.co.uk/nol/shared/bsp/hi/pdfs/14_07_04_butler.pdf [accessed 5 January 2019]
"Report of the Inquiry into the Circumstances Surrounding the Death of Dr David Kelly C.M.G", known as the Hutton Inquiry. (2004) [online] Available at: https://irp.fas.org/world/uk/huttonreport.pdf

the source remained unproven
The Butler Inquiry, p.139

was not shown to the DIS experts who could have commented on the credibility and validity of the 'unproven' intelligence
Chilcot Inquiry, 4.2, para 418

such obvious bullshit
Shoard, C. (2016). 'It was such obvious bullshit': The Rock writer shocked film may have inspired false WMD intelligence. [online] Available at: https://www.theguardian.com/film/2016/jul/08/it-was-such-obvious-bullshit-the-rock-writer-shocked-film-may-have-inspired-false-wmd-intelligence [Accessed 4 Jun. 2022].

the entire reporting had been invented
Chilcot Inquiry, 4.3, para 514

still in the balance
Chilcot Inquiry, 4.3, para 138

SIS concluded that its source was a fabricator who had lied from the outset.
Chilcot Inquiry, 4.3, para 532

which relies on cross-checked media reporting.
www.iraqbodycount.org. (n.d.). Iraq Body Count. [online] Available at: https://www.iraqbodycount.org [Accessed 4 Jun. 2022].

This may be the least transparent war in recent American history.
Khan, A. and Gopal, A. (2017). The Uncounted - The New York Times. The New York Times. [online] 16 Nov. Available at: https://www.nytimes.com/interactive/2017/11/16/magazine/uncounted-civilian-casualties-iraq-airstrikes.html.

battlefield executions, murders in detention centres, and coverups organized by the state
Taub, B. (2019). Iraq's Post-ISIS Campaign of Revenge. [online] The New Yorker. Available at: https://www.newyorker.com/magazine/2018/12/24/iraqs-post-isis-campaign-of-revenge [Accessed 17 Oct. 2019].

antiquities from Iraq and Syria
MacDonald, B.F., Georgi Kantchev and Alistair (2017). The Men Who Trade ISIS Loot. Wall Street Journal. [online] 6 Aug. Available at: https://www.wsj.com/articles/the-men-who-trade-isis-loot-1502017200.

According to a US Department of Justice filing
Justice.gov. (2017). United States Files Civil Action To Forfeit Thousands Of Ancient Iraqi Artifacts Imported By Hobby Lobby. [online] Available at: https://www.justice.gov/usao-edny/pr/united-states-files-civil-action-forfeit-thousands-ancient-iraqi-artifacts-imported.

As Tony Blair recalled later
Blair, 2010

Saddam Hussein recently sought significant quantities of uranium from Africa
President Delivers 'State of the Union', The White House, 28 January 2003, https://georgewbush-whitehouse.archives.gov/news/releases/2003/01/print/20030128-19.html [accessed 7 February 2019]

This visit has been confirmed
The Status of Nuclear Inspections in Iraq: an Update, Mohamed ElBaradei, Director General of International Atomic Energy Agency, 7 March 2003

I think that was the most scandalous part.
Evidence of Hans Blix to Iraq Inquiry, 6 February 2013 https://webarchive.nationalarchives.gov.uk/20130206045444/http://www.iraqinquiry.org.uk/media/51945/20100727-blix-final.pdf [accessed 7 February 2019]

there's simply too much oversight over too small an industry for a sale [of uranium] to have transpired
Wilson 4th, J.C. (2003). Opinion | What I Didn't Find in Africa. The New York Times. [online] 6 Jul. Available at: https://www.nytimes.com/2003/07/06/opinion/what-i-didn-t-find-in-africa.html.

Since the 1980s Iraq has been self-sufficient in uranium production, with significant uranium reserves on its own territory.
Cirincione, J. (n.d.). Niger Uranium: Still a False Claim. [online] Carnegie Endowment for International Peace. Available at: https://carnegieendowment.org/2004/08/28/niger-uranium-still-false-claim-pub-1595.

there's no question in my mind that the intelligence is correct
Evidence of Sir Richard Dearlove to the Iraq Inquiry, 9 August 2012. https://webarchive.nationalarchives.gov.uk/20120809215147/http://www.iraqinquiry.org.uk/media/50694/20100616-Dearlove.pdf (accessed 8 February 2019)

to give Iraq the margin of democracy
Chulov, M. and Pidd, H. (2011). Defector admits to WMD lies that triggered Iraq war. The Guardian. [online] 15 Feb. Available at: https://www.theguardian.com/world/2011/feb/15/defector-admits-wmd-lies-iraq-war.

our social attitudes and vanities
John Le Carré's introduction to The Sunday Times Insight Team's study of "The Philby Conspiracy" (1968)

Chapter 4

this attack was planned prior to September 2001
Zelin, A. (2017). Fifteen Years after the Djerba Synagogue Bombing. [online] Available at: https://ctc.westpoint.edu/fifteen-years-after-the-djerba-synagogue-bombing/ [Accessed 4 Jun. 2022].

It's our experience of Northern Ireland that makes us so good.
Storer, J. "The Tory peer who went to war." (2003). news.bbc.co.uk. [online] 20 Jun. Available at: http://news.bbc.co.uk/2/hi/uk_news/politics/2966470.stm [Accessed 4 Jun. 2022].

clear evidence of external support for the insurgents
IISS. (2019). Iran's Networks of Influence in the Middle East. [online] Available at: https://www.iiss.org/publications/strategic-dossiers/iran-dossier [Accessed 4 Jun. 2022].

Maliki never trusted the British again
Ledwidge, F. (2012). Losing small wars : British military failure in Iraq and Afghanistan. New Haven Conn. ; London: Yale University Press.

they failed to take account of their history there.
Martin, M. (2014). An Intimate War: An Oral History of the Helmand Conflict, 1978-2012. Oxford University Press.

fully commit to the ISAF plan rather than their narrower counter-terrorist objectives
Cavanagh, M. (2012). Ministerial Decision-Making in the Run-Up to the Helmand Deployment. The RUSI Journal, 157(2), pp.48–54. doi:10.1080/0307184 7.2012.675798.

It's use them or lose them
Written evidence of Sir Sherard Cowper-Coles, (23 December 2010), https://publications.parliament.uk/pa/cm201011/cmselect/cmfaff/514/514we10.htm [accessed 4 Jun. 2022]

Afghanistan provides an opportunity.
Sungupta, K. (2009). 'Army fury at refusal to bolster Afghan campaign'. The Independent [online] Available at: https://www.independent.co.uk/news/uk/home-news/army-fury-at-refusal-to-bolster-afghan-campaign-1693827.html [Accessed 4 Jun. 2022].

Ahmed Wali Karzai, brother of the President Hamid Karzai
Filkins, D. (2011). Death of an Afghan Godfather. [online] The New Yorker. Available at: https://www.newyorker.com/news/news-desk/death-of-an-afghan-godfather [Accessed 4 Jun. 2022].

they were being used to settle a private feud.
Martin, 2014

you can have one if you want one
Ledwidge, 2012.

major error of judgement
Dannatt job 'error of judgement'. (2009). news.bbc.co.uk. [online] 15 Oct. Available at: http://news.bbc.co.uk/2/mobile/uk_news/politics/8308669.stm [Accessed 4 Jun. 2022].

There's no place we won't go.
Chandrasekaran, R. (2013). The war within the war for Afghanistan. London: Bloomsbury.

and this was news
Nissenbaum, D. "McChrystal calls Marjah a 'bleeding ulcer' in Afghan campaign", McClatchy, (16 June 2015) https://www.mcclatchydc.com/news/nation-world/world/article24583621.html [Accessed 4 Jun. 22]

We threw out the COIN playbook
Chandrasekaran, 2013.

seemed to know loads of people
Martin, 2014

non-combatants killed by poor targeting or pure error
Gopal, A. (2021). The Other Afghan Women. [online] The New Yorker. Available at: https://www.newyorker.com/magazine/2021/09/13/the-other-afghan-women.

You have got to address Biden's intellectual fitness
Averre, D. (2021). Kabul evacuation is at 'very high risk of terror attack from ISIS'. [online] Mail Online. Available at: https://www.dailymail.co.uk/news/article-9926357/Kabul-evacuation-high-risk-terror-attack-ISIS.html [Accessed 4 Jun. 2022].

Chapter 5

execution is the fate of anyone who forms a political party
Asser, M. (2011). The Muammar Gaddafi story. BBC News. [online] 21 Oct. Available at: https://www.bbc.com/news/world-africa-12688033.

In one case, Nuri Al-Mismari
Jamestown Foundation, "A Man with No Limits or Restrictions": New Revelations From The Court of Mu'ammar Gaddafi, 26 July 2012, Terrorism Monitor Volume: 10 Issue: 15, available at: https://www.refworld.org/docid/50505f7e2.html [accessed 4 June 2022]

London's Pall Mall
Beaumont, P, Ahmed, K, Bright, M. (2003). The meeting that brought Libya in from the cold. [online] Available at: https://www.theguardian.com/world/2003/dec/21/politics.libya [Accessed 4 Jun. 2022].

this was the least we [Britain] could do for you
Corera, G. (2012). MI6: life and death in the British Secret Service. London: Phoenix.

Eagerly being managed by Western consultants
Libya looks to the future. (2010). Financial Times. [online] 7 Jun. Available at: https://www.ft.com/content/715e41e6-6fc6-11df-8fcf-00144feabdc0.

a successful effort to stave off widespread unrest.
Ertl, V. (2015) "Saudi Arabia's Response to the Protests in 2011 Analysis of Authoritarian Regime Survival Strategies". [online] Available at: https://www.sciencespo.fr/kuwait-program/wp-content/uploads/2018/05/KSP_Paper_Award_Spring_2015_ERTL_Veronika.pdf.

nerve centre of Libya's revolution
Chulov, M. (2011). Benghazi the nerve centre as Libya protest turns to revolution. The Guardian. [online] 24 Feb. Available at: https://www.theguardian.com/world/2011/feb/24/libya-benghazi-muammar-gaddafi.

Britain launched a secret operation
The Sun. (2011). Brit held with SAS in Libya was spy. [online] Available at: https://www.thesun.co.uk/archives/news/413680/brit-held-with-sas-in-libya-was-spy/ [Accessed 4 Jun. 2022].

It also caused great difficulties for MI6, which had plans to turn some key figures in Qadhafi's inner circle.
Urban, M. "Inside story of the UK's secret mission to beat Gaddafi". (2012). BBC News. [online] 19 Jan. Available at: https://www.bbc.com/news/magazine-16573516 [Accessed 4 Jun. 2022].

He said he felt forced into it.
Cameron, D. (2019). For the record. London: William Collins.

in televised scenes both men will hope play well back home
Logan, J, Farge, E. "Sarkozy, Cameron hailed in Libya, offer help." (2011). Reuters. [online] 15 Sep. Available at: https://www.reuters.com/article/libya-idUSL5E7KF3VB20110915 [Accessed 4 Jun. 2022].

only if we really seize it
David Cameron, Speech to the UN General Assembly, 22 September 2011, https://www.newstatesman.com/global-issues/2011/09/arab-world-region-libya-act (accessed 28 February 2020)

the alliance remains an essential source of stability.
Daalder, I.H. and Stavridis, J.G. (2012). NATO's Victory in Libya: The Right Way to Run an Intervention. Foreign Affairs, [online] 91(2), pp.2–7. Available at: https://www.jstor.org/stable/23217215.

Libya's implosion post-2011
Pack, J. (2021). Libya and the global enduring disorder. London: Hurst & Company.

Goldberg, J. (2016). President Obama's Interview With Jeffrey Goldberg on Syria and Foreign Policy. [online] The Atlantic. Available at: https://www.theatlantic.com/magazine/archive/2016/04/the-obama-doctrine/471525/.

distracted by a range of other things
Goldberg, J. (2016). President Obama's Interview With Jeffrey Goldberg on Syria and Foreign Policy. [online] The Atlantic. Available at: https://www.theatlantic.com/magazine/archive/2016/04/the-obama-doctrine/471525/.

in less than a page and blames the UN
Cameron, 2019

A British parliamentary inquiry in 2016.
House of Commons - Libya: Examination of intervention and collapse and the UK's future policy options - Foreign Affairs Committee. [online] Available at: https://publications.parliament.uk/pa/cm201617/cmselect/cmfaff/119/11902.htm.

I've never known a relief like it
Cameron, 2019

the Foreign Office's budget has received a progressively lower proportion of government expenditure almost every year since the 1970s.
HC 665 The Role of the FCO in UK Government Seventh Report of Session 2010-12 Volume I. (2011). [online] Available at: https://publications.parliament.uk/pa/cm201012/cmselect/cmfaff/665/665.pdf.

such elite schools as Eton, Harrow and Winchester
Buchan, L. (2019). "Tory ministers spend £91m on private school fees for top diplomats and military personnel." The Independent [online] Available at: https://www.independent.co.uk/news/uk/politics/tory-ministers-private-school-fees-children-diplomats-military-mod-foreign-office-a9181211.html [Accessed 4 Jun. 2022].

David Miliband recently pointed out
"Running out of credit?" British Foreign Policy Group, June 2019, https://bfpg.co.uk/wp-content/uploads/2019/06/Running-out-of-Credit-HR.pdf (accessed 5 March 2020)

in Mozambique in the early 1990s or in South Sudan as recently as March 2020
Vines, A. (2018). Elite Bargains and Political Deals Project: Mozambique Case Study. [online] Available at: https://assets.publishing.service.gov.uk/government/uploads/system/uploads/attachment_data/file/766037/Mozambique_case_study.pdf.

the nature of the power that we hold
Wintour, P. (2019). "UK no longer makes running on world stage, says ex-No 10 adviser". The Guardian [online] Available at: https://www.theguardian.com/politics/2019/dec/12/uk-no-longer-makes-running-on-world-stage-says-ex-no-10-adviser [Accessed 4 Jun. 2022].

In the same report
BFPG, 2019

we have no legal reason to hold this information
Foreign and Commonwealth Office, FOI Request Ref 0180 – 19

Greg Shapland, former head of Foreign Office Research Analysts, explained to me
Author's interview with Greg Shapland, 8 May 2020

Chapter 6

ASMA AL-ASAD empties a box of fondue mix into a saucepan for lunch
Buck, J. J. "Asma al-asad: A Rose in the Desert", Vogue, March 2011. Vogue has attempted to remove the article from the internet, but it can be found here: https://gawker.com/asma-al-asad-a-rose-in-the-desert-1265002284 (accessed 26 March 2020)

hold in their hands the crucial threads of power
Batatu, H. 'Some Observations on the Social Roots of Syria's Ruling, Military Group and the Causes for Its Dominance,' Middle East Journal, Vol. 35, No. 3 (Summer, 1981), pp. 331-344

needy families indentured their daughters to domestic servitude
Faksh, M.A. (1984). The Alawi community of Syria: a new dominant political force. Middle Eastern Studies, 20(2), pp.133–153. doi:10.1080/00263208408700577.

God has concocted a tremendous sin
The Qu'ran 4:48 (English text taken from 'The Qu'ran', Oxford World's Classics, trans. M. A. S. Abdul Haleem (2004) p.55)

a contemporary jihadist website
Nibras Kazmi, Syria through jihadist eyes: a perfect enemy, Hoover Press (2010), pp 13-14

the Syrian Observatory for Human Rights
The Syrian Observatory For Human Rights. (2020). Syrian Revolution NINE years on: 586,100 persons killed and millions of Syrians displaced and injured • The Syrian Observatory For Human Rights. [online] Available at: https://www.syriahr. com/en/157193/.

the problem is going to exist forever in Jabla
Shadid, A. (2011). Syria Escalates Crackdown as Tanks Go to Restive City. The New York Times. [online] 25 Apr. Available at: https://www.nytimes.com/2011/04/26/ world/middleeast/26syria.html [Accessed 4 Jun. 2022].

beheaded a captured child
Chulov, M. (2016). Syrian opposition group that killed child 'was in US-vetted alliance'. [online] Available at: https://www.theguardian.com/world/2016/ jul/20/syrian-opposition-group-which-killed-child-was-in-us-vetted-alliance [Accessed 4 Jun. 2022].

warmer relations with the Libyan Arab Jamahiriya
UN Security Council, report of meeting on 4 October 2011

More were to follow
Lister, C. (2017). Syrian jihad - the evolution of an insurgency. C Hurst & Co Publishers Ltd.

it's hard to see a rational motivation
The Guardian. (2013). An attack on Syria will only spread the war and killing | Seumas Milne. [online] Available at: https://www.theguardian.com/commentisfree/2013/ aug/27/attack-syria-chemical-weapon-escalate-backlash [Accessed 4 Jun. 2022].

The Ghouta attack represented the full development of that chemical weapons capability
Dan Kaszeta interview with the author, 16 April 2020

it is inconceivable that any Government would in practice depart from this precedent
Hansard, 15 May 2007

the necessity of consulting Parliament on military action
Hansard, 21 March 2011

on the side of Vladimir Putin and Bashar Al-Assad
Cameron, 2019

I am disappointed and I am slightly apprehensive
Watt, N. (2013). UK-US special relationship in danger, warns Philip Hammond. [online] Available at: https://www.theguardian.com/politics/2013/aug/30/uk-us-special-relationship-danger [Accessed 4 Jun. 2022].

that was the way we do something like that
C-SPAN.org. (n.d.). Secretary John Kerry Reflects Foreign Policy Successes and Challenges. [online] Available at: https://www.c-span.org/video/?421184-1/secretary-john-kerry-reflects-foreign-policy-successes-challenges [Accessed 4 Jun. 2022].

some mistakes could have been avoided
Author's interview with Shapland, May 2020

In the northern summer of 2014, in less than a hundred days, ISIS launched its blitzkrieg in Iraq
Kilcullen, D. (2016). Blood Year : Islamic State and the failures of the War on Terror. London: Hurst And Company.

It's a small number
www.c-span.org. (n.d.). U.S. Strategy Against ISIS | C-SPAN.org. [online] Available at: https://www.c-span.org/video/?328129-1/hearing-military-operations-islamic-state [Accessed 4 Jun. 2022].

taken out by Russia's airstrikes on 30 September 2015
Private conversations with the author. One of the sources was a former British government official. Another was a Syrian former rebel fighter.

more than 31,000 civilians
(2020). VDC - Violations Documentation Center. [online] Available at: https://vdc-sy.net [Accessed 4 Jun. 2022].

Welcome to the Middle East and have a nice day.
Financial Times, August 2013

Chapter 7

This is wrong
Cusick, J. (2019). Revealed: Boris, the Russian oligarch and the Page 3 model. [online] Available at: https://www.opendemocracy.net/en/opendemocracyuk/revealed-boris-russian-oligarch-and-page-3-model/ [Accessed 5 Jun. 2022].

wandering around an Italian airport, quite alone, seemingly wearing the clothes he had slept in and looking very much worse for wear
Hopkins, N. (2019). Morning after: Boris Johnson recovers from Lebedev's exotic Italian party. [online] Available at: https://www.theguardian.com/politics/2019/jul/26/boris-johnson-security-evgeny-lebedev-perugia-party [Accessed 5 Jun. 2022].

among its members were Vladimir Putin and Alexander Lebedev
Kovalev, A.A. and Levine, S.I. (2017). Russia's Dead End An Insider's Testimony from Gorbachev to Putin. Potomac Books. p. 81

I have been an opposition figure for a decade...
Pickard, J. and Ivanova, P., "Canadian sanctions put Lebedevs back in the UK spotlight." (2022). Financial Times. [online] 21 May. Available at: https://www.ft.com/content/c9fe610a-f4ec-413c-8f0d-fd9a86eca9dd [Accessed 5 Jun. 2022].

Johnson overrode the House of Lords Appointments Commission and, according to widespread reports, the advice of Britain's security services
Sweeney, J.. (2020). SWEENEY INVESTIGATES: What Changed to Make Evgeny Lebedev No Longer a Security Risk? [online] Byline Times. Available at: https://bylinetimes.com/2020/08/20/sweeney-investigates-what-changed-to-make-evgeny-lebedev-no-longer-a-security-risk/ [Accessed 5 Jun. 2022].

Lubov Chernukhin
O'Neill, S. (2018). Lubov Chernukhin: Quiet Russian's £1.7m makes her top female Tory donor. www.thetimes.co.uk. [online] Available at: https://www.thetimes.co.uk/article/lubov-chernukhin-quiet-russians-1-7m-makes-her-top-female-tory-donor-z2c00bcxl [Accessed 5 Jun. 2022].

Alexander Temerko
Belton, C. (2019) "Special Report: In British PM race, a former Russian tycoon quietly wields influence." Reuters. [online] 19 Jul. Available at: https://www.reuters.com/article/uk-britain-eu-johnson-russian-specialrep-idUKKCN1UE0WY [Accessed 5 Jun. 2022].

Aston Chase, 150,000 Russians live in Londongrad properties worth a total of £8 billion.
Lewis, N. (2022). Ending London's reliance on Russian wealth will be hard, suggests report. [online] Available at: https://thenegotiator.co.uk/ending-londons-reliance-on-russian-wealth-will-be-hard-suggests-report/ [Accessed 5 Jun. 2022].

the Ham & High discovered when it reported a major oligarch on its doorstep and then had to delete the report after legal threats
Richard Brooks, "Looting with Putin", Private Eye special report, https://www.private-eye.co.uk/pictures/special_reports/looting-with-putin.pdf (2018)

We regret their unwillingness to engage with our inquiry
Foreign Affairs Committee, (2018) "Moscow's Gold: Russian Corruption in the UK", UK Parliament [online] Available at https://publications.parliament.uk/pa/cm201719/cmselect/cmfaff/932/93204.htm#footnote-062 [Accessed 5 Jun. 22]

Russia's invasion of Ukraine is reprehensible and it is right that we stand together in condemning it
www.linklaters.com. (n.d.). Update on Linklaters' Russia-related work. [online] Available at: https://www.linklaters.com/en/about-us/news-and-deals/news/2022/january/update-on-linklaters-russia-related-work [Accessed 5 Jun. 2022]. Compare with Feb. 22 archived version at https://web.archive.org/web/20220201152543/https://www.linklaters.com/en/locations/russia

the imposition of direct rule over the British Virgin Islands in response to the corruption and mismanagement there
Loft, P., (2022) "Will the UK impose direct rule in the British Virgin Islands?" [online] Available at: https://researchbriefings.files.parliament.uk/documents/CBP-9538/CBP-9538.pdf [Accessed 5 Jun. 22]

in the period 2008–2018, a staggering £68 billion from Russia was lodged in these varied jurisdictions, according to the anti- corruption organisation Global Witness
Global Witness. (n.d.). Missing the bigger picture? Russian money in the UK's tax havens. [online] Available at: https://www.globalwitness.org/en/blog/missing-bigger-picture-russian-money-uks-tax-havens/ [Accessed 5 Jun. 2022].

it was the stamp of approval they'd been working for, and allowed them to deepen their infiltration of international markets
Belton, C. (2020). Putin's People. Harper Collins UK.

From 2002–2011, $39 billion was raised by Russian companies
PWC. (2012) "Equity sans frontières". [online] Available at: https://www.pwc.com/gx/en/audit-services/ipo-centre/assets/pwc-cross-border-ipo-trends.pdf [Accessed 5 Jun. 22]

a tragic mistake
Friedman, J. "Opinion | Foreign Affairs; Now a Word From X." (1998). The New York Times. [online] 2 May. Available at: https://www.nytimes.com/1998/05/02/opinion/foreign-affairs-now-a-word-from-x.html.

The answer he received was a devastating, life-changing shock
Bowlby, C. Vladimir Putin's formative German years. (2015). BBC News. [online] 27 Mar. Available at: https://www.bbc.co.uk/news/magazine-32066222 [Accessed 5 Jun. 2022].

a blistering speech at the Munich Security Conference
President of Russia. (2007). Speech and the Following Discussion at the Munich Conference on Security Policy. [online] Available at: http://en.kremlin.ru/events/president/transcripts/24034.

'very rash'
John Lough speaking to the author on the Doomsday Watch podcast, kite.link/doomsday (6 Mar. 2022)

Article 5
NATO (2021). Collective defence - Article 5. [online] NATO. Available at: https://www.nato.int/cps/en/natohq/topics_110496.htm.

a complex spy swap involving Russia and the USA
RadioFreeEurope/RadioLiberty. (n.d.). The Big Spy Swap: The U.S.-Russia Secret Agent Exchange 10 Years Ago. [online] Available at: https://www.rferl.org/a/the-big-spy-swap-the-major-u-s--russia-secret-agent-exchange-ten-years-ago/30713842.html [Accessed 5 Jun. 2022].

Skripal's wife, son and older brother had all died in questionable circumstances
Russian spy: Sergei Skripal collapsed alongside daughter. (2018). BBC News. [online] 6 Mar. Available at: https://www.bbc.co.uk/news/uk-43297638.

Alexander Litvinenko
Owen, R. (2016). The Litvinenko Inquiry Report into the death of Alexander Litvinenko. [online] Available at: https://assets.publishing.service.gov.uk/government/uploads/system/uploads/attachment_data/file/493860/The-Litvinenko-Inquiry-H-C-695-web.pdf.

Theresa May, at that time Home Secretary, confirmed that she had blocked a public inquiry in order not to offend the Russians.
The Independent. (2013). Alexander Litvinenko death: Theresa May admits 'international. [online] Available at: https://www.independent.co.uk/news/uk/politics/alexander-litvinenko-death-theresa-may-admits-international-relations-affected-ruling-8720405.html [Accessed 5 Jun. 2022].

We got rid of the Advanced Research and Assessment Group, which did the basic Russian analysis, we sacked our Ukraine desk officer and the defence intelligence service reduced its Russian analysis
Aston, S. (2020). UK lacks capacity to effectively tackle Russian threat – Rory Stewart. Civil Service World [online] Available at: https://www.civilserviceworld.com/professions/article/uk-lacks-capacity-to-effectively-tackle-russian-threat-rory-stewart [Accessed 5 Jun. 2022].

Putin's contention was that Ukrainians and Russians are one people
Putin, V. (2021). On the Historical Unity of Russians and Ukrainians. [online] President of Russia. Available at: http://en.kremlin.ru/events/president/news/66181.

should not 'close London's financial centre to Russians'
Watt, N. (2014). UK seeking to ensure Russia sanctions do not harm City of London. The Guardian. [online] Available at: https://www.theguardian.com/world/2014/mar/03/uk-seeks-russia-harm-city-london-document [Accessed 5 Jun. 2022].

'That arguably should have attracted the attention of the regulators, given that the EU has sectoral sanctions on the Russian defence sector.'
Moscow's Gold, UK Parliament (2018)

MI6 regarded it as a 'scandal'
Coughlin, C., Swinford, S., Ambrose, J., Withers, I. and Field, M. (2018). MI6 raises concerns after energy oligarch linked to Vladimir Putin makes £1bn on London Stock Exchange. The Telegraph. [online] 6 Feb. Available at: https://www. telegraph.co.uk/politics/2018/02/06/mi6-raises-concerns-energy-oligarch-linked-vladimir-putin-makes/ [Accessed 5 Jun. 2022].

Lord Barker, En+'s executive chairman, was paid a $4 million bonus by Deripaska for his work
British Lord Barker Got $4 Million Bonus on Deripaska Sanctions Deal. (2019). Bloomberg.com. [online] 1 May. Available at: https://www.bloomberg.com/news/articles/2019-05-01/en-chair-barker-said-to-get-4-million-bonus-on-sanctions-deal [Accessed 5 Jun. 2022].

an official report by the Intelligence and Security Committee of Parliament on Russian influence
Intelligence and Security Committee of Parliament Russia. (n.d.). [online] Available at: https://isc.independent.gov.uk/wp-content/uploads/2021/03/CCS207_CCS0221966010-001_Russia-Report-v02-Web_Accessible.pdf.

was a vocal advocate of the policy of sending only non-lethal equipment to Ukraine
Dollimore, L. (2022). Ukrainian leaders pleading for weapons were rejected by three UK PMs. [online] Mail Online. Available at: https://www.dailymail.co.uk/news/article-10747419/Ukrainian-leaders-desperate-buy-UK-weapons-defend-against-Russia-Crimea-invasion.html [Accessed 5 Jun. 2022].

several European countries have supplied more weapons and aid
The Economist. (n.d.). Which countries have pledged the most support to Ukraine? [online] Available at: https://www.economist.com/graphic-detail/2022/05/02/which-countries-have-pledged-the-most-support-to-ukraine [Accessed 5 Jun. 2022].

We repeatedly asked the Foreign Secretary what the FCO and the Government more broadly could do to help stop the flow of corrupt money into the UK
Moscow's Gold, UK Parliament (2018)

safe haven for corrupt individuals, their allies and assets
Transparency International UK. (n.d.). Transparency measures must be fast-tracked to kick-start dirty money crackdown. [online] Available at: https://www.transparency.org.uk/russia-sanctions-UK-latest-news-property-dirty-money-suspect-wealth [Accessed 5 Jun. 2022].

Chapter 8

In practical terms, this means three things
Parton, C. (2020). Towards a UK strategy and policies for relations with China x THE POLICY INSTITUTE About the author. [online] Available at: https://www.kcl.ac.uk/policy-institute/assets/towards-a-uk-strategy-and-policies-for-relations-with-china.pdf.

it took a publicly hostile stance on the referendum
www.globaltimes.cn. (n.d.). Scotland referendum shadows UK future - Global Times. [online] Available at: https://www.globaltimes.cn/content/880485.shtml [Accessed 5 Jun. 2022].

a pure mercantilist, unprincipled, self-serving decision aimed at attracting short-term investment
Britain's red-carpet welcome for Xi baffles traditional allies. (2015). Financial Times. [online] 18 Oct. Available at: https://www.ft.com/content/3e5a866a-7579-11e5-933d-efcdc3c11c89 [Accessed 5 Jun. 2022].

potentially sensitive intellectual property
Owen, G. (2020). Advisers investigated amid fears Beijing using Covid to own benefit. [online] Mail Online. Available at: https://www.dailymail.co.uk/news/article-8233229/China-advisers-investigated-amid-fears-Beijing-using-Covid-commercial-benefit.html [Accessed 5 Jun. 2022].

Lord Chadlington
Pickard, J. and Payne, S. "David Cameron pushes ahead with troubled $1bn China fund". (2020). Financial Times. [online] 15 Jun. Available at: https://www.ft.com/content/a0b3858e-4e92-4db2-83fd-a6550d0b1427 [Accessed 5 Jun. 2022].

donations
These can be found on the Electoral Commission website https://www.electoralcommission.org.uk/who-we-are-and-what-we-do/financial-reporting/donations-and-loans/view-donations-and-loans

Nirj Deva, then MEP for the Southeast of England
Baldwin, L and Geoghegan, P. (2019). Senior Tory revealed as Huawei cheerleader in Brussels. [online] Available at: https://www.opendemocracy.net/en/senior-tory-revealed-huawei-cheerleader-brussels/ [Accessed 5 Jun. 2022].

a safe haven for cyber criminals in exchange for those criminals being 'on call' to work for the benefit of the state
www.justice.gov. (2020). Two Chinese Hackers Working with the Ministry of State Security Charged with Global Computer Intrusion Campaign Targeting Intellectual Property and Confidential Business Information, Including COVID-19 Research. [online] Available at: https://www.justice.gov/opa/pr/two-chinese-hackers-working-ministry-state-security-charged-global-computer-intrusion.

A major online leak of the resumes of Huawei employees revealed startling connections
Hamilton, I. (2019). Researchers studied 25,000 leaked Huawei resumes and found troubling links to the government and spies. [online] Available at: https://www.businessinsider.in/researchers-studied-25000-leaked-huawei-resumes-and-found-troubling-links-to-the-government-and-spies/articleshow/70128784.cms [Accessed 5 Jun. 2022].

Huawei Cyber Security Evaluation Centre
OFFICIAL HUAWEI CYBER SECURITY EVALUATION CENTRE (HCSEC) OVERSIGHT A report to the National Security Adviser of the United Kingdom. (2019). [online] Available at: https://assets.publishing.service.gov.uk/government/uploads/system/uploads/attachment_data/file/790270/HCSEC_OversightBoardReport-2019.pdf.

we will have to reassess the ability for us to share information and be connected with them in the ways that we are today
U.S. will rethink cooperation with allies who use Huawei: official. (2019). Reuters. [online] 29 Apr. Available at: https://www.reuters.com/article/us-usa-huawei-tech-idUSKCN1S517H [Accessed 5 Jun. 2022].

The endeavour to build China into a prosperous, strong, democratic and highly civilized modern socialist state [...] a foreign policy of independence and peace
www.china.org.cn. (n.d.). 16th National Congress of the Communist Party of China, 2002. [online] Available at: http://www.china.org.cn/english/features/45461.htm.

the official ideology of the state
en.pkulaw.cn. (n.d.). Constitution of the People's Republic of China (2018 Amendment). [online] Available at: http://en.pkulaw.cn/display.aspx?cgid=7c7e81f43957c58bbdfb&lib=law [Accessed 5 Jun. 2022].

South China Sea
Asia Maritime Transparency Initiative. (n.d.). Home. [online] Available at: https://amti.csis.org [Accessed 5 Jun. 2022].

According to official Chinese leaked documents
Data leak reveals how China 'brainwashes' Uighurs in prison camps. (2019). BBC News. [online] 24 Nov. Available at: https://www.bbc.co.uk/news/world-asia-china-50511063.

organs harvested for transplants
China Tribunal. (n.d.). China Tribunal: Final judgement detailed, the hearings records, submissions etc. [online] Available at: https://chinatribunal.com.

mandatory surveillance software is installed on residents' mobile phones to scan for Islamic keywords and pictures
Feng, E. (2018). Inside China's surveillance state. [online] @FinancialTimes. Available at: https://www.ft.com/content/2182eebe-8a17-11e8-bf9e-8771d5404543.

Huawei's involvement in surveillance in Xinjiang is a confirmed fact
Cave, D. (2019). Mapping more of China's tech giants: AI and surveillance. [online] Aspi.org.au. Available at: https://www.aspi.org.au/report/mapping-more-chinas-tech-giants.

escapees from the concentration camps in Xinjiang began to give first-hand testimony of their terrible experiences and videos emerged of mass prisoner transfers on railways
Mauk, B. (2021). Inside Xinjiang's Prison State. [online] The New Yorker. Available at: https://www.newyorker.com/news/a-reporter-at-large/china-xinjiang-prison-state-uighur-detention-camps-prisoner-testimony [Accessed 4 Mar. 2022].

China threatened to retaliate to the Huawei decision by taking business away from other British firms
Beijing, S.S., Deputy Political Editor | Lucy Fisher, Defence Editor |Didi Tang (n.d.). China threatens to make British companies pay for Huawei ban. www.thetimes.co.uk. [online] Available at: https://www.thetimes.co.uk/article/china-threatens-to-make-british-companies-pay-for-huawei-ban-3tdbhxok5 [Accessed 5 Jun. 2022].

Boris Johnson was accused of operating a deliberate 'strategic void' on China
The Guardian. (2021). PM accused of deliberate 'strategic void' on China to prioritise trade. [online] Available at: https://www.theguardian.com/politics/2021/sep/10/pm-accused-of-deliberate-strategic-void-on-china-to-prioritise-trade [Accessed 5 Jun. 2022].

Chapter 9

In 1932, the Al-Saud's established rule of the current kingdom began
Madawi Al- Rasheed (2014). A history of Saudi Arabia. Cambridge Cambridge University Press.

the Saudi-Wahhabist state was based on violent repression of its opponents and firm religious support for the Al-Saud rulers
Simon Ross Valentine (2015). Force and fanaticism : Wahhabism in Saudi Arabia and beyond. London: Hurst & Company ; New York.

the French scholar Gilles Kepel
Gilles Kepel (2020). JIHAD : the trail of political islam. S.L.: Bloomsbury Academic.

A leaked US diplomatic cable from 2010
This comes from a Wikileaks leaked diplomatic cable: https://wikileaks.org/plusd/cables/09JEDDAH443_a.html. Whilst I am not normally in favour of using Wikileaks, this cable contains no sensitive material from a national security perspective.

Saudi Arabia exported Wahhabism
Pandith, F. (n.d.). Extremism Is Riyadh's Top Export. [online] Foreign Policy. Available at: https://foreignpolicy.com/2019/03/24/farah-pandith-saudi-how-we-win-book/.

9/11 Commission Report
United States. Government Printing Office (2004). 9/11 Commission report : the official report of the 9/11 Commission and related publications. Washington, D.C.: U.S. G.P.O.

Al-Jarrah's role was a closely guarded secret until May 2020 when the FBI accidentally revealed his name in a sloppily-redacted document
Rotella, T.G., Sebastian (n.d.). The Justice Department Accidentally Released the Name of Saudi Official Suspected of Helping the 9/11 Hijackers. [online] ProPublica. Available at: https://www.propublica.org/article/the-justice-department-accidentally-released-the-name-of-saudi-official-suspected-of-helping-the-9-11-hijackers [Accessed 5 Jun. 2022].

William McCants, an expert on terrorism has observed, the Saudis are 'both the arsonists and the firefighters'
Shane, S., "Saudis and Extremism: 'Both the Arsonists and the Firefighters'." (2016). The New York Times. [online] 25 Aug. Available at: https://www.nytimes.com/2016/08/26/world/middleeast/saudi-arabia-islam.html.

The human rights situation in Saudi Arabia reflects widely held conservative social values and, as such, needs to move at a pace that is acceptable to its society
Hansard, 5 January 2016.

Saudi Arabia has historically been the 'swing producer' of oil
Column: Saudi Arabia resumes familiar role as swing producer. (2019). Reuters. [online] 21 Feb. Available at: https://www.reuters.com/article/uk-oil-prices-kemp-idUKKCN1QA1AO [Accessed 5 Jun. 2022].

the largest proportion of GDP of any country on its military
Roser, M., Ortiz-Ospina, E., Ritchie, H. and Mathieu, E. (2013). Military Spending. Our World in Data. [online] Available at: https://ourworldindata.org/military-spending#military-spending-as-share-of-gdp.

Saudi Arabia has one of the world's best-equipped airforces, its pilots are notoriously incompetent and often crash in undemanding situations
Cooper, H., "Attacks Expose Flaws in Saudi Arabia's Expensive Military". (2019). The New York Times. [online] 19 Sep. Available at: https://www.nytimes.com/2019/09/19/us/politics/saudi-military-iran.html.

there's nobody in the Iranian General Staff that's afraid of Saudi Arabia on the ground
Barany, Z. (2021). Armies of Arabia : military politics and effectiveness in the Gulf. New York, Ny Oxford University Press.

Margaret Thatcher had played a prominent role
Harding, L. (2016). Declassified papers reveal real reason for Thatcher's dash to Riyadh. The Guardian. [online] 23 Aug. Available at: https://www.theguardian.com/uk-news/2016/aug/24/declassified-papers-reveal-real-reason-for-thatchers-dash-to-riyadh.

biggest sale ever of anything to anyone
Barker, A. (2010). Outside Edge: You are spoiling us, Sir Alan, Financial Times
bribes of £600 million had been paid in 1985

The Guardian. (2011). Secrets of Al Yamamah. The Guardian. [online] Available at: https://www.theguardian.com/baefiles/page/0,,2095831,00.html

BAE pleaded guilty to criminal charges and paid a fine of almost $450 million for allegations of corporate bribery in an unusual joint Transatlantic corruption investigation
www.justice.gov. (2010). BAE Systems PLC Pleads Guilty and Ordered to Pay $400 Million Criminal Fine. [online] Available at: https://www.justice.gov/opa/pr/bae-systems-plc-pleads-guilty-and-ordered-pay-400-million-criminal-fine.

Certainly I never knew No 10 to come up with any decision that would be incommoding to BAE
Coates, S. (2006) The weapons company with influential friends at the highest level. www.thetimes.co.uk. [online] Available at: https://www.thetimes.co.uk/article/the-weapons-company-with-influential-friends-at-the-highest-level-m76d6d9gsr0 [Accessed 5 Jun. 2022].

John Walker Lindh
Bergen, P.L. (2008). Holy War Inc Inside the Secret World of Osama Bin Laden. Paw Prints.

Iran was entirely opposed to the Huthi-Salih alliance
HuffPost UK. (2015). Iran Warned Houthis Against Yemen Takeover. [online] Available at: https://www.huffingtonpost.co.uk/entry/iran-houthis-yemen_n_7101456.

23 civilians in Sana'a, including women and children, according to Human Rights Watch
Human Rights Watch. (2016). Human Rights Watch submission to the Committee on the Rights of the Child regarding Saudi Arabia. [online] Available at: https://www.hrw.org/news/2016/09/02/human-rights-watch-submission-committee-rights-child-regarding-saudi-arabia [Accessed 5 Jun. 2022].

By late 2020, the Saudi-led coalition had carried out more than 20,000 airstrikes, killing nearly 9,000 civilians and injuring many more
Just Security. (2022). US Military Support to the Saudi-Led Coalition in Yemen Amid Civilian Toll: Mapping the Connections. [online] Available at: https://www.justsecurity.org/81754/us-military-support-to-the-saudi-led-coalition-in-yemen-amid-civilian-toll-mapping-the-connections/ [Accessed 5 Jun. 2022].

independent groups have judged that Saudi air attacks have amounted to war crimes
War Crimes Committed by Both Sides in Yemen, U.N. Panel Says. (2019). The New York Times. [online] 3 Sep. Available at: https://www.nytimes.com/2019/09/03/world/middleeast/war-crimes-yemen.html.

General John Deverell, remarked: 'The Saudi bosses absolutely depend on BAE'
Merat, A. (2019). 'The Saudis couldn't do it without us': the UK's true role in Yemen's deadly war. [online] the Guardian. Available at: https://www.theguardian.com/world/2019/jun/18/the-saudis-couldnt-do-it-without-us-the-uks-true-role-in-yemens-deadly-war.

They couldn't do it without us
www.channel4.com. (n.d.). Britain's Hidden War: Channel 4 Dispatches | Channel 4. [online] Available at: https://www.channel4.com/press/news/britains-hidden-war-channel-4-dispatches.

BAE sold £15 billion worth of arms and services to Saudi Arabia
Anon, (n.d.). CAAT - True value of UK arms trade to Saudi Arabia worth over £20 billion since 2015. [online] Available at: https://caat.org.uk/news/true-value-of-uk-arms-trade-to-saudi-arabia-worth-over-20-billion-since-2015/.

no UK-supplied cluster weapons have been used, and that no UK-supplied aircraft have been involved in the use of UK cluster weapons, in the current conflict in Yemen
"The use of UK-manufactured arms in Yemen", UK Parliament, September 2016

House of Lords International Relations Committee concluded that arms sales to Saudi Arabia were unlawful
Brooke-Holland, L. and Smith, B. (842AD). UK arms exports to Saudi Arabia: Q&A. [online] Available at: https://researchbriefings.files.parliament.uk/documents/CBP-8425/CBP-8425.pdf.

the Saudis have literally been digging in
Anon, (n.d.). Digging Up Diplomacy: The Salwa Canal and the Saudi-Qatar Stalemate – Young Professionals in Foreign Policy. [online] Available at: https://www.ypfp.org/digging-up-diplomacy-the-salwa-canal-and-the-saudi-qatar-stalemate/ [Accessed 5 Jun. 2022].

It looks like the FCA is consulting on amending the existing listing rules to accommodate the peculiarities of one company, which is not a very effective strategy for regulating the market as a whole London reforms set to open door for Saudi Aramco listing
(2017). Financial Times. [online] 13 Jul. Available at: https://www.ft.com/content/aeeb636e-67a7-11e7-9a66-93fb352ba1fe [Accessed 5 Jun. 2022].

BP Energy Outlook
Energy Outlook 2020 edition. (2020). [online] Available at: https://www.bp.com/content/dam/bp/business-sites/en/global/corporate/pdfs/energy-economics/energy-outlook/bp-energy-outlook-2020.pdf.

Possibly as many as 500 new jobs could be attributed to a growth in trade with the Kingdom
AP NEWS. (n.d.). AP FACT CHECK: Trump inflates value of Saudi arms deal. [online] Available at: https://apnews.com/article/jamal-khashoggi-north-america-donald-trump-economy-politics-2b4799b3d3ca4f6781efe1e70f207392 [Accessed 5 Jun. 2022].

unsuccessfully tried to arrange calls between President Biden and the de facto leaders of Saudi Arabia and the United Arab Emirates
Cloud, D.N., Stephen Kalin and David S. (2022). WSJ News Exclusive | Saudi, Emirati Leaders Decline Calls With Biden During Ukraine Crisis. Wall Street Journal. [online]

9 Mar. Available at: https://www.wsj.com/articles/saudi-emirati-leaders-decline-calls-with-biden-during-ukraine-crisis-11646779430.

We assess that Saudi Arabia's Crown Prince Muhammad bin Salman approved operation in Istanbul, Turkey to capture or kill Saudi journalist Jamal Khashoggi
Assessing the Saudi Government's Role in the Killing of Jamal Khashoggi Classified By: Derived From: Declassify On. (2021). [online] Available at: https://www.dni.gov/files/ODNI/documents/assessments/Assessment-Saudi-Gov-Role-in-JK-Death-20210226v2.pdf.

the Saudis had 'kompromat' on Johnson
Steerpike (n.d.). Did MBS kompromat Boris? | The Spectator. [online] www.spectator.co.uk. Available at: https://www.spectator.co.uk/article/did-mbs-kompromat-boris- [Accessed 5 Jun. 2022].

star pupil of Saudi deradicalisation left Saudi Arabia to join the Islamic State in Syria
The Guardian. (2014). 'Living suicide bomb' rejoins al-Qaida after Saudi deprogramming. [online] Available at: https://www.theguardian.com/world/2014/jan/18/suicide-bomb-al-qaida-saudi-ahmed-al-shayea [Accessed 5 Jun. 2022].

Chapter 10

They told us that everything should be finished within two-three hours
web.archive.org. (2015). Tehelka: Free. Fair. Fearless. [online] Available at: https://web.archive.org/web/20151030025253/http://archive.tehelka.com/story_main35.asp?filename=Ne031107We_dragged.asp [Accessed 6 Jun. 2022].

Many respected scholars
See for example Brass, P.R. (2005). The production of Hindu-Muslim violence in contemporary India. Seattle, Wash.: University Of Washington Press ; Chesham.

Indian Special Investigative Team found in 2013
Times of India (2013). Special Investigation Team: Is SIT hiding proof in Gujarat riots case? | India News - Times of India. [online] The Times of India. Available at: https://timesofindia.indiatimes.com/india/is-sit-hiding-proof-in-gujarat-riots-case/articleshow/21132148.cms [Accessed 6 Jun. 2022]. Also Harris, G. and Kumar, H. (2012). 32 People Convicted for Roles in Gujarat Riots. The New York Times. [online] 29 Aug. Available at: https://www.nytimes.com/2012/08/30/world/asia/32-people-convicted-for-roles-in-gujarat-riots.html?module=inline [Accessed 6 Jun. 2022].

in 2018 the Supreme Court of India recommended that parliament enact specific legislation to outlaw the problem
Mahapatra, D. (2018). Mob lynching: 'Draft new legislation to stop people taking law into own hands', says SC to Parliament | India News - Times of India. [online] The Times of India. Available at: https://timesofindia.indiatimes.com/india/mob-

lynching-draft-new-legislation-to-stop-people-taking-law-into-own-hands-says-sc-to-parliament/articleshow/65019261.cms?utm_source=contentofinterest&utm_medium=text&utm_campaign=cppst [Accessed 6 Jun. 2022].

This language has repeatedly been used by Modi's right-hand man Amit Shah
Amit Shah vows to throw illegal immigrants into Bay of Bengal. (2019). Reuters. [online] 12 Apr. Available at: https://www.reuters.com/article/india-election-speech-idUSKCN1RO1YD.

Assam led to two million people, almost all of them Muslims, finding themselves stateless and required to prove to Foreigners Tribunals that they were in fact Indian citizens
Sur, P. (2020). A Year After Rendering Millions Stateless, India Has Yet to Hear a Single Appeal. [online] Foreign Policy. Available at: https://foreignpolicy.com/2020/09/10/2-million-people-india-assam-stateless-year-nrc/ [Accessed 6 Jun. 2022].

Johnson had given a rambling speech in favour of Modi for which he was paid more than £100,000
Suroor, H. (2019). Boris Johnson paid £40, 000 an hour for three hours in New Delhi. [online] National Herald. Available at: https://www.nationalheraldindia.com/international/boris-johnson-paid-pound40-000-an-hour-for-three-hours-in-new-delhi [Accessed 6 Jun. 2022].

This will swing the actual election result
The Guardian. (2019). 'Divisive tactics': WhatsApp messages urge Hindus to vote against Labour. [online] Available at: https://www.theguardian.com/politics/2019/nov/08/british-hindus-urged-whatsapp-messages-vote-against-labour [Accessed 6 Jun. 2022].

As Jafri's son Tanveer explained to me when we spoke in late 2020
Author's conversation with Tanveer Jafri, 29 November 2020

expressing astonishment that he was still alive
web.archive.org. (2016). Ehsan Jafri called Modi for help, I heard Modi abuse him: Gulberg survivor. [online] Available at: https://web.archive.org/web/20160603213058/http://www.catchnews.com/india-news/ehsan-jafri-called-modi-for-help-i-heard-modi-abuse-him-gulberg-survivor-1464888144.html [Accessed 6 Jun. 2022].

disfigured and burned beyond recognition
There are numerous consistently harrowing eyewitness accounts of the Gulberg Society massacre, both from survivors and perpetrators. These include the Tehelka material, interviews in Rakesh Sharma's 2003 film Final Solution as well as testimony in the Special Investigation Tribunal and the Concerned Citizens Tribunal.

Modi had incited reaction by driving the charred bodies burned in the Godhra train across the state in a motorcade
www.sabrang.com. (n.d.). Concerned Citizens Tribunal - Gujarat 2002: An inquiry into the carnage in Gujarat. [online] Available at: https://www.sabrang.com/tribunal/ [Accessed 6 Jun. 2022].

After three days, he asked us to stop and everything came to a halt...
Tehelka Haresh Bhatt transcript, June 1 2007

life, liberty, equality, and dignity of the people of the state
Department Of State. The Office of Electronic Information, B. of P.A. (n.d.). Issue of Gujarat Chief Minister Narendra Modi's Visa Status. [online] 2001-2009. state.gov. Available at: https://2001-2009.state.gov/p/sca/rls/rm/2005/43701.htm [Accessed 6 Jun. 2022].

I came out of the interview shaken
India-seminar.com. (2022). 513 Ashis Nandy: Obituary of a culture. [online] Available at: https://www.india-seminar.com/2002/513/513%20ashis%20nandy. htm [Accessed 6 Jun. 2022].

core values of democracy, pluralism and tolerance
Available online at https://assets.publishing.service.gov.uk/government/uploads/ system/uploads/attachment_data/file/264173/India-UK_core_script.docx [Accessed 6 Jun. 2022]

We have to get out of this post-colonial guilt
Murphy, J., Sands, S. (2012). William Hague: I came back to be the Foreign Secretary... that's. [online] Evening Standard. Available at: https://www.standard. co.uk/news/politics/william-hague-i-came-back-to-be-the-foreign-secretary-that-s-what-i-m-doing-8099138.html [Accessed 6 Jun. 2022].

An elderly Sikh gentleman stood and said he'd been jailed for campaigning for democracy and independence. Why hasn't Britain apologized for that?
Nelson, D. (2013). David Cameron's India trade trip: why we owe a debt to India. [online] Available at: https://www.telegraph.co.uk/news/worldnews/asia/ india/9876387/David-Camerons-India-trade-trip-why-we-owe-a-debt-to-India. html?onwardjourney=584162_c1 [Accessed 6 Jun. 2022].

Britain was making more consequential decisions for its relationship with India
The Economist. (n.d.). The politics of apologising for Amritsar. [online] Available at: https://www.economist.com/britain/2019/04/04/the-politics-of-apologising-for-amritsar [Accessed 6 Jun. 2022].

India had to 'take back' its existing nationals that had overstayed their visas, before any question of liberalising the migration regime
The Independent. (2016). Theresa May says India has to 'take back' nationals before more can get visas for Britain. [online] Available at: https://www. independent.co.uk/news/uk/politics/theresa-may-says-india-has-to-take-back-its-nationals-from-britain-before-it-is-given-more-visas-a7402511.html [Accessed 6 Jun. 2022].

he encouraged attendees in advertisements claiming the festival was 'clean' and 'safe'
Scroll (2021). Modi is a 'super spreader' of coronavirus, says IMA vice president. [online] Scroll.in. Available at: https://scroll.in/latest/993413/modi-is-a-super-spreader-of-coronavirus-says-ima-vice-president [Accessed 6 Jun. 2022].

It can be said with pride that India not only defeated Covid...
Resolution passed in BJP National Office Bearers meeting, 21 February 202.,

the consistently well-connected Westminster journalist Alex Wickham wrote
Wickham, A. (2021). POLITICO London Playbook: Bordering on farce — V.O.C.'d it up — Burger bunfight. [online] Available at: https://www.politico.eu/newsletter/london-playbook/politico-london-playbook-bordering-on-farce-v-o-c-d-it-up-burger-bunfight/ [Accessed 6 Jun. 2022].

Chapter 11

Blair dismissed the French president's views as 'dangerous' and 'pathetic'
Watt, N. (2005). PM attacks Chirac's 'pathetic' power vision. [online] Available at: https://www.theguardian.com/uk/2005/jan/29/eu.france [Accessed 6 Jun. 2022].

All is not well... the rules-based international system is under greater strain than for many decades – and the evidence is all around us
Hunt, J. (2019). Foreign Secretary Hunt: Britain's role in a post-Brexit world. [online] Available at: https://www.gov.uk/government/speeches/foreign-secretary-hunt-britains-role-in-a-post-brexit-world.

through 'gritted teeth'
Gordon, M.R. and Trainor, B.E. (2007). Cobra II : the inside story of the invasion and occupation of Iraq. New York: Vintage Books.

The circumstances in which it was decided that there was a legal basis for UK military action were far from satisfactory
Iraq Inquiry, John Chilcot's public statement.

the National Security Agency intercepted the calls of 35 world leaders, including Germany's Angela Merkel
Mazzetti, M. and Sanger, D.E. (2013). Tap on Merkel Provides Peek at Vast Spy Net. The New York Times. [online] 31 Oct. Available at: https://www.nytimes.com/2013/10/31/world/europe/tap-on-merkel-provides-peek-at-vast-spy-net.html [Accessed 6 Jun. 2022].

For more than two centuries we have stood together in friendship
Obama, B. (2011). Remarks by President Obama In Honoring the Alliance Between the United States and France. [online] Available at: https://obamawhitehouse.archives.gov/the-press-office/2011/11/04/remarks-president-obama-honoring-alliance-between-united-states-and-fran [Accessed 6 Jun. 2022].

so special that only one side knew that it existed
Timothy Garton Ash (2005). Free world : America, Europe, and the surprising future of the West. New York: Vintage Books. p. 199

Obama, who appeared to have picked up a stack of DVDs
Drury, I. (2009). To my special friend Gordon, 25 DVDs: Obama gives Brown a set of classic movies. Let's hope he likes the Wizard of Oz. [online] Mail Online. Available at: https://www.dailymail.co.uk/news/article-1159627/To-special-friend-Gordon-25-DVDs-Obama-gives-Brown-set-classic-movies-Lets-hope-likes-Wizard-Oz.html [Accessed 6 Jun. 2022].

A trade deal isn't going to change the fact that we aren't very good at making things to export to the Americans
This data comes from the IMF website, available at: IMF.org [Accessed 6 Jun. 22]

very difficult position, in the words of Peter Ricketts
Newsweek. (2017). Trump's planned U.K. state visit puts the Queen in a 'very difficult position'. [online] Available at: https://www.newsweek.com/donald-trump-state-visit-puts-queen-very-difficult-position-foreign-office-550480 [Accessed 6 Jun. 2022].

Trump's visit was downgraded but was still largely a disaster
The Sun. (2018). I told May how to do Brexit but she wrecked it — US trade deal is off! [online] Available at: https://www.thesun.co.uk/news/6766531/trump-may-brexit-us-deal-off/.

A dim if not dismal future' awaited NATO members
Shanker, T. (2011). Defense Secretary Warns NATO of 'Dim' Future. The New York Times. [online] 10 Jun. Available at: https://www.nytimes.com/2011/06/11/world/europe/11gates.html [Accessed 6 Jun. 2022].

With Britain, there is no need. We know their constant opportunism. So there is no need to bring our ambassador back to explain
France 24. (2021). PM Morrison rejects French accusation that Australia lied over cancelled submarine deal. [online] Available at: https://www.france24.com/en/europe/20210919-france-accuses-australia-and-us-of-lying-over-cancelled-submarine-contract [Accessed 6 Jun. 2022].

such an agreement was unlikely to be reached in President Biden's first term
The Independent. (2021). UK would be 'lucky' to strike trade deal in Biden's first term, says former ambassador. [online] Available at: https://www.independent.co.uk/news/uk/politics/biden-brexit-us-uk-trade-deal-b1788756.html [Accessed 6 Jun. 2022].

Within minutes of a vote for Brexit the CEO's of Mercedes, BMW, VW and Audi will be knocking down Chancellor Merkel's door

Davis, D. (2016). David Davis responds to Moody's threat to downgrade the UK following Brexit. [online] Available at: https://www.daviddavismp.com/david-davis-responds-to-moodys-threat-to-downgrade-the-uk-following-brexit/ [Accessed 6 Jun. 2022].

continue to challenge ill-founded arguments and muddled thinking
'A tremendous wrench': Sir Ivan Rogers' resignation email in full. [online] Available at: https://www.theguardian.com/politics/2017/jan/04/quote-sir-ivan-rogers-resignation-eu-brexit-email-in-full [Accessed 6 Jun. 2022].

The day after we vote to leave we hold all the cards and we can choose the path we want
Gove, M. (2016). THE FACTS OF LIFE SAY LEAVE: WHY BRITAIN AND EUROPE WILL BE BETTER OFF AFTER WE VOTE LEAVE. [online] Available at: http://www.voteleavetakecontrol.org/assets-d3n8a8pro7vhmx.cloudfront.net/voteleave/pages/271/attachments/original/1461057270/MGspeech194VERSION2.pdf [Accessed 6 Jun. 2022].

the easiest in human history. EU trade deal 'easiest in human history'
(n.d.). BBC News. [online] Available at: https://www.bbc.co.uk/news/av/uk-40667879.

In 2019, the EU's GDP (stripping out the UK) was €14 trillion. The UK's in the same year was €2.4 trillion
Ward, M. (2019). Statistics on UK-EU trade. commonslibrary.parliament.uk, [online] 7851(1). Available at: https://commonslibrary.parliament.uk/research-briefings/cbp-7851/.

no British Conservative government could or should sign up to any such arrangement
News Letter. (2018). Watch Boris Johnson tell the DUP in 2018 he would never put border in the Irish Sea - today he put a border in the Irish Sea. [online] Available at: https://www.newsletter.co.uk/news/politics/watch-boris-johnson-tell-dup-2018-he-would-never-put-border-irish-sea-today-he-put-border-irish-sea-816300 [Accessed 8 Dec. 2021].

I will direct them to throw that form in the bin Johnson tells Northern Ireland businesses to 'bin' customs forms
(2019). belfasttelegraph. [online] Available at: https://www.belfasttelegraph.co.uk/news/northern-ireland/johnson-tells-northern-ireland-businesses-to-bin-customs-forms-38674258.html [Accessed 6 Jun. 2022].

remained in the EU's single market NI Direct
(2018). EU exit and the Northern Ireland Protocol. [online] Available at: https://www.nidirect.gov.uk/articles/eu-exit-and-northern-ireland-protocol.

globally unique opportunity
Brandon Lewis, Twitter, 2 January 2021

not, 'compatible with the result of the referendum'
Brandon Lewis MP. (n.d.). Why I am backing the Brexit Deal. [online] Available at: https://www.brandonlewis.co/news/why-i-am-backing-brexit-deal [Accessed 6 Jun. 2022].

This is the first step in an infringement procedure
European Commission - European Commission. (n.d.). Press corner. [online] Available at: https://ec.europa.eu/commission/presscorner/detail/en/ip_20_1798.

How can we reproach Russia, China or Iran when their conduct falls below internationally accepted standards, when we are showing such scant regard for our treaty obligations?
Quoted in Gillespie, S. (2021). English Legal System. S.L.: Oxford Univ Press. p. 121

In speech after speech, both Putin and [Russian Foreign Minister Sergei] Lavrov
Remler, P. (2020). Russia at the United Nations: Law, Sovereignty, and Legitimacy. [online] Carnegie Endowment for International Peace. Available at: https://carnegieendowment.org/2020/01/22/russia-at-united-nations-law-sovereignty-and-legitimacy-pub-80753.

Conclusion

Britain must find a sensible means of living alongside its larger neighbour and main trading partner
Ricketts, P. (2021). HARD CHOICES : britain and the new geometry of global power. S.L.: Atlantic Books.

China to position its nationals at the head of a wide range of UN agencies, as Politico reported in April 2020
Lee, K. (2020). It's Not Just the WHO: How China Is Moving on the Whole U.N. [online] POLITICO. Available at: https://www.politico.com/news/magazine/2020/04/15/its-not-just-the-who-how-china-is-moving-on-the-whole-un-189029.

Finding themselves well represented in these senior positions gives the Nordic countries an opportunity to exercise power over international institutions
Novosad, P. and Werker, E. (2018). Who runs the international system? Nationality and leadership in the United Nations Secretariat. The Review of International Organizations, [online] 14(1), pp.1–33. doi:10.1007/s11558-017-9294-z.

INDEX

The first biography of Ukraine's leader written for a Western audience

ZELENSKY
Ukraine's President and His Country
By Steven Derix with Marina Shelkunova
256 pages
August 2022
Hardback £16.99. ISBN 9781912454778
Ebook £9.99. ISBN 9781912454785

www.canburypress.com